Locating Publics

Florian Grote

Locating Publics

Forms of Social Order in an Electronic Music Scene

Springer VS

Florian Grote
Berlin, Germany

Dissertation of the Zeppelin University, Friedrichshafen 2013
First Reviewer: Dirk Baecker
Second Reviewer: Martin Warnke
Third Reviewer: Karen van den Berg
Date of the Disputation: September 11, 2013

ISBN 978-3-658-05406-9 ISBN 978-3-658-05407-6 (eBook)
DOI 10.1007/978-3-658-05407-6

The Deutsche Nationalbibliothek lists this publication in the Deutsche Nationalbibliografie; detailed bibliographic data are available in the Internet at http://dnb.d-nb.de.

Library of Congress Control Number: 2014934691

Springer VS

Printed on acid-free paper

Springer VS is a brand of Springer DE.
Springer DE is part of Springer Science+Business Media.
www.springer-vs.de

Acknowledgments

The world of electronic music is a fascinating place. It relies on sounds that can be created freely, without limitations imposed by acoustic instruments and their rules of operation. Its musicians are versatile masters of their instruments nevertheless, only the notion of the instrument has changed drastically. Pieces of software or a device connected to a computer, microphones and loudspeakers as well as small applications on mobile devices are all being used in a wide variety of styles and genres. Acoustic instruments are not forgotten, though. Many of the musicians I was in contact with during my research have a background with and profound training on one or several acoustic instruments, some of them even relying on them as their main way of creative expression, all the while remaining firmly rooted in the world of electronic sound. While the creation of electronic music has always embraced new technologies, the same is true for its reception. Much of electronic music is consumed by playing back digital files, using all sorts of different devices. Outside of artistic practice, electronic music scenes have gone through major shifts brought about by new technologies used for organizational purposes, mainly utilizing different means of online communication. This openness to try out and make use of new technologies has been a very visible common trait in most of the members of the scene in which I had the privilege to conduct my research. First and foremost, I have to thank these artists and organizers, who remain anonymous in this book, for supporting my research in their creative field and for taking the time to patiently explain to me the inner workings of their practice from their own perspectives. Their dedication to live their love of music was the inspiration for my work.

I want to thank my promotors, Prof. Dr. Dirk Baecker and Prof. Dr. Martin Warnke, for encouraging me to embark on this endeavor, and for the continued support throughout the years I worked on it. I also want to thank Prof. Dr. Karen van den Berg for assessing my dissertation and pointing me in very interesting new directions. To these academic supervisors, I am deeply thankful for the many long discussions and the in-depth feedback, as well as the guidance they provided, but also for repeatedly challenging me to rethink my methods and theses, all of which have made this undertaking an incredibly enriching experience.

I want to thank my family, Marie Beyeler and my parents, Irmgard and Dr. Klaus Grote, for their continued support throughout the years. Their strength was my main encouragement.

In this study, I lay out an account of structures and processes as I see them, and I describe the methodology that led me to these results. For me as for any observer, the step out of the relative security of keeping things ambiguous, and to really sketch out an account of the very diverse situations I experienced, was the most critical part. It would not have been possible without the many people who reviewed my work while I collected all the bits and pieces, providing input that sometimes stopped me on a wrong path, but more often sparked new ideas and new possibilities to observe things happening in the field. For this, I want to especially thank Jan Beyeler, Dr. Hendrik Buhl, Prof. Dr. Rolf Grossmann, Prof. Dr. Michael Harenberg, Thaddeus Herrmann, Dr. Athanasios Karafillidis, Prof. Dr. Maren Lehmann, Takeshi Nishimoto, Andreas Otto, Dr. Silke Seemann, Dr. Christina Weiss, and my colleagues at Native Instruments.

Contents

Introduction

In the old, run-down center of Berlin-Kreuzberg, the streets are lined with international call shops and small cafés, Turkish banks have their branch offices, and the overground metro rail cuts through a landscape dominated by the concrete tower blocks of 1970s social housing initiatives. Right here, in one of the hotspots of old West-Berlin, every month, participants of a small electronic music scene converged in small venues where artists played music from their latest releases on a specialized music label. Most visitors and the artists traveled to these venues from other parts of the city or from other cities in Europe. The performance events held here were not local, but rather located in the sense of being deliberately placed here, with visitors and organizers who did not usually spend their evenings in this area. The placement of these and similar performance events was viewed as playing an important role by the participants, and great care was taken in the selection of venues and the organization of the events themselves.

This study investigates how this small electronic music scene organized its activity through public communication. This was not the scene of high-profile music events, which drew thousands of tourists to Berlin every weekend, but its participants were prolific and highly engaged nevertheless. Online communication played an important role in the scene's activity, so I integrated in-depth case studies of these phenomena with my research on located events.

Why the music scene? What qualifies this field of cultural and artistic practice for a study on forms of social order? The answer lies in the position this scene holds in the face of the large-scale changes as society moves from industrialized modernity to its next state, predicted by Peter F. Drucker as the "Next Society" (Drucker 2001). Here, instead of production jobs, knowledge work is key, set in the context of all-encompassing computer networks. This change is only in its beginning stages, yet some areas of society are already affected much more than others. The music scene is among the most affected areas: Most of both its means of production and its "commodities" in the form of recorded music are, for all practical purposes, available as pure information, more or less decoupled from any physical substrate. Both can be used and distributed on computers, so that the most important physical objects in the music scene have become software objects. As such, they are subjected to falling prices, which at the time of writing are trending towards zero. The huge studios, icons of the music industry, are no longer needed, nor do most artists have the funds to book them. Other forms of cultural and artistic practice gain relevance again, for example the concert and the DJ performance, even though they do not provide monetary compensation for decreasing revenue from sales of recorded music. Most importantly, the electronic musician has to understand his own role differently now, and this promises a rich field for empirical exploration.

The field of this study is defined by the focus on a particular music label. The artists in the center of my observations all have at least one release on this label. Stylistically, the music released here can be subsumed under the term "electronica", a genre where electronic sounds are combined with broken beats originating in hip hop and jazz, with occasional acoustic or electro-acoustic instruments mixed in. The reach of the label was global, releasing music by artists from all over the world. Even so, many of the international artists had moved to Berlin, in part because of the collaboration with this music label.

This study is not primarily an investigation into the aesthetic and stylistic aspects of the music created and performed by field participants, although they play a significant role in the analysis as well. I deliberately chose to rather focus my investigation on the details of the communicational process, in an effort to find out more about how the scene organizes itself under changing circumstances.

The main method of analysis applied throughout this study is what I refer to as form analysis. It is an attempt to look at the very fine-grained forms of communicational constructions, for example when a statement is offered or a reaction to something that was communicated takes place. This approach is based on sociological systems theory, where communication is described as multiple chains of singular events, which can be observed as streams of the communicational process. Each event can be analyzed as an individual form, while being embedded in semantics of broader topics spanning across different events. In the form, the arrangement of distinctions between the different references can be observed on the process level, while at the same time including the cultural relevance of the form in the analysis by remaining sensitive to the references made.

As a part of society, musicians and the cultural practice surrounding them always had to deal with the changes and challenges prevalent in the wider contexts of social life. This can be observed for singing at campfires, just as well as for the music mega stars of the 20th century. Music scenes emerged as realms of social action focused on a specific type of artistic practice, and with them, certain forms of organizations came into being, catering to the artistic practices and the public interest in them.

As with other artistic and cultural practices, the industrialization of music over the course of the 20th century has produced certain forms of trade, of institutions and organizations, of expectations and standards and the various roles associated with them. Industries are economies of scale, and the mass adoption of their products therefore presupposes and creates the notion of a mainstream media culture, where tastes are not differentiated in too many niches to still be profitable. The resulting musical artifacts can be subsumed in the term "popular music" (e.g. Kusek / Leonhard 2005).

As the economical basis for this industrial, mass-market business model has largely ceased existence with the advent of free online content towards the end of the 20th century, institutions and roles of the old system do not disappear overnight, if at all. Products of the industrial form are still released, yet in very different economical contexts. This has implications for the ties among different roles associated with the artistic and cultural practice of music. Already while the industrial economy was still viable, certain sub-groups defined themselves as opposition to the one-size-fits-all mass market. These so-called "independent" (e.g. Millard 1995) scenes did, however, mostly copy the institutional structures and role schemes of the mainstream practices they narratively separated themselves from, only that their versions were scaled down so they could be steered either by the musicians themselves or by people they knew and trusted.

Institutionalized structures of both mainstream and independent music economies included forms such as the multiplex studios, record labels, distributors, nationwide music retailers, and royalty collection societies. All these forms emerged with the mass audiences and their markets during the central decades of the 20th century. As these markets fragmented from the last decade of the 20th century on, the above and similar forms of institutionalized structures continued to exist, even though some individual organizational installments vanished and a larger number of them slimmed down in size. This organizational change altered the ecology of operation for artists, both in mainstream and independent scenes. In terms of the installments of artistic and cultural practice, institutions had been in control throughout the era of industrial success. Albums were created in large studios and concerts often placed in extensive venues like stadiums and arenas.

With the availability of the MP3 format, it has become not only possible but also convenient to treat music recordings as pure information. For all practical purposes, copying recorded music is not bound to physical representations of recordings any more, and the quality of the copies has reached a standard that is sufficient to satisfy the vast majority of listeners. For a recording industry built on the foundation of physical scarcity of their products, this has posed enormous problems. Sales numbers have gone down for individual releases, and with them, revenues and production budgets have decreased. As a result, releases with major record labels have lost much of their appeal, which had been gained by the promise of artistic fame coupled with economical wealth. The releases in the field of this study did not generate enough revenue to support a larger organization, let alone one of an industrial scale. Rather, the focus of economical considerations surrounding a release laid on supporting the lifestyle of the recording artists. This brought with it the need for the artists to take over tasks which had previously been handled by others. Now, they needed to organize large parts of their public communication themselves, and get involved in almost all aspects of recording and releasing music. While some artists in the field had to cope with this change, it was the only mode of practice known to many others, who had started their artistic career already in the context of the wide availability of networked computers.

The traditional music industry of a few big players has been losing ground against a fragmented market landscape of many small actors. Nevertheless, scalability is still provided for theoretically, i.e. in the case of a big success for one of the releases in a smaller scene, the mass-production mechanisms of the old industry model would still be available. The manufacturers of CDs and vinyl records have adapted to the smaller sales volumes, and production costs are reasonably low even for relatively small pressings in the hundreds or low thousands. At the same time, it would still be easy to place an order of a hundred thousand copies, if a label or an artist suddenly saw a demand for them.

In this study, we analyze the public communication strategies of artists and institutions in a specific music scene. The artists' work falls within the broad realm of electronic music on the fringes of academic and popular techno and hip hop music, as well as media art. The artists, related events, and organizations were chosen on the basis of their involvement with a particular record label, which used to be run from both Berlin and Manchester. The partner in Manchester dropped out of the label during the period of field research, leaving the Berlin partner in charge of the label. All of the artists included in this study have at some point released music through this label, although none of them used it as exclusive outlet for their music work.

The focus of observation rested on the emergence and the function of publicly accessible communicational events in the field. An event can be any manifestation of communication taking place, i.e. an observable entity of signs connecting different references to meaning. The underlying research interest of this study can be summarized in the question why participants of a scene who have access to networked computers in all their stationary and mobile forms and who could, therefore, communicate with the publics interested in their work regardless of their location, still arrange for located interaction at public concerts and performance events to address a variety of topics. Methods of data collection included interviews with field participants, the structured collection of phenomena observable online, a survey, and multiple accounts of participatory observation. The interviews conducted included questions about spatial arrangements of locatable objects relevant to the music work of an artist. This could mean questions about accessibility and placement of relevant elements such as studios, record stores, venues, and organization offices, but also about the media used for communication between artists and their fan base as well as peer artists, and the efforts at controlling the artists' and the label's own representations in these forms of media.

The study starts with an overview of the social and economical contexts in which the field participants operated. The first chapter also introduces the core epistemological concepts that built the foundation of the collection and analysis of my data. Chapter 2 introduces the field and the methods used in the empirical work. In this chapter, I already start to build an analytical overview of the operative relations in the field utilizing methods from network theory, which are also explained here. Chapter 3 is focused on the public use of online communication media in the field, with detailed analyses of presentations and communicational processes involving the online platforms MySpace and Facebook. Chapter 4 follows with in-depth accounts of my participatory observation efforts at performance events. The analysis examines ways in which the parties involved in the performance events collaborated and communicated with their relevant publics. Finally, Chapter 5 explores a theoretical model of how the field participants integrated the different approaches to publicly communicate in their cultural and artistic practices.

The observations in this study are a momentary snapshot of a changing cultural field. The label from which my explorations started has stopped to release new music as of late 2012, while one of its sublabels continues to release small runs of vinyl singles. On the other hand, most of the artists are still active. Some of them release their music on other labels, while many act primarily on their own, releasing their music directly to online platforms and curating their own artistic identity in social networks. As the change continues, the broad electronic music scene remains a fascinating field for empirical research.

A note on citation: I will cite from my data throughout the study, even before the data types and the methodology of their collection and analysis are introduced in Chapter 2. The citations state the entries in the research database, beginning with "P" (for primary document) followed by their assigned number. The research database cannot be published for copyright reasons and to protect the anonymity of the field participants. It can be made available upon request for scientific purposes.

Chapter 1: Social and Economical Contexts

1.1 The Notion of the Network

Social theory at least since the 20th century has shown a tendency to import paradigms and metaphors from technological advances or scientific language of other fields. This was true for the mechanistic concept of stimulus/response in behavioristic models, and has proven vital in cybernetics with its neurobiological background. Network theory as one of the most recent theoretical developments in social science came about roughly at the same time as the public, and with it social science, took note of the prevalence of computer networks. This happened even before the deep social impact these networks and their successors would have could be estimated, and so social science had time to adapt the paradigm and use it in its efforts at understanding the social effects evolved technological networks have had on society.

The similarities between computer and social networks, however, only go so far. While computer networks rely on actual permanent connections via cables or wireless protocols in order to send and receive information, networks in the social realm are not made of such more or less tangible relations. A social tie cannot be unplugged and put to use elsewhere, like a network cable can. Social ties are ephemeral, as the network theorist Harrison C. White has pointed out (White 2008). They exist only in the moment when they are actualized in communication, and one can never be sure that a tie will work again the next time. Ties can be strong, as in close family relationships, or they can be weak, as in remote friendships or acquaintances. The social scientist Mark Granovetter has shown (in Granovetter 1973) that weak ties can actually be more productive in getting certain action than the strong ties of a strict hierarchy. In any case, regardless of whether ties are weak or strong, they are less reliable than an average network cable or wireless connection. This is because they depend on social and, in addition, individual contexts.

The social contexts of ties emerge out of the complexity that ties are usually embedded in. No social tie exists under laboratory conditions, where it could connect two, and only two, spots of social action. Instead, both sides that are interested in a tie accumulate a multiplicity of other interests and requirements, so that the actualization of any one tie is subjected to triage, the selection of its importance to be used to trigger action. In addition, individual contexts, such as bodily health of persons involved, can have an influence on social ties, although they are not observable in the realm of the social. That is why sickness makes for such a great excuse in social relations.

Because of the ephemeral nature of social ties, White has suggested to refrain from the notion of basic stability in social networks altogether. Social networks can be relatively stable, as working hierarchies and functional families show. But this is owed to their construction and operation, rather than to a basic, inherent reliability of underlying ties. Breaking away would never be a technical, but more likely a social problem for all participants. Therefore, instead of referring to ties and knots or hubs, as in classical graph theory (for an introductory overview, see for example Barabási 2003), White suggests (for example in White 2008) a notion of networks as being constructed out of identities struggling for control. Any entity that is observable in the social realm, i.e. that can be described in themes of communication, can be viewed as an identity. Exactly how it is described and in which thematic contexts it is triggered is of essential importance to an identity. It is in such occurrences that the overall notion of an identity and with it its capabilities to be embedded in social action evolve. Therefore, identities engage in a never-ending struggle to control their representations in other communicational contexts and thereby, network positions.

On the operational level, struggles for control have to rely on observations and selections. An identity gets triggered, for example that of an artist in a comparison between two artists. In order to be triggered, the identity of the artist had to be selected for the comparison. And in order to establish the relation between itself and the other artist's identity, both had to be observed in the context of the other. From these observations an explicit selection could be derived, such as "identity x is preferred over identity y", or "identity x is similar to identity y". These selections were again subject to observations in other contexts, and from these other observations, yet other explicit selections could be generated. They could have a positive or a negative form, such as "identity x is indeed better than identity y", or "identity x is not really better than identity y". It is crucial to note that in all these cases, the selections are affirmed on the operational level of communication, i.e. they are accepted as valid communicational statements. Even a negative statement is positive in that it positively communicates its negativity. The addition of a positive or a negative evaluation requires a separate operational step, based on an observation that takes contexts into account. Since an observation can only ever take on one perspective at any one instance (we will come back to this), a process like the one described necessarily generates sequentiality, which itself can be observed and selected as time.

1.1.1 The Next Society and its Cultures

The idea of the "Next Society" was brought to the table by the American economist Peter F. Drucker, who coined the term in an article published in 2001 by The Economist (Drucker 2001). Drucker later expanded on these ideas in his book "Managing in the Next Society" (Drucker 2002). The main concept in this idea stems from the observation that society, thought as one society that spans across all parts of the world, has been undergoing such drastic changes at the outset of the 21st century, that it will indeed transform into an entirely new state, which Drucker calls the Next Society.

Drucker makes out a variety of factors driving the change in the industrialized countries. This change, he argues, will not halt until society has altered its state profoundly enough to be recognized as "next". One of the main factors, and one which brings changes in many, very different fields, is demographic change. Drucker points out that, in most developed countries, the birthrate has long since fallen below the reproduction threshold of 2.2 children per woman, which means that the older generations will soon become the largest age group (Drucker 2001: p. 1; Drucker 2002: pp. 250). This development could only be countered with either a higher birthrate, or with accelerated immigration from developing countries. But even if this was achieved, society would not look the same any more.

One of the most obvious changes is the transformation of the job market. The regular full-time jobs that have been the mainstay of the job market since the dawn of industrialization will not go away, according to Drucker, but there are an increasing number of alternatives, including part-time employment, as well as freelance and consulting contracts. These models of working could benefit especially the senior workers, who may not have a choice but to keep on being productive for far longer than their parent generation (Drucker 2002: pp. 249). On the flipside, this brings flexibility for the organizations as they have more freedom in the design of processes than they would have relying only on full-time employees. Drucker predicts that, in the company of the Next Society, most of those working on the processes will not be members of the company's organization. The organization may well only consist of its management board, with all operational tasks sourced out to skilled external "knowledge workers", as Drucker calls them (2001: pp. 1; 2002, pp. 87). The few executives would give such a company its identity, and design the processes needed to offer products or services accordingly. The external knowledge workers would then do the actual work involved with these products or services.

Such distributed cooperation would be unthinkable without the ability to communicate instantaneously with anybody from almost anywhere in the world. Without the internet and mobile communication devices, companies could not hope to reorganize their processes with the best available knowledge workers in the world. Rather, they would be restricted to the knowledge of their local workers, of the members of their organization, which cannot necessarily be enlarged with more employees only to increase the quality of a part of a process. With the internet and mobile devices available, companies can harness specific skills wherever they may be situated, thereby creating the very notion of the knowledge worker (Drucker 2002: pp. 252).

The knowledge worker, as Drucker characterizes the type, is engaged in a never-ending process of training and learning, but has passed a certain point where he or she can claim to have a set of sophisticated skills in a certain field. The actual tasks of the knowledge worker would mostly be completed manually, as they would be highly specialized and not repetitive. Much of that manual work, it can be added, would be done on the computer mouse, keyboard, touchscreen gestures, and other, more specialized input methods. But it could still be considered manual work, albeit requiring detailed knowledge and sophisticated skills. "Knowledge", Drucker states, "has become the key resource, and the only scarce one. This means that knowledge workers collectively own the means of production." (Drucker 2002: p. 254)

The internet enables these knowledge workers to be involved in projects regardless of their location. This also means that they can work on more than one project at once. The cooperations Drucker describes as the future of the lean company in the Next Society are not all-inclusive for either persons or organizations, but rather very selective and very disposable at the same time. A knowledge worker in the Next Society may either carry a selection of two to four or five different business cards, or make a point of having none at all.

While the labor carried out by Drucker's knowledge workers may not be site-specific, the manufacturing of the technology they rely on certainly is. Mobile computers and the entire technological back-end of the (mobile) internet – servers, hard drives, cables, satellites, data centers, air conditioners, components for cellular towers, all have to be manufactured in industrial processes that require huge machines and large amounts of relatively low-skill manual work (see for example Dean 2007). Therefore, the industrial era will not go away, but we can rather see how a new mode of working and collaborating emerges in the wake of the ubiquitous accessibility of information relevant to the processes one is embedded in.

1.1.2 Cultures

The notion of the Next Society, as Peter F. Drucker has introduced it, is focused on the demographic and economic changes this new state of society will bring about. However, implications such as the ability to work regardless of location also point in the direction of a profound change of lifestyle. The difference in how things can and will be done in the Next Society will inevitably bring about noticeable changes in all areas of social life.

Being part of communication, the evolution of cultures is closely linked to the evolution of communication itself. Niklas Luhmann has described different stages of society being formed by their respective dominant communication media (Luhmann 1997a: pp. 190). In principle, communication emerges in a situation where two participants have to acknowledge that neither of them can foresee how the other will react to something that was offered in communication. Both have expectations towards the reactions of the respective other, and in their own actions, they will typically select reactions anticipating the other's expectations.[1] Thus, communication ensues.

With Erving Goffman (e.g. 1963) and Niklas Luhmann (1995a: pp. 412), interaction is a mode of communication where participants can observe each other as present in a face-to-face situation. This means that any reaction to a communication offer made by one of the participants in the interaction can be observed directly by this participant, and he can in turn react to these reactions immediately. In interactions, spoken language and bodily expressions usually take the role as primary media. Other communication media, such as writing, print, electronic devices, and networked computers, allow for non-interactional modes of communication that do not have to rely on face-to-face situations. This brought about profound changes with regard to how and what can be communicated. Participants do not have to be immediately present for each other any more, which leads to the possibility of asynchronous communication, i.e. modes where communication offers and subsequent reactions are separated and reactions to offers cannot be observed directly.

Nevertheless, interaction remains an important mode of communication. Written letters, telegraphy, the telephone, email and chat systems have not rendered face-to-face communication obsolete. Instead, many new means to organize and to enrich face-to-face communication have been introduced with these media. They enabled participants in interaction to pull in information from sources outside of the immediate realm of the interaction, while also making it easier to arrange situations of face-to-face communication. I made the same observation in the field at the outset of this study, and I will explore in the following chapters how situations of interaction were integrated with non-interactional communication utilizing networked computer systems in the public communication of this specific electronic music scene. But first, to offer a perspective, some remarks on the co-evolution of communication media and forms of society.

1 Luhmann (1995a: pp. 103) introduces this as the concept of double contingency, which is a condition for communication, i.e. a situation in which no participant can predict the communication offers and reactions of the other participants. At first sight, this would make it highly improbable that something like an understanding would be possible at all.

Historically, the first state of what could later be called a society came to life with the introduction of spoken language. All of a sudden, meaning did not have to be immediately apparent any more, as language offered a buffer, a repository for signs (Luhmann 1997a: pp. 205). Thereby, it introduced the first catastrophic overflow of meaning – much more meaning was accessible through language than without language – and the societies confronted with language had to find ways to deal with this. Niklas Luhmann has described these ways of dealing with the overflow of meaning introduced by a new dominant medium as culture forms (Luhmann 1997a: pp. 409). They are mechanisms that allow a society to create order out of what would otherwise be the noise of unstructured, seemingly superfluous meaning. The reach of spoken language was limited to the situation at hand, and only including those who could directly listen and hear what was being said. Nevertheless, the ability to tell stories about actions already brought about what Paul Watzlawick has called metacommunication (Watzlawick / Beavin / Jackson 2003: pp. 53), the ability to communicate about communication. Such an ability would have been enough to place hierarchies that did not count on it in danger. In reaction to this, the groups that now had to deal with the medium of spoken language developed a culture form, specifying their way to handle the uncertainties introduced by the new overflow of meaning. Dirk Baecker (2007b) has suggested boundaries as the culture form of societies having to deal with language, as they serve as references in communication, arbitrarily limiting what could be said and to whom it could be said. The type of society that emerged making use of spoken language was the tribal society (Luhmann 1997b: pp. 634), a form of society that was able to generate order out of the reach of spoken language as its dominant medium of communication.

The next drastic change came about with the introduction of written language, as meaning did not have to be spoken any more in order to be accessible. Instead, with writing, signs of signs became available, later to be called symbols (Luhmann 1997a: pp. 249; Peirce 1955, pp. 98). Again, the overflow of additional meaning in any social situation was catastrophic for the existing structures. A new culture form had to be found that could deal with this. New forms of narratives emerged that could only survive as written communication, such as hierarchies including absent people, as well as stringent and detailed histories. Such innovations were bound together, according to Luhmann, by an overarching, all-encompassing culture form of purpose, or telos, as the Greek named it. The idea of serving a purpose allowed individuals to include themselves in hierarchies that had no immediate control over them, and it supported the idea of linear historical developments. All of this gave rise to what we now commonly refer to as the antique society (Luhmann 1997b: pp. 663).

The next major development in the field of communication media was the invention and mass implementation of the printing press. Although it did not introduce a new meta level in terms of signs of symbols, it drastically increased the accessibility of writing and copying, and with it, the availability of written language (Luhmann 1997a: pp. 291). This made it feasible to include even more participants in communication, participants who were not part of direct face-to-face control. The promise was that with writing, and especially with printed writing, the reach of the writer's control could be expanded to those who had access to the written and printed artifact. All bureaucratic organizations were based on this idea, whether they were industrial complexes or political administrations. This promise came at the loss of the ability to observe if and how the communicational offer made in writing was understood by the recipients, and to react accordingly in a timely manner. Communication based on written and especially printed language could directly address and inform multiple interaction systems. As a way to deal with this, Luhmann (1997a: pp. 410) describes a communicational mode of constant balancing of different outside influences that try to exert control via written statements in each interaction. This translates into a culture form of restlessness that tries to establish equilibria wherever it can (see also Baecker 2007b: p. 16).

Another aspect of this is the potential independence of the spreading of information made possible by the adoption of the printing press, which gave birth to the news press, echoing the close relation with the technology in its name. As a counterpart to the press, Dirk Baecker (2007a: pp. 80) describes the rise of the public, which emerged together with the press as a forum for opinions on the information conveyed by it. Through narration, the public allowed for the outside observation of realms that would otherwise have been private. Different interests, e.g. in sports or religion, led to the formation of different publics. This age of printed written language is what Luhmann describes as the modern society (Luhmann 1997a: pp. 291).

One thing to keep in mind is that neither of these technologies were invented for the massive social impact they eventually had, nor were the new states of society they propelled direct and unavoidable results of their technological innovation. Instead, it took decades or even centuries of social adoption of these technologies for the profound impacts we are now attributing to them retrospectively to emerge. Technological innovation is for the most part a social process, and therefore, we have to see the advancements in technology and in the paradigms of social order as different sides of one and the same, coherent co-evolutionary process.

Advancing on Niklas Luhmann's notions of the different forms of society in different eras of dominant media of communication, Dirk Baecker (e.g. 1997b) has suggested that Peter F. Drucker's Next Society may indeed be the next stage that society is currently entering, ushered in by the new forms of social structuring that have been made possible by the introduction of the computer into almost all aspects of social life. As these stages of society are not discrete switches – one day we have a modern society, the next day the Next Society –, we can only observe the social changes in different kinds of phenomena and draw conclusions from there. Also, no society is ever entirely over: We can still observe phenomena that originate in the cultural form of a tribal society today, and the same is true for phenomena of the antique society. We can only assume that these as well as the modern society will retain their social relevance once we have fully entered what we now call the Next Society. The notions of boundaries, of purposes, and the restless balancing of influences continue to influence how society operates even as new communication media such as the networked computer are introduced and find their way to dominance. Like the other dominant media, the networked computer in all its various forms introduced an overflow of meaning. At the time of writing this study, society already dealt with this overflow in various ways; however, so far no single dominant strategy seems to have gained the upper hand. In this study, I will investigate how new forms of communication are dealt with, and how they are integrated with older, established forms. The scope of the study is limited to a specific field of artistic and cultural practice, and so I will not look for the single, overarching culture form of the Next Society. Instead, I will venture into the realm of one music scene in search of basic communicational structures that are valid in its specific context. Whether or not these structures play a significant role in other contexts of the Next Society will be left up to further investigation.

Nevertheless, when we look at specific music scenes or artistic cultures in general, we have to first understand them as derivatives of the respective form of society they are a part of. In the modern society, for example, the practices of music cultures have to take into account that newspapers and, in its later stage, other mass media will potentially write about it, pulling it into the area of judgment that is the public opinion. This potential informs the way music is being produced, perceived, and talked about in the modern society. It can be seen as a positive chance or as a risk by the participants in artistic and cultural practice, but, as long as they want their culture to be part of society, it cannot be avoided.

At the same time, the printing press gave rise to the mass distribution of musical scores, and thus granted large numbers of musicians and their audiences access to works published in this medium. The mass media newspapers established the role of the professional critic, while separate publications dedicated to music culture featured texts by music journalists. Thereby, the implications of the dominant communication medium of written and printed language created important roles participating in artistic and cultural practice. Their positions have been important ever since. The risk, however, is obvious as well: Critics and music journalists have the power to broadcast an opinion into the public sphere, where it can be hard to counter for musicians or their agents. Therefore, they will try to anticipate and influence the reactions and the publications by these critics and journalists as good as they can.

Niklas Luhmann has suggested to look at cultures as functions of comparisons (Luhmann 1995c). In this view, culture is rooted in lifestyle, as it emerges from the observation of how something is done in different ways. There are different ways to eat, to work, to discuss, and, in the cases we will take a closer look at in this study, to produce and listen to music. Thus, there are eating cultures, work cultures, discourse cultures, and music cultures. The notion that a specific way of doing something could be called a culture stems from the observation that it could also be done differently. In this regard, culture can also be called a memory function of society, as it also allows comparisons between how something is done today and how it has been done before.

If Niklas Luhmann is right about the basic functionality of cultures, then it is home to self-observation and categorization in light of comparisons with similar, but different ways of doing things. This becomes very important in the assessment of works of art and their production. Although we do have working cultures and eating cultures, when we use the term culture on its own, it usually serves as a reference to the practice and assessment of art. Culture, in this sense, seems to mark the culmination of all that is specific to a certain part of society.

Cultural practice, on the other hand, is a term used to describe the social processes surrounding works of art, i.e. their being handled by society, including their presentation and their trade (Luhmann 2000: pp. 133; Baecker 2007c: pp. 315). Therefore, the notion of cultural practice is genuinely social, as all activities that can be subsumed under this term are observable in society. Works of art themselves are different: As artifacts, they are objectifications outside of society. They are ecological phenomena that have to be brought back into communicational processes by means of description, which includes comparison and critique. The production of art, however, is a social process as well. It involves interaction among members of a group, for example, but also the artist's use of instruments for his or her productive work. This, too, can be seen as a social process, where the instrument's designers and builders – guitar luthiers just as well as software programmers – make offers which the artist reacts to.

Unlike cultural practice, artistic practice is primarily focused on aesthetical considerations. That is not to say artistic practice is entirely decoupled from outside influences, as it has to take into account its own contexts as well. Artistic and cultural practice entail each other, as artists can get involved in the cultural activities surrounding their work, while cultural practice regularly references artistic work in discussions, promotional statements, and journalistic writing. The focus of my work in this study is on the interrelations between artistic and cultural practice, investigating how artists and other participants in the field get their actions ordered and react to each others' communicational offerings.

1.1.3 Cultural and Artistic Practice

Following Niklas Luhmann's description of cultural practice as the multitude of possibilities in social processes surrounding works of art (Luhmann 2000: pp. 133), its form can be expected to depend on the standing and the valuation of the works of art it is concerned with in greater processes of society. Especially when we look at economical aspects of cultural practice, the dependence on the valuation of the works becomes clear. Artistic practice, on the other hand, is often surrounded by narratives of freedom and independence. As we will see in the analysis in this study, artists in the field were heavily involved in the cultural practice of promoting their own work, as well as in other areas of similar activity. The realm of artistic practice, where an artist or artist group can focus primarily on aesthetic decisions, had to be carved out of the day-to-day business of cultural practice the artists were involved in.

In music cultures of societies before the modern society, and especially prior to industrialization, music had been offered as a service almost exclusively. Musicians were paid directly for individual compositions or as instrumentalists.[2] Because of this, compositions often had direct dedications, linked to the occasion they were commissioned to be played at. Another model was the institutionalization of musicians' roles, for example employments in orchestras or as orchestra directors. Composers who held such positions could produce their compositions on the side, while fulfilling their duties as directors.[3] Often, in such symbiotic relationships, the reputation of the composer as a producer of original works of art was relevant for the institution's selecting him for the well-paid post of musical director of their opera house or concert orchestra.

With the technological advancements of the industrial age, in the late 19th century, recording the actual sound of a musical performance onto a physical object became technologically possible (Bruch 1983a). For the first time, this created the opportunity to offer music not as a service, but as a commodity. At first, every physical object holding a recording had to be produced individually (Millard 1997: pp. 37). Audio recording had been invented to make office work easier, to save dictations and record telephone calls (Ibid.).

Soon enough, mass copying of recordings was invented as well (Ibid.: pp. 44), opening up the door for an entire industry. Recorded music was now available to the economies of scale, which had been emerging since the beginning of the industrial age. This meant that, as a commodity, recorded music could be sold to as many buyers as it could find, being completely decoupled from the actual musical performance given by the recorded musicians. Economically, this was only possible because the

2 See for example W. A. Mozart's case, described in Gutman 1999.
3 Perhaps most famously Gustav Mahler, described in Müller 1988, pp 80.

price of creating a copy that would sell as a product was low enough in relation to the price it could achieve on the market.

All of this has shifted since computers in their various forms have taken over as the primary devices for music production and listening. In the industrial age, before the pervasion of computers into social life, the production of copies of recorded music was technologically bound to a physical limit. The production of copies for the market required an industrial setup, while the copies which consumers could make – mostly on magnetic tape – degraded significantly with each generation of copying (Bruch 1983b). Recorded music was coupled to the physical substrate of its medium, and thus could be kept scarce by the industry selling it. On computers, however, this coupling to the physical substrate, despite being still existent, gained enormous flexibility. For all practical purposes, recorded music could be treated as pure information on computers.[4]

This development has undermined the notion of recorded music as a commodity. Following the famous expression that "information wants to be free" (Brand 1988: pp. 202), recorded music, once it has become publicly accessible information, cannot be contained in a mode of scarcity any more. Efforts at creating synthetic scarcity, such as digital rights management technologies, have been highly unsuccessful in the marketplace (Stone 2009). Therefore, one of the earliest and clearest changes the advent of the Next Society has brought about was that music could no longer be seen as a commodity (see also Warnke 2011). Similar developments can potentially be expected for all other commodities that can be treated as pure information when handled with computers. Especially movies, journalistic writing, and books seem to be subject to a very similar development. As soon as the information becomes practically decoupled from the physical substrate of its medium, it potentially loses its economical base as a commodity.

I have been using the notion of the flexible coupling of recorded music to the physical substrate of its medium with care, and consciously added the limitation "for all practical purposes", because indeed, even on computers, information is still dependent on a physical substrate (see Warnke 2004). Computers are devices that have to be manufactured, and which require a certain amount of material assembled in a certain way in order to function. This process is deeply embedded into an industrial economy, where a few manufacturers of the basic computer components serve the brand-name companies that focus on the marketing of their devices (see Dean 2007). This industry certainly is an economy of scale, and without it, the proclaimed free exchange of information in the Next Society could not happen. In addition, the tech-

4 For the immediate practical implications of the adoption of the MP3 format, see for example Renner 2004: pp. 138.

nological standards to which computers adhere have always been subject to control efforts by political and industrial entities.[5]

In this context, how does the artistic and cultural process, how do the habitual actions involved with being a musician or running a music label change? How can it be that even though information could be spread and exchanged efficiently using nothing but online media, the live music scene is still alive and thriving, perhaps more than ever? How does a scene integrate artistic musical practice with both online communication and the interaction at live music events? What are the social functions of the different modes of communication employed within these realms? Those are some of the questions I try to cover in this study, focusing on a specific field of artistic and cultural practice, where musicians, label managers, members of the public, and organizations such as music technology manufacturers and music magazines were engaged in various constellations. I try to lay out the details of the products of this quite heterogeneous social action, in the hope to shed some light on the state of the cultural communicational processes within this specific field. One of the starting points for this venture is the suspicion that as the products which made the music part of the cultural industry so successful – the physical releases of recorded music – were becoming less and less important, musicianship became also less about releasing music in the formats dictated by the industry, and instead refocused on its network function as artistry, finding the interest of publics, and drawing audiences. The ability to draw attention within the realm of a certain scene could become a value in itself, which other actors in the vicinity of the musicians could try to utilize for their own interests. Such cases are analyzed in detail in this study, in an attempt to understand the roles fulfilled by the participants, and to lay open the underlying social structures giving the cases their formats. The cases themselves integrate online communication and instances of interactions located in social space.

1.1.4 Social Space

The notion of space has undergone drastic changes in the course of theoretical discourse in philosophy and social sciences. From the Kantian (1770 / 2006) concept of an a priori space that precedes and contains objects and cognition, the opposing view emerged, understanding space as the very product of the placement of objects and subsequent cognitive processes related to them. Many definitions of space are based on phenomena that are understood as tangible, as belonging to a physical reality. Outside of such materialistic assumptions, philosophical and sociological discourse have evolved the concept of social space. I follow this notion, with the focus of my

5 For an overview regarding internet protocols, see Coy 1998.

field research on social phenomena that relate to the concepts of space laid out in the theoretical discourse.

The definition of space as social space has kindled a dynamic discourse of its own within sociology. Perhaps the best known approach is that by Pierre Bourdieu (1985), who suggests a notion of space as arrangement of social elements, and therefore as structure of social action. With reference to art practice, Henri Lefebvre (1974) describes the social production of space and investigates the possibilities to make this very process of production observable – and to disturb it – through artistic re-definitions of spaces. More recently, Martina Löw (2001) suggests a notion of the social construction of space as a synthesis of the locating (Ver-Ortung) of social elements and the establishing of relations between them. In her theory, space has the primary function to allow for the simultaneous construction of places and of embodiments. Following Löw, space could be seen as being a social function in itself, instead of being a container allowing for a function.

Sociological systems theory is only occasionally concerned with the notion of space. Niklas Luhmann (1984; 1995a; 1997a; 1997b) describes space as a substrate of interaction systems, therefore playing a major role in historic societies that were built primarily upon interaction. In the contemporary world society that integrates interaction, organization, and the high-level functional systems of society, interaction itself is still relevant, but only as one type of social formation among others. Thus, space does not have the same relevant function in Luhmann's theory of the functionally differentiated society.[6] Rather, this society allows for the negligence of space for participation in the functional subsystems. Luhmann does not assume space to be a category of meaning next to the categories of the social, the temporal, and the factual (see section 1.3.2). Referring to this, Dirk Baecker (2003a) suggests that space functions as an ordering mechanism for the other categories, and therefore is often left unobserved in the analysis of phenomena in these three dimensions. Markus Schroer (2006) hints at a renaissance of the notion of space in Luhmann's late main work "Die Gesellschaft der Gesellschaft" (Luhmann 1997a; 1997b). According to Schroer (2006: pp. 135), this is primarily connected to the role of success media in the modern society, where a topology of center/periphery defines social status (see also Lippuner 2008). Secondly, the importance of inclusion/exclusion schemes can again be seen as a function of social topology, where space can be used to control who gets included in social action (Stichweh 2005).

The resulting notions of space might seem rather fixed at first sight. However, all types of spatial differentiations described by the authors have to be constructed out of social operations, and can therefore be understood as temporal forms. As such, I

6 For a specific discussion, see also Stichweh 2008.

will follow Dirk Baecker's (2005a) approach to create abstract descriptions of them using George Spencer-Brown's calculus of indications (Spencer-Brown 2008), which I describe in section 1.4.1. From this, I will develop the argument that space can indeed be understood as a network function, where social relations deliberately constitute the possibility of interaction, i.e. communication under the impression of mutual observation.

1.2 Electronic Musicians in the Age of Networks

In the following sections, I will investigate the changes in production and distribution methods that have profoundly influenced how artistic and cultural practice operated in the field.

1.2.1 Computers: Ubiquitous Production Machines

The evolution of computer technology has introduced enormous changes into the landscape of semi-professional and professional music production. Although the basic technological components involved in recording music have remained almost unchanged over the years, their availability to amateurs and semi-professionals with budget restrictions has increased dramatically.

Technological innovation has a long history of making a variety of sounds available at lower and lower efforts. Pipe and reed organs, for example, were designed to emulate a whole brass, reed, or even string section of an ensemble, thus replacing the manual work of several players with the interpretation by just one organist (Ashdown Audsley 1988: pp. 465; Harenberg 1999). However, although these instruments may have been designed with their capabilities at emulating existing tonal and sonic possibilities in mind, this has not become their main function in artistic practice. Instead, they have inspired composers to write music dedicated to the specifics of these instruments, and thus, both instruments have amassed a huge variety of literature in a broad selection of musical genres.

Electronic music as a genre is directly linked to the technology required to make electronic sounds. Again, the first electronic devices that were being used as musical instruments in their own right were not designed for this task, but were rather a part of the vast array of technological inventions that had been sparked by the development of radio technology. Radio had its first use in military communications, before it became available for civil use and, eventually, also came into the hands of musicians (Kittler 1986). Electronic music developed into a variety of genres over the course of the 20th century, spanning from abstract, non-repetitive music to pattern-based minimal and techno music, in addition assimilating all harmonic and rhythmic paradigms that had established a cultural presence before the inception of electronic sound generation.

The digital computer became available to a wider institutional audience in the late 1940s, yet it took two decades before it was (mis)used for musical purposes (Ruschkowski 1998: pp. 266). Lejaren Hiller, employed at the University of Illinois, used his university's mainframe computer to calculate the score for his Illiac Suite based on probability values in Markov chains (Ibid.). This composition was still played by human players using traditional acoustic instruments, as the direct synthesis of sound was not yet possible with the computers of this era. The computer scientist Max Mathews pioneered the area of direct sound synthesis in the late 1950s (Ibid.: pp. 287), but it would still take more than ten years until computers could generate even simple sounds in realtime (Ibid.: pp. 292). Until the 1990s, expensive dedicated computer hardware was required to synthesize sounds with computers.

Another string of technological innovation developed the ability to record and play back recordings of concrete sound as "samples" from a keyboard (Ruschkowski 1998: pp. 336). This allowed for the recording of individual instrument voices that could then be played melodically without having the instrument and its player present. While devices like the Mellotron (Brice 2001: pp. 108), achieving this using analog-mechanical technology, remained largely experimental and exclusive, the computer made this ability available to the broad mainstream of musicians. At first, the devices allowing for the immediate and direct playback of samples were mainly specialized computers, such as the Fairlight system or other dedicated hardware "samplers" (Ruschkowski 1998: pp. 355). Again, as with the direct synthesis of sound, the revolution of availability in the mass market happened in the 1990s, when, for the first time, the playback of sampled sound in good quality became possible on general-purpose personal computers (Walker 1998b). From then on, no dedicated and expensive hardware was required any more, and the personal computer that many musicians had access to anyways could now be used as a full-featured, yet self-contained music production device. The features were now a function of software packages that could be loaded onto any computer.

While this already helped to bring the cost of a good-quality music recording and production system down significantly, the evolution did not stop there. Music recording and production software became more and more capable over the years, adding advanced functionality that could not be replicated with analog or mechanical devices any more. At the same time, prices for recording and production software packages decreased considerably over the years. One of the widely used production softwares by the time of research, Apple Inc.'s "Logic Studio" (Apple 2011a), started out in the late 1980s as a software built by Emagic, a German company, to arrange control data for dedicated audio hardware, and, upon integration of the new developments in computer-based audio production that came about in the 1990s, eventually evolved into a self-contained system, meaning that no other software was needed for full-blown music productions (P. White 1995). A capable personal computer and adequate loudspeakers were still required, as were good microphones in case acoustic instruments or the human voice were to be recorded. The price of Logic's full version had remained at a steady level throughout different versions after reaching a certain mature feature set, i.e. becoming a full, self-contained music production solution. This price point remained at around 1,000 EUR while the software was still produced independently by the company its inventors built (Wherry 2007). In 2002, Apple Inc. bought Emagic and continued to employ most of the development and management team (Bell / Wherry 2002). Two versions under the reign of Apple later, version 8 was released, and its retail price was halved (Wherry 2007). The new price point of 500 EUR meant that many more musicians were able to afford the new version. Already since version 6, Logic Studio did not run on computers by other manufacturers than Apple any more (P. White 2003), so the musicians that were enticed to buy into Logic Studio at the new low price point had to either invest in a new Apple computer, or, if they already had one, their choice of this platform now became a dependency.

With the know-how Apple had bought by acquiring Emagic, the company also developed the software "GarageBand", a music production and recording package aimed at beginners and hobby musicians (Walker 2006). This software shipped for free with every new Apple desktop or laptop computer as part of Mac OS's "iLife" package (Apple 2011b). While GarageBand did not incorporate many of the features that professional users relied on, and which they found in Logic Studio, it came to be recognized as an easy-to-use, yet adequately capable software that offered much of the possibilities of computer-based music production essentially for free – if the musician owned an Apple computer. On the competing Windows platform, free software packages did not match the capabilities of Apple's GarageBand. On the other hand, inexpensive solutions were available (Kremp 2006), and the use of illegal software was much more common among users of Windows PCs.

The widespread availability of key production methods to the mainstream of musicians has been called a "democratization" (e.g. Price 2008). After the price reduction for Apple's version of Logic Studio, other manufacturers reacted and reduced the retail prices for their software packages significantly. This also benefited the users of Windows PCs, as most of the other products continued to work cross-platform. At the time of research, the major full-featured software packages for music production were available in a price range between 300 and 600 EUR (Thomann 2011). Since then, the price of the full-featured Logic Pro has continued to fall even further (Apple 2013). While this was a considerable difference to the free-with-computer-purchase offering of GarageBand, these software packages were still much less of an investment than previous versions, or even a setup consisting of dedicated hardware. The cost for such hardware-based systems of amateur or semi-professional quality typically ranged in the tenths of thousands of dollars or Euros, while the equipment for a truly professional-grade studio could not be had for less than one hundred thousand dollars or Euros, not factoring in the construction of acoustically optimized rooms. Many functions of the professional-grade studio could now be performed in the ~500 EUR software packages, which gave them a potential to function as social equalizers, or, in other words, really foster the democratization of music production. And indeed, the large studios widely experienced economical challenges from the 1990s onward, with several of them having to close entirely or slim down their operations.[7]

At the same time, some of the larger studios were able to continue working successfully. This is especially true for those studios that managed to build a strong identity for themselves, such as Abbey Road Studios in London or Hansa Studios in Berlin (Abbey Road 2012; Hansa Tonstudio 2012). In both cases, the studios were able to focus public attention on their history, with legendary recordings by the Beatles having been produced at Abbey Road, or David Bowie's album productions at Hansa. Such studios with a respected name were regularly presented in the relevant publications (see for example Sound On Sound 2012), and they were frequented by many of the musicians who had benefited from the so-called democratization of music technology. The main difference was that these were not full productions on site any more, where musicians would go into the studio for weeks or even months, fine-tuning their compositions in full-scale pre-productions. Instead, the majority of musicians now booked these studios only for very specific parts of the entire production process, especially for parts where either high-end equipment could not be substituted by software, or where special know-how of a studio operator was desired (Olivarez-Giles 2009). The first case included amenities such as the availability of an excellent recording room, perhaps coupled with a selection of top quality vintage microphones for the recording of voice or instruments (Abbey Road 2012). The second case could be observed mostly in later stages of a production process, and especially when it came to mastering, where the final changes were applied to the production, which nevertheless could have a great effect on its overall sound (Katz 2007). At this stage, knowledge of the fine details of the composition of a good overall sound was crucial, and some also thought it beneficial to have someone else do the mastering (P1175: 80), as the musicians or original producers themselves were usually too attached to the mix they had produced to alter it drastically (Herrmann 2006). Another aspect that brought clients into the remaining full-size professional studios was that, for mastering purposes, an excellent monitoring system consisting of a set of high-end studio loudspeakers and

7 For examples from the Los Angeles area, see Olivarez-Giles 2009.

amplifiers was highly desirable. It did not end with the availability of the technological components, though. The room in which the loudspeakers were placed had to be carefully designed to match them and the position from which the mastering engineer and the customers could listen and monitor the sound of the production. In addition, the experience of the mastering engineer, who may have heard thousands of productions on this very monitoring system, was an invaluable asset in the assessment of the fine details of a mix.

In my researched field, the owner of the label I observed usually invited the artists to a mastering session at Dubplates & Mastering, a dedicated mastering studio near Kottbusser Tor in Berlin that had a very good reputation especially with artists in the field of electronica, but also in the area of the typical Berlin techno style (Herrmann 2006). Next door from the studio was the legendary record store Hardwax, a hallmark in the Berlin techno scene. The store was owned by the former label heads of the dub techno label Basic Channel, which had been among the actors dominating the Berlin techno scene in the 1990s (Stenton 2006).

1.2.2 A Typical Production Setup

During the time of data collection, in the years between the beginning of 2007 and the end of 2010, the so-called democratization of music production setups had already reached a proficient level of maturity. Most of the available software packages had high version numbers, and additional hardware to control the software had begun to break musicians free from the tedious task of performing some of the most repetitive functions in their software systems with the computer's regular mouse and keyboard.

While the typical computer-based music production setup would have included a desktop computer in the 1990s, this changed more and more to incorporating laptop computers in the early 2000s. The typical setups I observed with the artists in the field involved a laptop – mostly a model made by Apple – as well as a dedicated external audio interface and a controller keyboard that combined anywhere from one to four octaves of traditional piano keys with at least eight knob dials. These dials could be used to control continuous parameters inside the software, such as volume levels or the threshold points of sound filters. In addition, many of the musicians used one or two dedicated pieces of non-computer music hardware, which they featured prominently both on stage and in their home studios. These devices could be analog synthesizers, or even acoustic instruments, such as a guitar. What joined all these devices was that they allowed for enhanced interactivity with the audience, and they all had something narratively "special" to them (P3178).

On the software side, most of the musicians I observed used a software by the Berlin-based company Ableton as a basis of their performances. Aptly named "Live", this software had started out as a system to arrange audio loops (Future Music 2011). The genuine innovation that Ableton Live brought to the table was that it broke with the traditional time-based linearity of arrangement software, which had dominated as a paradigm ever since the continuous recording or playback techniques of mechanical pianos, Edison's wax cylinders, record inscription systems, or tape recorders (Bruch 1983a; Bruch 1983b). This paradigm had remained in a dominant position even as the technological possibilities of computer-based music production lifted its technologically determined necessity. Ableton Live was the first software that became successful in breaking with this paradigm, and instead offering immediate access to all the loops that were preselected for a performance. The layout was in the form of a spreadsheet, and loops were represented visually as blocks that could be clicked to start their playback.

A key feature for the prevalent pattern-based music styles of Ableton Live's users was the automatic sync function: In order to match new pattern loops to those that were already playing, the user did not have to manually start the playback at the correct time, rather, the software determined when to start the playback so that the rhythm of the new loops was synchronized (Future Music 2011). This seemingly simple functionality had been impossible to implement without computers.

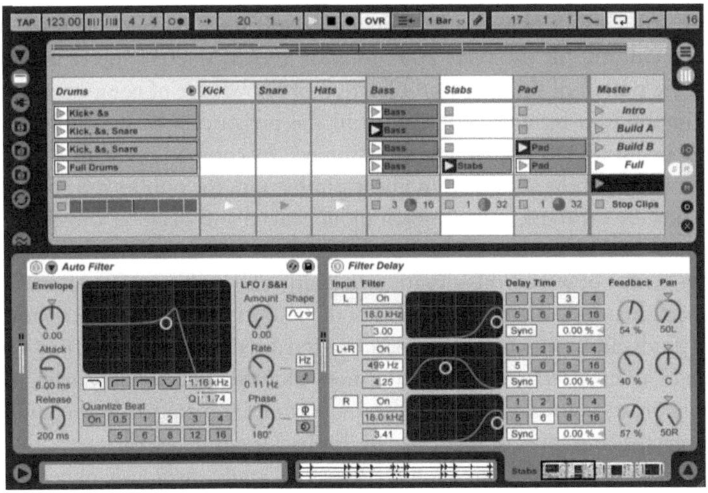

Screenshot of Ableton Live 8 (Archive FG).

Almost all of the musicians I observed were heavy users of Ableton Live. There was, however, a distinction between software packages like Logic Studio and Ableton Live:

Although Ableton Live had gained almost all of the core functions of the full-scale production systems, it was not regarded as a true alternative to these systems. There was a widespread opinion among musicians that described Ableton Live's audio quality as inferior to that of the older systems (documented e.g. on Gearslutz 2011), and, while they relied on Ableton Live for huge parts of their live performances in front of audiences, many musicians would not use it to produce music for public release. The typical setup of a musician in this scene would therefore incorporate Ableton Live for performance aspects, and at least one other package, often Apple's Logic Studio, for production tasks.

Usually, these different software packages were not installed on separate computers, but the musicians often used one laptop computer for all music-related tasks. As this computer was at the heart of their setup, there was not much difference between production and performance setups any more. Most parts of the production setup were mobile anyway, and so the musician could bring the setup he was most accustomed to onto the stage.

1.2.3 Producer Publics

The percentage of people who have had some music education and/or owned an instrument which they played at least once a month was anywhere between 30-50% in Western cultures for the years 2007 to 2009 (NAMM 2011: pp. 136). Merging this with the notion of the broad proliferation of knowledge of computer-based production methods, a fundamental change in the preconditions that influenced any judgment in the public sphere can be assumed: In comparison with the situation before the advent of the computer in music production, the publics musicians catered to could now be expected to have much more general and detailed knowledge of the technologies used by the musicians.

In the field, I observed this situation in nearly all instances of publics. At events hosting performances, a large proportion of the visitors I knew had some background in music production, which could in part be accredited to my network position as an employee of a music technology manufacturer. However, through my acquaintances, I was more or less connected with the largest part of the members of the public visiting these events, and most of them shared this background as well.

Computers had made production methods that could previously only be accessed in professional – and expensive – studios readily available to musicians at all levels of professionalism. As the software packages matured, hobby musicians as well as music educators and students became an increasingly interesting target group for software manufacturers looking to make use of the knowledge they had built and expand their sales potential. Almost all of the manufacturers of professional production systems released separate versions with a limited feature set – leaving out the features only required by professionals – at a smaller price (e.g. Ableton 2011; Apple 2011d). In addition, music software was widely proliferated through illegal copying among amateurs (IMSTA 2011).

The market for music production products could generally be segmented into the areas of professionals, semi-professionals or "enthusiasts", and amateurs or hobby musicians (Grote / Klauer / Thoma / Werner 2011). The professionals were the only group that earned all or the largest part of their living with the production of music. Most of them had a studio, although the term "studio" did not necessarily refer to multi-room arrangements with separated spaces for mixing and acoustic recording; rather, in many cases it referred to a single room with good acoustics and a high-end technical setup, of which the computer was often the centerpiece. If high-quality acoustic recordings needed to be done, they could be accomplished using facilities that were either shared with other studio professionals or that were rented per day.

The semi-professionals or enthusiasts earned most or all of their income from other sources than music production, but their methods copied those of the professionals. They, too, often had dedicated rooms at their disposal, and an advanced technical setup – although not necessarily as high-end as that of a professional – was a basic requirement for this group. However, most of them did not have dedicated rooms for acoustic recordings. If they wanted to record vocals or acoustic or electro-acoustic instruments, they would usually do that in the same room with their technical setup. The setup of a semi-professional was often even more centered around the computer than that of a professional, because a professional usually had more dedicated hardware devices with specific functionalities, which the semi-professional could mirror in pieces of computer software, without the need to make the often significant investment in additional hardware gear. The main difference between the professionals and the semi-professionals or enthusiasts was that the professionals actually followed a release schedule, while the enthusiasts worked on their material in the time they were free from other work, releasing music, if at all, whenever they themselves were happy with it.

The third group in the market were the amateurs, or hobby musicians. They differed from the other groups in that they earned no money from music, and also did not delve into production methods with the goal of releasing music to the public. Instead, they produced the music for their own enjoyment, sometimes also for that of their family and friends. If the latter was the case, the line separating a hobby musician and a semi-professional providing some of his music for free could sometimes blur, since both often used the same methods for distribution: MySpace, Facebook, and YouTube. In terms of their technical setup, the hobby musicians typically used an instrument they had learned to play in the past in conjunction with a personal computer they owned anyway, adding an entry-level external audio interface in order to be able to make recordings of their instruments or their voice.

Among all of the groups, music educators were increasingly integrating computer-based methods into their teaching curriculum. This led to music students potentially getting in touch with the uses of computers in music at a relatively early stage. For this reason, music educators were a valued target group for the music software manufacturers, as the products they used could be expected to be used by many amateurs, future semi-professionals, or even professionals.

A new level of wide availability of music production methods was reached when Apple started to ship a free copy of its low-end music software package GarageBand in 2004 preinstalled on every computer they sold (Pogue 2004; Walker 2006). This put many of the basic methods of computer-based music production into the hands of non-musicians, who were not per se interested in these methods, but who would, at least to a large extent, learn about these methods through trying out their computers. By this time, GarageBand had already become a benchmark for entry-level music production software. Other software programs with a smaller feature set existed, but they mostly catered to a niche of users with special needs. Any software product that was designed to support the production of a broad variety of music styles and genres, including the recording of vocals and acoustic instruments – provided the necessary external hardware was available – had to be positioned against GarageBand, especially if it was sold commercially. Even though GarageBand was only available on Apple computers, its effect as a benchmark reached across into the realm of the Windows platform.

GarageBand, however, did not hinder the further development of low-end music production software by Apple's competitors. If a hobby musician or music student wanted to record vocals or an acoustic or electric guitar, for example, they needed to buy an audio interface in the form of a dedicated hardware extension to their computers. Catering to these low-end markets, manufacturers produced a large variety of products in all price ranges. Notably, many of these products, especially those targeting beginners, were bundled with an entry-level version of a semi-professional music production software package (IMSTA 2011). This way, almost everyone interested in producing music on a computer had access to the basic set of features in this area, often in the form of two or more separate software programs that shipped together with pieces of hardware. Interestingly, even in the face of a market that was largely saturated, innovative new products catering to the semi-professionals managed to carve a niche for themselves, partly through technological advancements, partly through aggressive pricing models.[8]

8 A good example is the audio workstation software Reaper, described in Walker 2007.

1.3 Communicating About Music

In this study, the focus is on the phenomena of artistic and cultural practice that could be observed in a variety of social situations. Aesthetical considerations are taken into account whenever their embeddedness in a social situation made them accessible for observation.

1.3.1 What Can and Cannot be Said About Music?

Discussions about music usually involve a great number of adjectives, such as "heavy", "light", "dark", "mellow", etc. These are all means to distinguish musical styles via categorizations. However, when it comes to the descriptions of feelings that music evokes, they are poor and faint images of what is presumably experienced in the individual mind. The words and definitions we have regarding music hint at potentially great effects that music can have on the mind. Yet, we cannot actually communicate these effects. If we follow sociological systems theory, the psychic system of the mind and the social system of communication are operationally closed for each other (see for example Luhmann 1995a: pp. 14). The words we can use, even when enriched with non-verbal information, such as the tone of our voices or our facial expressions, are always generalizations and cannot express the apparently existent true depth of the perception of music. Actual modes of perception cannot be communicated, which also means that their very existence can neither be verified, nor ruled out entirely.

Therefore, for all practical considerations in communication, there is no right or wrong in how music can be perceived. If a group wishes to agree on certain features of perception, it has to reach this agreement in communication. Its members have to find external terms that can be observed and understood, thereby necessarily including a level of generalization. Such processes can lead to more or less formal structures. Dancing, for example, has rather formal terms, involving generalized rhythmical or choreographed body movement, while descriptions in language such as "mellow" or "deep" have much less formal implications.

What follows from this is that processes of the mind and processes of communication have to be considered as separate. Niklas Luhmann (1995a: pp. 255) has described exactly this situation, and suggested to look at minds and processes of communication as separate operational systems: On the one hand, psychic systems, i.e. individual minds, and on the other, social systems, consisting of communicative processes. Such systems are autopoietic, meaning that they reproduce their own elements and do not import information from the outside. They can, however, be disturbed by outside occurrences, and then find internal representations for the processes they assume are going on outside of themselves, causing the disturbance. In the case of music perception, the descriptions we have in communication to grasp individual perception – e.g. "harsh", "soft", "happy" – are such representations. They are estimations, and they can be – and regularly are – contradicted by others. It may be common for communication to be disturbed by psychic systems, but there is nothing deterministic in this relation. It remains a disturbance from the outside that communication has to deal with, but by its own means and on its own terms. This works the other way around as well: Psychic systems have to deal with disturbances which they perceive as being induced by communication, the realm of the social. Yet they can never be entirely sure whether there really is communication, or if the disturbances are caused by other processes. Thus, whenever we analyze social phenomena, we take up a perspective of observation that cannot be proven right, or even existing. It is at the reader's discretion to either follow this perspective or object to it.

Since this writing in anticipation of your reading is part of communication, I cannot venture into considerations of how the music that the artists produce is being perceived by specific individual minds. All I can discuss is what can be observed in communication: Indications signifying that perception has taken place at all, and indications signifying how it went. Therefore, the frame of reference for my observations and analysis is communication and its multiple and complex phenomena. I will not try to draw conclusions about psychic systems beyond the assumption that their processes cannot be observed directly within communication.

However, without asserting to be able to observe or understand the actual individual perception of music among members of its audience, we can look at aesthetic choices made by the artists in our field, and the cultural semantics that go along with them, either explicitly or implicitly. Then, it becomes interesting how certain aesthetic choices are dealt with in concrete performances. For example, we can observe a focus on hip hop beats in the productions by some of the artists in our field (see sections 3.1.2 and 4.1.4). The aesthetic choice to use these beats is then countered by the choice of sounds with which to build them.

In this study, I will rely on my own account of perceptions that cannot necessarily be observed directly within communication, either. For example, I will share observations on whether music playback was loud or unusually quiet in certain situations. I will attempt to ground such accounts in observations of their disturbances to communication in general, such as loud music suppressing the ability to hold conversations in a room. Similarly, I will analyze the interactions between musicians as they performed on stage, and try to draw some careful conclusions on aesthetic considerations in the artistic practice carried out in the respective situations.

1.3.2 Art and Meaning

Communication has to somehow limit what can possibly be understood as communication, otherwise it would run the risk of drowning in noise. Through this limitation, we can anticipate that what is being communicated may actually and against all odds have a chance of being understood (Luhmann 1995a: pp. 107). In any medium of communication, there is redundancy, which is necessary to maintain a basic structure on which actual information can build. In the case of language, this redundancy can be found in both words as combinations of letters that get used over and over again, and in grammar as combinations of words that get used over and over again. From this, sentences can arise that are more flexible to carry fresh, i.e. less redundant information. However, the vast majority of accounts of novelty in communication are handled via recombinations of existing elements. New names can be assigned to phenomena, but have to be introduced using known elements in order to assume a place in communication.

Niklas Luhmann (1995a: pp. 59) has described the relation between current, actual offerings of utterances, information, and what else could potentially be offered as meaning. Furthermore, he has suggested to look at what is actually communicated in relation to the situation in which it is being communicated and what is possible in this situation, as the relation of medium and form. The potentialities offered by the specific social configuration of a situation serve as medium for the actual form the communicational process takes on in this situation. Reaching back to Fritz Heider's (1926 / 2005) notion of coupling of elements to construct a thing, actual communication happens in forms that are constructed out of the potentials available in meaning. These forms include references that reach beyond what they actually express, e.g. to what is intended by their statement, and what is negated by it. These implicit references provoke the next communicational steps, where either the same participant or another participant needs to make a selection of some aspect of the previous form and react to it.

Niklas Luhmann (1995a: p. 75) has further suggested that meaning can be differentiated into three dimensions: the factual, the social, and the temporal. Actual forms in communication are always forms in at least one of these dimensions, separating on the lowest level areas of social, factual, or temporal meaning. On the higher levels of social constructions, such distinctions into the separate dimensions of meaning are not always apparent, yet, following Luhmann, they can be made out in the analysis of the communicational phenomena at hand. Meaning, then, is the medium of all communication, with its forms consisting of factual, social, and temporal statements.

As a medium, meaning remains transparent, though, and can never be observed in its entirety, especially as it is a dynamic potentiality that continuously integrates novelty. Meaning is, as communication goes on, constantly developed further. The elements and their possible forms are not static sets, but rather evolve dynamically. The development of meaning has its own ways to introduce new elements: Metaphors, for example, can serve as a means to introduce definitions of new disturbances into communication by relating them to similar forms (Lakoff / Johnson 1996). We can observe this happening regularly in communication about music and technology, for example. I have described in section 1.2 how music production technology regularly was designed to resemble already established workflows. A development of meaning can take an ongoing process of society dealing with new disturbances, in this case the implications of using computers in music production, and develop means to deal with these disturbances, i.e. discuss them, in the available media of communication. Such a process, however, can only happen gradually and over time.

Whenever I refer to art or music as cultural scenes, it is meant as a reference not to specific works of art or music, but to communication that at least in part describes either the perception of such works or the modes and contexts of their production. Niklas Luhmann (2000) has described this as a system of its own, as communication about and around art builds up its own dedicated elements of meaning to be re-used and developed further over time. One of the core theses is that communication about art is coded in the sense that all communication offers having art as a theme are evaluated with regard to the works fitting or not fitting the cultural context they are situated in (Luhmann 2000: pp. 118). This makes the social processes surrounding art sensitive to implausible placements of works in non-fitting contexts, but it also empowers cultural practice to maintain strict regimes of judgment in the evaluation and critique of works of art and their production.

1.4 Preconditions for Observation

The observations that serve as the basis of all analyses in this study came about in many different situations and contexts. In the following section, I will detail the preconditions and theoretical considerations that influenced my empirical work.

1.4.1 The Notion of Distinction

We begin with the notion of distinction. This notion is as simple as it is complex, and it will provide a veritable outset for the observations and analyses we undertake. Distinction is simple, because all it denotes is the act of separating something from that which it is not. It allows us to separate and differentiate things, for example by distinguishing a certain record by our favorite artist from all the similar recordings, that are close to it, but just not quite the same. Distinction is the introduction of a divide within something that was heretofore in unity, even if this unity was empty. This happens, for example, when we have to explain to someone the differences between two performances by an artist, who that someone did not even know existed. Distinction, however, is also complex, as it implies that one side of the distinction has to be marked, i.e. indicated, in order to be able to separate it from everything it is not. Such a distinction separating an indication on one of its sides from the unspecified other side can serve as a sign for that which it indicates. Sticking with the example of the music release, a new album has to be named and actively separated from the previous releases by the artist in order to be successfully marketed. The situation gets more and more complex as more than one distinction and indication is involved – different albums have to be distinguished from one another, and, adding an additional level of complexity, they also relate to each other in distinguishably different ways. The traditional brick-and-mortar record store is a representation of this complexity, where only experts really know their way around in the depths of the cases with hundreds of releases from a variety of labels and in many different styles.

I use the notion of distinction and indication as the basis of my analysis, because it provides me with a means to observe processes below the level of actions. Distinctions and indications make up the preconditions from which we can construct actions, relations, and all other social phenomena. They will enable us to look beyond dominant memes in the field, and provide the building blocks for my attempts at modeling the basic processes of communication that are observable here.

To gain an understanding of how the interplay of distinctions works in a very general way, I will utilize the theoretical basis laid out by George Spencer-Brown. In his book "Laws of Form" (Spencer-Brown 1972 / 2008), he attempts nothing less than a fundamental rebuilding of logic and mathematics, based on the notion of distinction. Since this undertaking requires the formulation of basic rules on how we can deal with distinctions, it provides us with the necessary means at the outset of our analysis in the realm of the social world. A distinction can be represented as follows:

$$\text{distinction} = \;\rceil\;.$$

Form equation 1.4.1.a: The form of distinction.

Spencer-Brown starts with the notions of distinction and indication already in place, i.e. he takes both for granted as ideas and does not deduct them from elsewhere (Spencer-Brown 2008: p. 1). Indeed, this would be impossible in itself, because there is no way to define a distinction without drawing one, nor without already implying an indication, as the fabrication of a specification against the backdrop of unspecific semantics is the very nature of a definition. Spencer-Brown does, however, explicate the notion of distinction in a more functional definition, stating that "distinction is perfect continence" (Ibid.), meaning that everything that belongs to either one of the sides is indeed completely framed by this distinction, and completely separated from the other side. In the equation above, we can point to the inside of the distinction, or to the outside, thereby specifying it – marking it with the term inside or outside – and thus creating an indication.

The distinction shown above is a simple instance of a form. A distinction form is a cleavage in something that had been in unity before. The distinction form, when it has been introduced, consists of an inside and an outside, and the cross separating the two sides. The cross can serve three functions: As a mark, it defines the inside of the form and thereby its realm in the world, creating an indication. As a tie, by separating the inside and the outside, it keeps both connected as well, as they both have to have something in common from where they can be separated. Finally, it serves as a call, enticing one to cross over from its inside to its outside, or back to its inside.

In addition, the distinction form itself is written on a background of its own, in the case of this study, white spaces on pages, framed by text. This again marks a difference, e.g. between text and the areas where the arrangements of distinctions are presented. In other cases, the backgrounds could be blackboards or slates of stone. George Spencer-Brown calls the separation between the background of the form and everything that is not the background of the form the "unwritten cross" (Spencer-Brown 2008: p. 6). Every form is framed by an unwritten cross. If we make the unwritten cross explicit, i.e. write the heretofore unwritten cross, it then becomes part of a new form, which again is framed by an unwritten cross. In the case of this study, when we write the cross that separates the background of a form from the text, then the cross between this study and everything that is not this study would be the unwritten cross framing the new form. This process could be continued eternally and for every conceivable form. Thus, every form is framed by an infinite number of unwritten crosses.

Two things can happen with distinctions: They can be used over again, or both sides of one distinction can themselves be included on one side of another distinction. These two possibilities are Spencer-Brown's Laws of Form. The first possibility, using a distinction over again, is named the Law of Calling. It states that "the value of a call made again is the value of the call" (Spencer-Brown 2008: p. 2), meaning that a mere repetition of a distinction does not change what is on both of its sides.

Form equation 1.4.1.b: The Law of Calling: The value of a call made again is the value of the call (Spencer-Brown 2008: p. 2).

This may appear counterintuitive, mostly because perception and communication rarely consciously employ singular distinctions, but rather usually rely on complex nested structures of distinctions. Reduced to one distinction, such as "art" distinguished from everything that is not art, this description may fit all or almost all works exhibited in a gallery in the very same way. With only this one distinction at hand, we could not distinguish between different works of art, because they would all just be "art" as opposed to "not art". Of course, this is an important distinction in the discourse about works of art, but it is not enough to operate in a network that deals with works of art. There, further distinctions are necessary to achieve various classifications and allow for conflicting perspectives without entirely negating that a given work is indeed art. However, further distinctions that might be used to specify a definition do not change the value of the basic distinction, in our case art / not art.

$\text{art} = \overline{\text{art}}\rceil\ \text{not art}$

Form equation 1.4.1.c: Art as the distinction of art from everything that is not art.

$\text{art} = \overline{\text{art}}\rceil\ \overline{\text{art}}\rceil\ \overline{\text{art}}\rceil\ \overline{\text{art}}\rceil\ \text{not art}$

Form equation 1.4.1.d: The distinction of art from everything that is not art used over and over and over again.

Crossing a distinction means to look at it from its other side. In our case, this would shift the focus to everything that is not art, with the knowledge that art needs to be distinguishable in order to get this focus. Crossing, just like calling, is a temporal process, as the two sides of a distinction can never be focused on at the same time, but only in successive steps. Thus, time is created. Nevertheless, even though a distinction may seem to primarily separate its sides, it also creates a relation between them, making a statement that the two sides are in some way similar enough to be distinguished – even if their sole similarity is being part of the same world.

The Law of Crossing states that crossing a distinction twice cancels it (Spencer-Brown 2008: p. 2). In our case, if we separate art from everything that is not art, then look at the outside of that which is not art and find out that what we had been referencing as "not art" was in fact conceived of in the context of art, the distinction in the middle can be canceled. This could for example be the case when we find out that the exhibition we had been walking through was not about the individual paintings on the wall, but instead the whole exhibition had been planned as a happening, an art performance in itself, with the visitors playing a part in it. In this case, the gallery space, even the cloakroom and the restrooms, and all the social interaction happening there, were not "not art", but indeed art. We would cross the same distinction we had made before between the paintings and the walls again, and thus it would have to be canceled.

$$\left.\overline{\left.\overline{\;\;}\right|}\right| \; = \quad .$$

Form equation 1.4.1.e: The Law of Crossing: The value of a crossing made again is not the value of the crossing (Spencer-Brown 2008: pp. 2, 5).

1.4.2 A Calculus of the Social

It is important to note that we are using Spencer-Brown's calculus in a context of social inquiry, not in a mathematical sense. In the conception of his calculus, Spencer-Brown does not use elements of natural language inside form arrangements. However, in Appendix 6 (Spencer-Brown 2008: pp. 181), he suggests exactly the kind of utilization we are employing here. The use of form arrangements in sociological theory was introduced by Niklas Luhmann (1995a: pp. 176; 1997a: pp. 60) to demonstrate the basic distinction between system and environment; a distinction that is the essential precondition for any system to gain existence. Dirk Baecker (2005a) then pioneered the use of form arrangements to demonstrate differentiation within the social system that is society. The elements of natural language used in the form arrangements can be seen as variables in a mathematical sense, being placeholders for actual definitions. This understanding is important, as language allows us to keep the exact definition of the terms we use vague, and generalize as we communicate. An exact definition would have to be made explicit by an observer, and would in any case have to rely on further generalizations. Any definition would have to leave at least some of the contexts in our observation out of the focus. Thus, generalizations serve communication well, and they ensure that observers do not have to expose themselves in detailed definitions of each and every term they use. Such a requirement would likely make communication too complex to operate, and all social activity would stall in total gridlock.

Also, as a variable in the mathematical sense, the term "art" can take on any value that is allowed in the calculus. However, the only value possible in the calculus introduced by Spencer-Brown is the marked state (Spencer-Brown 2008: p. 3). Thus, while any variable using language refers to further definitions that lay outside the realm of the form at hand, with Spencer-Brown we have to presuppose that it consists of further differentiation structures that can theoretically be reduced to their state being either marked or unmarked, using the methods stated in the Laws of Form. However, such a process, when executed on a definition from social language, would give up relevant information with every step, reducing complexity until, at the end, the answer whether art can be reduced to the marked or the unmarked state is completely irrelevant. It is important to note that this is indeed only one value, the mark, which can be present or absent. Since we are discussing this matter in language, we can only resort to positive statements, and only hint towards the void that is the unmarked state.

Any hypothetical outcome of such a reduction that gets reintroduced into social processes, e.g. by discussing the result being either the marked or the unmarked state, would change the process of its own calculation, in our example because the notion of art would have to take this calculation into account. For the participants, it would become part of the definition of art, thereby potentially changing the outcome in unpredictable ways. Any attempts at factoring in this uncertainty would just add to it. Therefore, I will not venture into attempts at reducing definitions of variables to a single state, as I see the information value of definitions in finding out more about the structure of interrelated distinctions used in the field. This notion of the variables does, however, do away with the idea of differentiating between syntax and semantic in the form arrangements. Variables are embedded in nested structures of distinctions, yet they are themselves nothing but placeholders for other nested structures of distinctions.

Keeping this context in mind, it is very well possible to understand the analysis of distinctions in social phenomena as the reconstruction of calculations in the realm of the social. For example, we can start with a simple distinction:

$$a = \overline{a\,|}$$

Form equation 1.4.2.a: a as the distinction of a from everything that is not a.

Observing *a* as the distinction of *a* from everything that is not *a* can serve as the first step in further analysis. We can carve out further areas to indicate, and to separate from everything they are not. However, in this process, we have to respect *a*, since we already indicated it. If we did not want to refer to it in our further analysis, we would have to switch to a new observation altogether, and create a new equation for it. As we expand our equation, *a* is always a reference, which can be further expanded on. For example, we can introduce *b* as a name for everything that is not *a*:

$$a = \overline{a\,|}\; b$$

Form equation 1.4.2.b: a as the distinction from everything that is not a, which is b.

Naming the outside *b* does not specify it in any way, though. It is simply a synonym for "everything that is not *a*", not meaning anything specific that is not *a*, but also something else. If we want to specify what *b* is, we need to separate it from everything that is not *b*, while *b* still remains the context of *a*:

$$c = \overline{\overline{a}\rceil\, b}\rceil$$

Form equation 1.4.2.c: c as the distinction of a from b, distinguished from the outside that is neither b nor a in the context of b.

By introducing and indicating the variable *b*, we have not just expanded our first equation, but indeed created a second, separate equation. The equation is not just about indicating *a* any more, but now can also serve to indicate *b*. Both equations can be considered correct in the sense that the equal sign connects the two sides of the equations. The fact that equation 1.4.2.c was constructed out of equation 1.4.2.a is only known to us at this point. Our assertion that equation 1.4.2.c can, taking additional analysis into account, be derived from 1.4.2.a, can in this context only be seen as a calculation step. In creating equation 1.4.2.b, we take 1.4.2.a into account. Further expanding the equation by differentiation, we take all previous equations into account. We can do this by referencing the last one, as all previous equations are contained within it.

When we now analyze equation 1.4.2.c, we can consider *a* in the context of *b*, but also, by crossing over to *b*, consider *b* as the context of *a*. However, we do so keeping in mind that *a* only exists in the context of *b*. This is our memory of the full equation. Thus, if we assert that each such operation of a crossing with something memorized creates a discrete step of time, we can rewrite our equation as follows:

$$c = \overline{\overline{\overline{\overline{a}\rceil\, b}\rceil\, a}\rceil\, b}\rceil$$

Form equation 1.4.2.d: c as the distinction of a from b, distinct from a, which is distinct from b, distinct from the outside.

As we continue to analyze the equation, time progresses, and we have to rewrite our equation again:

$$c = \overline{\overline{\overline{\overline{\overline{\overline{a}\rceil\, b}\rceil\, a}\rceil\, b}\rceil\, a}\rceil\, b}\rceil$$

Form equation 1.4.2.e: c as the distinction of a from b, distinct from a, which is distinct from b, distinct from a, distinct from b, distinct from the outside.

This process would continue for as long as we continue to concern ourselves with the equation, which is potentially endless. The mathematician Louis H. Kauffman has described this mechanism as the process of adding a potentially unlimited number of additional frames to the current observation (Kauffman 2009: p. 125). The new frames can be added on the outside of the current observation, looking at additional contexts. Or they can be added on the inside of the observation, when a finer-grained differentiation of the operation in the focus is being observed. In the Laws of Form, the following rewrite signifies this potentially infiniteness of the equation:

$$c = \underline{\overline{\overline{a}\rceil\; b}\Big\rceil}$$

Form equation 1.4.2.f: c as the unity of the difference between a and b, distinct from the outside.

This step is called re-entry. The distinction separating the part to the right of the equal sign in equation 1.4.2.e from everything it is not is re-entered at position *a*. In plain words, this demonstrates the unity of the difference between *a* and *b*, meaning that we can consider *a* and *b* separately, but only while keeping in mind their being connected by the distinction between them. Implicitly, we are therefore always considering the entire distinction arrangement, even when explicitly observing only a specific part of it.

The calculation step between equation 1.4.2.a and equation 1.4.2.c can be made explicit through an additional observation. I did this in the previous paragraph, and it can also be done using the same formalism as for the other equations that are models of observations:

$$\text{equation } 1 = a = \overline{a}\rceil$$

Form equation 1.4.2.g: equation 1 as a as the distinction of a from everything that is not a.

$$\text{equation } 2 = c = \overline{\overline{a}\rceil\; b}\Big\rceil$$

Form equation 1.4.2.h: equation 2 as c as the distinction of a from b, distinguished from the outside that is neither b nor a in the context of b.

The two equations are separated in distinct areas as they refer to different observational analyses, even though some parts of them appear to be identical. However, since the definition of each variable depends on its position in the arrangement of distinctions, the variables in these two equations are not necessarily equal, i.e. they cannot necessarily be substituted for each other. This also means that none of the equations can be reduced or expanded to the other out of itself. The calculation step including us as the outside observers – knowing how we constructed the equations – is required to get from one equation to the other. There is no inherent relation between the two, but rather, looking at them and making the connection is a reconstruction of the calculation step with the observer.

Since an observer is required for this calculation step in any case, no mathematical rule can be constructed to get from equation 1.4.2.a to equation 1.4.2.c. On the other hand, we could argue that the observer is indeed an integral part of the calculus. She is included in every equation, as her arrangement of distinctions and variables, and her assertion of an equal sign indeed indicates his identity. It is the observer who ventures from distinction to distinction, form arrangement to form arrangement, and equation to equation. It would therefore seem appropriate to call this process social calculation.

$$\text{calculation}_X = \overline{\overline{\text{equation 2}}\big|\ \text{equation 1}}\Big|$$

Form equation 1.4.2.i: calculation X as the unity of the difference between equations 1 and 2.

The difference between social and mathematical calculation lies in the realms of reference. Whereas a mathematical calculation creates terms that are all consistent with the same underlying set of static axioms, social calculation is not based on a similarly static foundation. In a mathematical term, variables are well defined by their data types, e.g. integers, floating point numbers, or boolean values. What a specific integer, floating point number, or boolean value is does not change during calculation steps. In social calculations, the variables reference social constellations and are usually presented in the medium of language. Their semantic, therefore, is volatile and prone to change, even during calculation steps. The situation gets even worse if we take our reading of an equation and our following of social calculation steps into account. The semantic of the variables included in these form equations may have changed considerably between the references the original observer intended and the references we read into them. Together with the semantics, the observers change as well. This brings up two additional reasons why it is impossible to claim semantic stability for a calculus of the social. Firstly, the original observer constructing the form arrangements and we as the readers approach the arrangements from different social positions, with different social backgrounds and being embedded in different contexts. Secondly, even if we were to read our own equations at another time, our social position would inevitably have changed, as the operative processes we are a part of or influenced by have continued while the artifact of the form equation remained unchanged in its arrangement.

What, then, is to be gained from the notion and the methods of a calculus of the social? Being a calculus, it allows us the precision of a formal system in the analysis of social constellations. While we have to deal with the instability of our variables' semantic, we can make clear and concise statements about the relations between these variables in a specific observation. The calculus allows us to deconstruct expressions by focusing on their inner differentiation. In the medium of form equations, we can give an account of these deconstructions and offer individual calculation steps to be considered by other observers. In terms of its usefulness for communication research, I see two main reasons to apply the calculus set forth in the Laws of Form to the analysis of social phenomena: On the one hand, it allows for the simultaneous representation of multiple contexts and areas of operation, without having to rely on the linearity of representation in language. Secondly, any form is equal to a specific observer perspective, and thereby inherently communicates that any stated form is only one among potentially many possible statements by different observers.

As a formalism, the calculus of indications seeks to offer a stable structure for the analysis and presentation of distinctions and thereby, relations. However, it is itself a genuinely social construction. Spencer-Brown himself used language to introduce his calculus in the Laws of Form, and all discussions of its implementation make use of the same medium as well. This is true for all of mathematics and any concepts derived from it, e.g. formal languages for computer programming, and modeling in various science and business applications. In the end, they are attempts to objectify statements by creating signs that are meant to exist outside of the semantic evolution of language. Their blind spot is that by their origin, they themselves are semantic constructions as well. If this is understood, objectifications of any sort can indeed be accepted to present statements with enhanced stability and conciseness, and by following the socially constructed rules of a formal system, certain relations and structures can become more accessible than what is achievable in language. For example, the precise presentation of distinctions which we gain by using Spencer-Brown's calculus could not be achieved in language. This additional value lies in the epistemological function of the form analysis. An understanding of social phenomena based on distinctions alone cannot be communicated solely using language, because language is based on its high-level preconditions, i.e. implicit subject-object relations, generalizations that are native to different languages, and other objectifications of social structures that are deeply embedded in language. Yet, we cannot make do without using language, either, as it is the necessary common ground from where we can discuss novel approaches. Using language in the captions below the form equations, I can introduce the abstractions of the form arrangements to you, the reader, having to leave it up to you to take up the epistemological approach suggested by them and embed them with the language of this study. My perspective on the phenomena in the analysis focused on the distinctions used in the field, and I tried to find a language for their descriptions that stays sensitive to them and does not obscure them with too many generalizations. As this is hard or even impossible to achieve to a satisfactory extent, I will use form equations to demonstrate the fundamental parts of the analysis and model some of my theses.

Returning to our previous example, the distinction between "art" and "not art" can then itself be included on the inside of another distinction. Keeping our example, this could be the case when an artist A's activity gets observed in a historical narrative, for example structured in decades. The distinction between "art" and "not art" could mean different things for artist A's work in the 1970s and the 1980s.

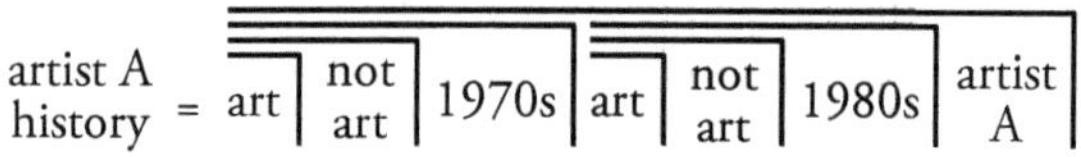

Form equation 1.4.2.j: The history of the artist A as the difference between his work in the 1970s and the 1980s, with the focus on the operative distinction between art and not art.

An arrangement of distinctions like the one seen in equation 1.4.2.j can only be made by an observer. It is this observer who selects the distinctions from the world as she perceives it, and arranges them in a certain order. Only an observer can declare something as art, or not art. Another observer may disagree and negate the statement, but he cannot negate that the first observer has indeed made a statement declaring something as art. We can negate a statement in communication, but we cannot negate that communication has taken place – otherwise there would be nothing to negate in the first place. Therefore, equation 1.4.2.j marks a statement by an observer who gives her account of observing the history of the work of a particular artist. This observer has to rely on certain generalizations, such as the notion of art in general, the knowledge that mentioning the 1970s and 1980s marks a succession, and the general concept of a history, bringing together some factual judgment and temporal markers, in this case certain decades. Yet the arrangement is constructed referring to a specific artist, not artists in general. This dealing with distinctions already creates a perspective: Whether we as observers look at actual works, or at them being art or not, or at which decade we are in within a historical narrative, or how it all fits in with the artist A's biography, puts us in different places within the form, if we take it as a representation of the distinctions we make.

In social life, a multitude of distinctions is often observed together, in conglomerates that are not usually separated. In our example, since we would know at least some of the historical narrative surrounding a specific work of art, we could not observe it without taking this narrative into account. If we go by individual distinctions, as soon as we would look at an actual work, we would also look at the historical narrative, perhaps the decade it was created in, and the identity of the artist, itself in the context of the historical narrative. In addition, in this section, we are not taking up the perspective of the observer ourselves, but we are rather analyzing the distinctions made and arranged by another – in this case, hypothetical – observer. The situation is similar to that at an art gallery, where visitors observe each other while they are perceiving works of art, and offer accounts of their perception in communication. Even just the act of standing in front of a picture and looking towards it, for example, can be observed in communication as a valuation of this picture being worth the attention. Later on in this study, I will analyze similar observations I made in the field.

If we extend the example to assert that the account given in equation 1.4.2.j was indeed observed by us in a gallery setting, for example in an exhibition about the artist A's work in the 1970s and 1980s, the complexity of the social mesh begins to unfold. We will then observe the statement in the context of the setting at the specific gallery B, without the ability to disregard this situation for any of its internal distinctions. For example, the choice what to include on the inside of the distinction where we had our observer place the variable "art" will have to be seen in the context of the gallery, and not just by itself. We would always remember in communication that we are observing this distinction there, and act accordingly. Any participation in communication would have to hold its ground there, in this social setting. Notably, though, we have now explicitly included another area of observation, as we are observing the statement made about the artist A's history in the defined social setting of gallery B. We can therefore distinguish the two as separate realms of meaning. However, both sides being brought together in a social setting, they may change any time we try to define them. For example, while we focus on observing the gallery setting in order to give a detailed account of it, the other observer, who is also our own construction, may have changed her statement about the artist's history on the basis of a work she has been looking at. Or, while we focus on the other observer's account of the artist's history, new visitors arrive at the gallery and change the social situation of the context. As long as the social activity continues, this oscillation of changing the focus back and forth never stops. Whenever observation seems to rest on one side, one realm of meaning, there will likely be topical links to the other side, or the necessity to supplement the current observation with aspects as seen from the other side. Thus, a state of resting is usually not maintained for long.

Our position as observers within the form would be oscillating back and forth endlessly. To accommodate for such cases, Spencer-Brown (2008: pp. 45) has introduced the notion of the re-entry of one distinction into another distinction. The implication for sociological analysis is that the one distinction cannot be observed without also observing the other distinction. In our case, if what we actually look at are works of art, for example at the exhibition on A's work at gallery B, the other distinctions would have to be re-entered into our distinctions between the individual works, effectively serving as our social memory. Notably, the situation of reception I am describing here is a specific, and not a generic situation, which is why I've called it "C".

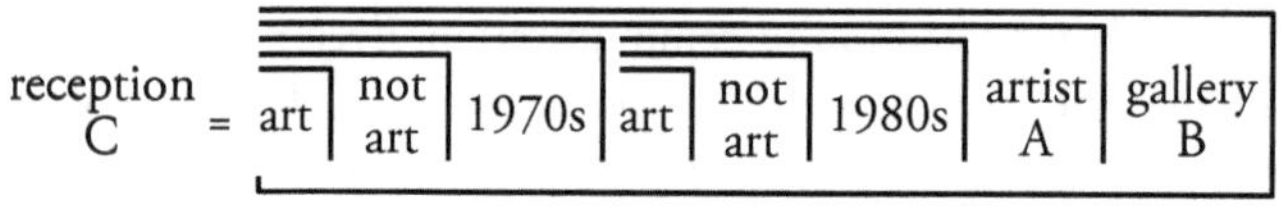

Form equation 1.4.2.k: Reception C as the unity of the difference between the artist A's work in the 1970s and the 1980s, with the focus on the operative distinction between art and not art, observed at the gallery B.

As I have mentioned above, there is a difference between general and specific accounts of arrangements of social distinctions. While specific accounts reference certain identities being involved, general accounts make proposals about how specific social differentiations work in principle. For example, there is a difference in stating that gallery exhibitions are boring, and that the gallery exhibitions one has experienced recently were all boring. Generalized statements are objectifications of specific observations. From observing a specific set of gallery exhibitions and evaluating them as boring, one can try to objectify the notion that all gallery exhibitions are boring. However, any observer making such a claim to have general knowledge of some social phenomenon will be held accountable if other observers choose to disagree.

Therefore, it follows that no general statements can be made on any social phenomenon, as there is no all-encompassing perspective of observation. Nobody has ever had the chance to directly observe all gallery exhibitions in the world, and even if this were the case, it would be impossible to also observe all other perspectives of other observers at these exhibitions. The same limitation is true for this statement as well: I as the writer of this statement can only make it based on my previous experiences, but it is impossible for me to rule out entirely that there is such an all-encompassing perspective. At the same time, you as the reader cannot know for sure whether or not I am in a position to know or not know about these things – which is, again, my guess.

This last paragraph shows how complicated avoiding generalizations is. For language in society, this would be impractical. Language would become overly complex if all statements had to be explicitly attributed to identities all the time. Therefore, society accepts and fosters generalizations in communication. Generalization can be described as the process of forgetting the attachments of social functions to identities, thereby generating the illusion of them existing independent from any social involvement. It is also the process of forgetting the observer's own involvement with the statement she makes: If all gallery exhibitions are boring, the observer who makes the statement does not have to assume personal responsibility for making it. Rather, she refers to it as if it was an established fact, existing independent from any individual judgment. Also, generalization does away with the internal differentiation of the structure it is applied to. In our example, if all gallery exhibitions are boring, the statement does not have to differentiate between specific gallery exhibitions any more.

If they are all equal in this regard, it becomes impossible to differentiate them based on the distinction between boring and not boring. As a method of social forgetting, generalization is an essential function of communication. It allows communication and its media to stay dynamic, gradually changing generalizations over time.

In addition to the perspectives visible in the form, the form itself is a manifestation of a perspective as well: The perspective of the observer arranging all of the distinctions in the form. In the forms shown above, I as the observer of my own example have to take over the responsibility for the arrangement of distinctions inside the form, and for the construction of the hypothetical observer. Therefore, the form as a whole is a manifestation of my perspective on the hypothetical observer's view on the phenomenon described in the example. Also, the form is not just an arrangement of distinctions, but it is given here as a form equation, with an equal sign and a term on the other side of it. Spencer-Brown suggests to read the equal sign as "can be confused with" (2008: p. 57), i.e. not in the mathematical sense of term equality, but in a sense that already includes an observer. In the mathematical understanding of the equal sign, the term quality of both sides is assumed to hold in all contexts, whereas the confusion of the two sides of a form equation is attributed to an observer: He is the one confusing these two sides. The potential for disagreement from other observers is implicit in this concept. The same holds true for all form equations in the following chapters of this study: I as their observer have constructed them as arrangements of distinctions which I confuse with a specific semantic entity. It is my hope that you, the reader, will benefit from the detailed demonstration of my observations, and that maybe you can follow my confusions.

Nevertheless, if one term can be confused with another, it should also be possible to substitute one term with the other. Substitutability is still covered in the use of the equal sign by the Laws of Form, as Spencer-Brown states in theorem 7 of the Laws of Form (Spencer-Brown 2008: pp. 17). Thus, we can replace a part of the term in the above form equation 1.4.2.k by the term this part can be confused with, according to form equation 1.4.2.j.

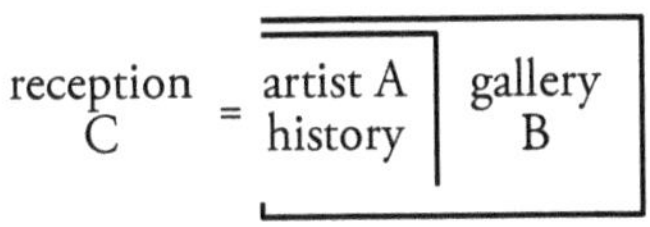

Form equation 1.4.2.l: Reception C as the artist A's history observed in the situation at the gallery B.

The form equations included here so far have all been accounts of observations of observations of an individual hypothetical observer. As a written statement, they are part of non-interactional communication between the hypothetical observer and myself, potentially also including you, the reader. In the field, I have observed numerous situations where participants observed each other's statements, and then stated accounts of their observations themselves, upon which the other participant reacted again, and so on. All of these participants operated as independent entities, in a mode of double contingency (Luhmann 1995a: pp. 103), i.e. without the ability to predict each other's upcoming reactions. Therefore, each participant was to be held accountable for his or her own statements. Nevertheless, having myself been a participant observer in these situations, I could – ex post – give my own account of the interaction I had observed there. Or, in other cases, where field participants published their statements on websites, I could study them and give an account of the path of recursive observations which had been rolled out there. Notably, any such observation knowingly takes into account that it integrates the operations of independent participants. It is therefore crucial to make this clear in the explication of the observation, e.g. in a form equation, where distinctions mark independent areas of social action. The analysis always puts an operational process into the focus of its arrangement of differences. Observing accounts of related communicational processes can be done by expanding the focus to an operational coupling, i.e. the nexus where two or more such operational processes directly reference each other (Luhmann 1997b: pp. 604; Karafillidis 2010: pp. 262). This principle is expressed in the following equation:

operational coupling = differentiation | observation |

Form equation 1.4.2.m: Operational coupling as the unity of the difference between a differentiation and its observation (equation taken from Karafillidis 2010: p. 265, transl. FG).

Expanding our example one last time, we could imagine a critic writing an article about the situation described above as reception C. Looking at this article and the context in which it was published, as well as our own observation of the situation it references, we can construct a form arrangement that manages to integrate these operationally coupled events:

$\text{critique}_{\text{reception C}}$ = art | not art | 1970s | art | not art | 1980s | artist A | gallery B | article D | newspaper E |

Form equation 1.4.2.n: Critique of reception C as the unity of the difference between the operative differentiation structure of reception C and article D in the context of newspaper E.

Form equation 1.4.2.n models the observation of the single communicative event when two separate operational processes and their respective differentiated contexts interlock in an observation referencing both areas of social action.

The form arrangements and equations constructed using Spencer-Brown's Laws of Form can be seen as operations, where the crosses serve as distinctions between operational boundaries. As such, they separate, yet they are incentives to be crossed. For example, if we consider art in the context of commerce, then we take both realms as separate, yet the phenomena we include in our consideration likely operate in at least these two realms. Also, as outsides of forms re-enter on their insides, we assert that the operation in the focus has to take these outsides into account at each step it takes.

At the same time, the arrangements are also testaments of observations. They are condensations of operations that unfold over time – or, rather, which unfold time. Certain parts of a form arrangement may never be made explicit in observable communication in the field, yet an outside observer can nevertheless attest them as being latent, but relevant for an operation. In our field, examples of such functions can be found in the communicational rationalizations of artistic work, where artists sometimes construct narratives of an idealized independence from economic considerations. It is then left up to observers within the scene to communicate accounts of the latent contexts and influences generated, for example, by considerations where to release a record or where to acquire funds for a production phase.

1.4.3 Networks From Distinctions

The field in which I situated my observations can be described as a social formation of various different identities, many of them artists, which are connected in various different ways. One connection they all have is with the label C, where all of the artists I included in the focus of my research had released at least one full-length album. The selection of artists who release on a label is called its roster (P84). Stylistically, the releases mostly fell into the realm of electronica, with variations including approaches towards the techno or electro-pop mainstream styles as well as in the direction of psychedelic rock (see also section 4.1.4). Electronica can broadly be described as being based on synthetic sounds, combined with broken beats taken from jazz and hip hop, often enriched with parts recorded on an acoustic or electro-acoustic instrument, such as a guitar or cello. Via the label's catalog, observers of the label could build up certain expectations about the stylistic realm of upcoming releases as well as other activities sponsored by the label.

The identity of the label C did not simply exist from the moment its owners started to operate it. It was established and maintained through its connections with other identities, such as the artists on its roster, the distributors, shops, venue owners, journalists, and opinion leaders within its public target group. However, the label identity as an entity was ephemeral; in the field, it could only be observed in the events when connections to other identities were actualized, i.e. became expressive and thus observable. The label identity was not observable in one place, where I simply could have gone and collected all information. Instead, statements providing information about the label, the artists, and the other entities mentioned above were distributed in various places and in different media.

Any identity in the field could only be observed out of the relations to other identities, never as a singularity on its own (see for example Barabási 2003). Any effort at describing the label, for example, would inevitably have to call on comparisons with other labels, or other styles of music. As observers, we have to relate our descriptions of the label to these other identities in order to embed any information. If information is taken as "a difference that makes a difference" (Bateson 1985: p. 488; see also Luhmann 1995a: p. 40), the difference has to be established through some sort of distinction between that from which the difference originates – without which there would be no difference – and that which is affected by the difference, that to which it matters. This attribution, however, has to be made independently from both perspectives. In information theory, these perspectives are described as sender and receiver, both being connected via a channel (Shannon 1963: pp. 34).

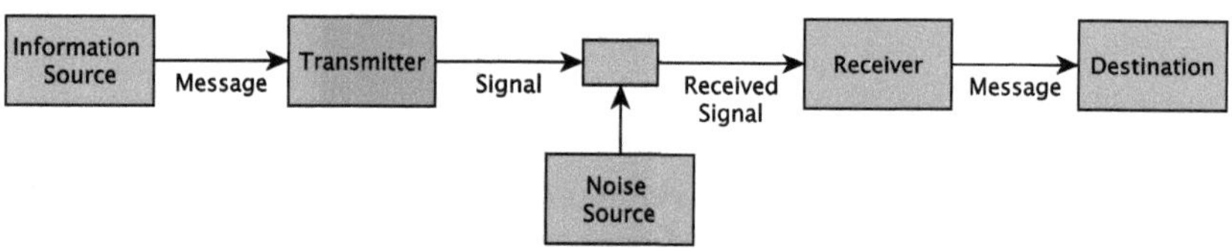

Shannon's mathematical model of communication (Shannon 1963, p. 34).

The catch with the channel is that it is not entirely reliable, i.e. that noise from the outside can interfere with the transmission and prevent the successful reception on the receiver's end. Important for us is the notion that sender and receiver are in fact disconnected for all purposes other than the particular transmission that connects them, and even then only momentarily and more or less unreliably. So, both sender and receiver have to deal with the information in their own, distinct ways. The sender takes up the task of condensing a bit of information in his own world of meaning, and the receiver then has to deal with this in his world, without actually having access to the sender's world. An understanding is thus highly improbable if there was no underlying similarity between the world in which the information was sent and the one in which it was received. For many practical purposes, such similarities may be assumed, but they can never be relied on entirely. In the realm of the social, sender and receiver both maintain their areas of crafting and of processing information independently (Baecker 2005b, pp. 61), and so communication always runs the risk of missing understanding. A point of observation can be introduced in such a system (Shannon 1963: pp. 68; Baecker 2005b: pp. 64), from where both sender and receiver and their processing of information can be seen, and from where the observer can exert influence on the communication channel. The observer can then compare the social operations in which the sending and the receiving of the message were embedded, and suggest corrections as he sees fit. Nevertheless, even such a system with a correction mechanism still operates in a mode of uncertainty, as now the observations and comparisons made as well as the suggestions for correction add another realm of social meaning: The observer's own background and social position. In addition, the observer has to rely on the stability of unstable communication channels again for his own observation, and also for the transmission of his potential suggestions. More observers would be needed to correct mistakes on each of these three channels, but they would again use channels themselves, needing further observers, and so on.

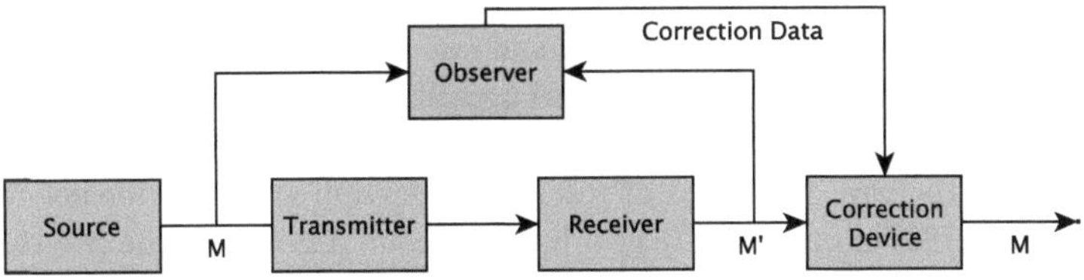

Shannon's mathematical model of communication including an observer who can correct errors in the transmission (Shannon 1963: p. 68).

Information is only one part of Luhmann's definition of communication (Luhmann 1995a: p. 147). In this theory, it is coupled with the message in which it is embedded, and the understanding of its meaning to synthesize an operation of communication. In line with the notion of information, both message and understanding are based on distinctions and connections between them. A message is a codification bridging two different realms of information – one realm instigating that which makes the difference, the other receiving and processing this fresh information as a difference. The message has to facilitate the distribution of the information so that it can make a difference in the receiving realm as well. Understanding, on the other hand, adds a second information to the first one, signaling that the first information was indeed received and that it is recognized and will be processed as fresh information, making a difference. I will analyze (in Chapter 3) how communication works in the field using online communication media. There, information is embedded into posts on websites, functioning as messages, while understanding can only be signaled and observed via further posts. This created a special situation in the field, where communication was on the one hand decoupled through relatively long response times, while at the same time relying on full accessibility of all previous posts at any time. Using the formalism introduced above, the definition of communication described here can be expressed in the following equation:

$$\text{communication} = \overline{\overline{\text{information}\,|}\;\text{message}\,|}\;\text{understanding}\,|$$

Form equation 1.4.3.a: Communication as the unity of the difference between information, message, and understanding (Karafillidis 2010: p. 209, transl. FG).

All elements of the threefold synthesis of communication as Luhmann has described it are based on the notion of at least two distinctions: The first one separating two realms of different informational levels, one having fresh information and embedding it in a message, the other receiving it and signaling its reception and processing as understanding. An example from our field would be the publication of information on an upcoming performance event or the release of an album. The second distinction relevant in communication is one that actually unites both realms separated by the first distinction as both belonging to the same system, which is separate from its environment. Thereby, both sides of the first distinction are operationally coupled (see Luhmann 1997b: pp. 604). That is, by this second distinction, the two elements separated by the first distinction are joined in being differentiated from everything that is not addressed by the message and could not be assumed to understand both message and information – and their difference. Coming back to our example, this would be the notion of both realms being joined in one music scene, embedding both the artist providing the original information and the interested member of the public processing it, potentially signaling understanding.

Thus, communication utilizes distinctions sequentially, as opportunities for continuity are offered and acted upon. Accumulating a set of distinctions used in communication, observers can describe this as a network of identities. Via analysis of the contexts in which the distinctions are being used in the process of communication, the observers can also draw conclusions on the relations between these identities and how they attempt to influence each other. Our field, or at least the material I have gathered in it, can therefore be analyzed as complex sets of distinctions, which I will try to condense into descriptions that are hopefully helpful in making some sense of it.

Harrison C. White (1992 / 2008) has described phenomena in which identities try to control social processes in order to reduce the uncertainty of their own persistence. The only way an identity can form and persist is through ties with other identities, observing how they observe itself and through this recursive operation adapt to its social surroundings, thereby surviving in society. This principle can be modeled as follows:

network = control efforts | identity

Form equation 1.4.3.b: The network as a set of control efforts embedded in the notion of identities (Baecker 2005a: p. 226, transl. FG).

One identity granting another the – possibly limited – freedom to pursue its own control efforts can itself be part of a control effort. For example, a primary identity can exert control by selecting which secondary identities it grants such freedom. Of course, the primary identity has to take care that its selection is enforceable and revocable should its status be disputed. Because the allocation of freedom to pursue control efforts is one of the most crucial and commonly disputed aspects in the observed cases of cultural practice, we will analyze in detail how control is assumed and exerted in certain distinct areas of cultural and artistic practice.

All of this is entirely the construction of the observer, in this case myself and you, the reader. Only the observer can rely on forms of description he has observed being used before, but cannot claim universal, transcendental truth for his constructions. Instead, descriptions given by an observer – such as this study – are themselves offerings in communication, to be neglected or to be acted upon, with the latter option reproducing social continuity. Nevertheless, it is possible for observers to draw conclusions on the social process and the networks in which it runs and which it reproduces continuously. However, the visualizations of networks we have grown accustomed to, showing connected dots and lines as hubs and their connections, only represent static snapshots of social formations that evolve dynamically in their own social time.

Artists are not always connected to the label, for example, but they can usually re-actualize a connection they had in the past without much effort. In the day-to-day dynamics of communication, artists and the label are actually disconnected most of the time, as their activities are embedded in different contexts. Harrison C. White (2008: pp. 36) warns against taking the relations between different identities as fixed and static connections. Rather, he advises, ties as relations should be observed as singular events. Such events, however, do not occur randomly. After all, the information available with reference to an artist in the electronica music scene allows for certain expectations towards a performance the artist announces, and as a potential member of the audience, an observer will adjust his behavior and dress code accordingly, for example. Social processes emerge around constructed identities, responding to expectations, and thereby influencing the probability of the recurrence of certain events.

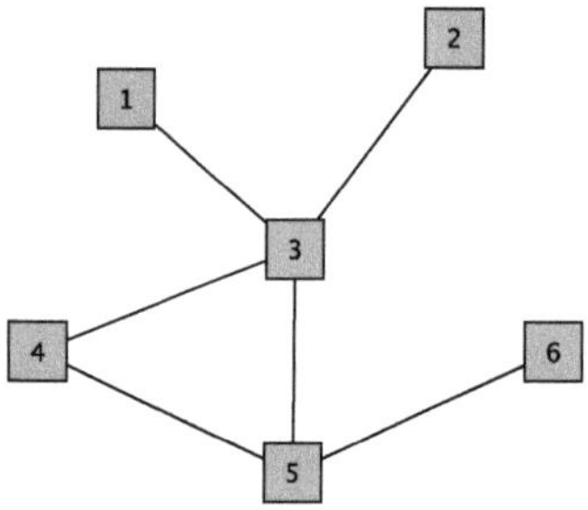

Visualization of a network graph, with nodes 3, 4, and 5 serving as hubs with different levels of connectivity.

1.4.4 Observing Observers

Distinctions are relations as seen from one observer's perspective. Such relations are transitive from one side only, i.e. in the direction in which the transmission of information can be observed. For example, when an information about an upcoming event was published in a post on a website, I could sometimes observe the signaling of understanding from a visitor to the website who had left a comment in which the information was referenced. This would hint at a tie in one direction. If the artist who had provided the original information then reacted to this in another posting, we could describe the tie as two-directional, i.e. double transitive. With the communication being decoupled into posts, the two directions were, however, actualized separately. Double-transitive ties, I would argue, have to be constructed on behalf of another observation adding to the first. In any regular observation, we can usually only observe the triggering of singular transitive relations. Having observed a sufficient number of such triggerings, we can construct dyadic, triadic, or higher-order relations – not because we have observed them directly, but because we think we have understood the social process insofar as to know which recursivities in relations between identities exist in our field.

This again brings into focus the problem of observation in communication. If any distinction separating something from everything it is not can indeed be considered an observation, then any indication that is separate from the first indication and also from everything that is not itself nor the first indication can be considered observing the first observation. With Heinz von Foerster (e.g. 2003: pp. 283), the first indication can be described as a first-order observation, one that introduces a new difference into the world.

$$\text{observer} = \overline{\text{indicated}\,}\rceil \quad .$$

Form equation 1.4.4.a: The observer as the function indicating something, thereby also separating it from everything it is not.

By doing so, the first-order observation directly observes operations in the social process, i.e. it marks events in the autopoiesis of society (see also Karafillidis 2010: pp. 186). It is this indication that declares something as something that can be communicated about, thus also defining the outside of itself as communication in the medium of meaning. This can be expressed in the following equation:

$$\text{observer}_{\text{social function}} = \overline{\text{meaning}\,}\rceil\ \text{meaning}$$

Form equation 1.4.4.b: The social function of the observer as the separation of meaning from meaning. This is similar to the definition given above, but since it applies to the realm of the social, we know that everything that is not indicated is also meaning.

For example, the statement "great music!" in response to a music piece offered for streamed playback on a website (see the analysis in section 3.1.2) can be seen as a first-order observation. It defines a certain operational realm – audio files linked from a website, playable through a computer setup, referencing a specific artist identity – as music, adding an individual evaluation to it. Via this first-order observation, the material becomes available to further communication. The world around the operational realm of a first-order observation would then be considered everything that is not indicated by the first-order observation, in our example everything that is not this music referenced in the first-order observation. I will analyze in Chapter 3 how such references are established by placing statements in certain spots on websites and online platforms. Further observations, taking the first-order observation into account, would be described as observations of observations, i.e. second-order observations (von Foerster 2003: pp. 283). The situation gets a bit complex at this point, as any second-order observation can only be introduced into the world as a first-order observation, separating itself from everything it is not. The first first-order observation is then part of this outside realm. At the same time, when we write down a first-order observation, we do so in a mode of observation ourselves, i.e. we are observing an observation. This, however, was just defined as a second-order observation. What follows from this is that first-order observations are only observable in second-order observations – which is their definition –, yet second-order observations are only possible in the mode of first-order observations. Therefore, when we observe observations, which we do in all parts of this study, we are always in both modes at the same time: I observe an observation in the field, but I do so by operating as observer of the first-order. This fundamental operation, however, has to remain unobserved, otherwise we would add another second-order observation, complete with its operative first-order observation on top. This additive process can theoretically continue to infinity, without ever introducing new information from the world.

$$\text{observer}_{\text{2nd degree}} = \overline{\overline{\text{indicated}_{\text{first}}}\;\text{indicated}_{\text{second}}}$$

Form equation 1.4.4.c: The second-order observer indicates the outside of what the first-order observer has indicated, and can therefore oscillate between the first and the second indication. Nevertheless, the entire form taken together is constructed in a first-order observation.

Observation can be seen as a function of communication. To focus on a specific observer means to concentrate on the social structure of the observation, trying to find elements in the meaning indicated by the observer that are static and somehow predictable. As a prerequisite for this, the outside of that which had been marked in the first-order observation has to be specified as well.

$$\text{observer}_{\text{social function 2nd degree}} = \overline{\overline{\text{meaning}}\;\text{meaning}}$$

Form equation 1.4.4.d: The social function of the second-order observer as the specification of the outside meaning.

Out of perceivable patterns, identities can be constructed. For example, if a participant in the field reacts to similar events in the same way over and over again, we can associate these reactions. Over time, we may generalize our expectations and construct a notion of identity behind the observer, attributing our further observations to this specific entity in our field. The perceivable bodily presence of people as observers can influence and prejudice such generalizations, but the attribution of being an observer is not limited to what can be constructed as persons. Any address in communication has the theoretical capacity to be observed as an observer, whether it be a car, computer, or dog. In any case, the generalization requires us to introduce another difference in our own observation, as it is reflected in equation 1.4.4.e.

$$\text{observer}_{\text{person A}} = \boxed{\text{observer}_{\text{social function 2nd degree}} \;\Big|\; \text{identity A}}$$

Form equation 1.4.4.e: The specific observer person A as the unity of the difference between A's constructed identity and the social function of the second-degree observer.

Luhmann has established the mutual recursive observation as precursory in any social action (Luhmann 1995a: pp. 103). The notion of recursion stems from cybernetics theory, especially the work of Heinz von Foerster (for example in von Foerster 2003: pp. 229), who propagated the distinction between observers of the first order and observers of the second order. The very act of drawing a distinction would theoretically be the purest form of a first-order observation: The observer who draws the distinction simply separates two areas of meaning. An observer of the second order then observes this first-order observer making his observation. Heinz von Foerster himself reacted on Luhmann's importing of his theory into sociology with the suggestion that all forms of social action indeed have to be recursive, that it takes a mutually recursive observation from at least two perspectives on any theme for social action to be established (Ibid.: pp. 305). However, such relations of mutual recursive observations are hard to observe in any given field. Even though all participants in interaction have to take into account that all of their communicative actions will be observed by all other participants, the flow of communication can nevertheless take on a directedness, as suggested by studies on turn-taking in discussions (Sacks 1995). Further examples include the self-presentations analyzed by Erving Goffman (e.g. in Goffman 1959 and Goffman 1979), who shows that participants in interaction can be quite innovative in finding ways to influence how other observers see them as persons, or to deal with undesired descriptions of their selves by others.

The inner differentiation of the models built in the analysis of social phenomena is an arbitrary arrangement set by the observer. In the construction of these arrangements, I often encountered contexts of varying relevance. Also, contexts regularly also came into the focus of the observation as operational realms in their own right. The result was that for any given social phenomenon, such as a performance event, different arrangements of differentiation could be constructed. Different participants in the field introduced different perspectives, and I as a participatory observer could certainly take different stances on the same occasions as well. For example, performance events as they are described in Chapter 4 involved various different operational realms, such as the artists preparing the stage and performing, the organization, which included planning, supervision of the setup, but also operating the bar and closing the venue at the end of the night. Finally, the public also had its own operational realm, with the visitors having to choose between engaging in interaction and listening to the performance at any point in time.

In all these possible arrangements of differentiation, I tried to make out those with relevance to the cultural scene. For example, the perspective of the barkeeper may have been of relevance for the barkeeper and his personal network, but for the scene, his role was typically limited to a very specific function, acting out decisions that had been taken before, in other social constellations, for example when the venue owner had calculated prices and decided where to place the bar. Of course, this limited role is not necessarily fixed, and as a researcher, I had to remain open for surprises, such as a barkeeper taking on a major role in the organization of a performance. References by relevant participants in the field served as a method of guiding further research and analysis. Certain roles in the different areas of operation were mentioned more often than others, and mostly in very specific relations. These roles and relations could be seen as attractors in the network that made the event possible, with certain configurations being more successful than others, by being referenced over and over again. Other configurations, for example centered around the barkeeper, were not referenced at all, at least in the communication I observed. Heinz von Foerster (e.g. in von Foerster 2003: pp. 261) has used the term "Eigenvalue" for such stable forms that emerge from dynamic complexity. In his theory, Eigenvalues of forms are a function of the system in which they emerge, as the system is engaged in the recursive processing of information, i.e. when the output of a system is fed back into the system itself. This was certainly the case in the field of this study, for example when the same participants who organized a performance event also discussed it repeatedly, during the performance as well as before and afterwards. The configuration they started with before the performance event already was an Eigenvalue of the system in the phase leading up to the performance event, while the configuration observable afterwards was an Eigenvalue taking the performance event into account. Louis H. Kauffman (e.g. in Kauffman 2005 and Kauffman 2009) has suggested to use the term "eigenform" for such forms that model Eigenvalues of a recursive process.

1.4.5 Analytical Strategy

During the analysis in this study, I try to regularly include self-observations. After all, the observations stated here are my sole responsibility, and it is my hope that clarity can be gained if I also set forth some of the circumstances under which they were acquired. If form equations as I present them here are an adequate means to model social activity, they should also be suitable to model my own perspective on the subject of the research and analysis. The sociologist Niels Aakerstroem Andersen has suggested (e.g. in Aakerstroem Andersen 2010) that for each analysis of social phenomena, the analyst should define the strategy for his endeavor. This includes a definition of the research topic that starts with a general realm of interest and then zooms in on the focus of the research by making explicit choices on which operational realms to include, and then differentiating them further until an adequately detailed definition of the topic is reached.

For this study, I have started to lay out my research interest in the introduction. I picked this field because it offered me the opportunity to observe processes within an artistic and cultural practice that was, at the time of research, advanced in its use of networked computer technologies, such as mobile computing devices, software-based production environments, and so-called “social networks”, online platforms like MySpace and Facebook, where the participants could be represented and communicate about their own as well as other representations at the same time. What makes this situation so interesting is the fact that numerous technologies were used that allowed for both synchronous and asynchronous communication regardless of the whereabouts of the participants, yet the very much located interaction at the performance events I attended was of great importance for the processes keeping the scene alive. The interaction was home to operative communicational events that could have been location-independent in other communication media, yet were deliberately located and grounded in the arrangement of the performance events. Thus, the focus of the analysis in this study is on the operational realm of communicational events, i.e. the ties between communicational offers and reactions. This is contextualized by the observation of their being located in different situations, yet being location-independent when taking the availability of networked communication media into account. Finally, the operational realm and the locational considerations are set in the context of the cultural scene they were a part of, and which defined the semantic horizon of the entire field. The unity of these differences is expressed in the following equation:

$$\text{analytical strategy}_{\text{this study}} = \overline{\overline{\overline{\overline{\text{operational events}}\,\Big|\;\text{located}}\,\Big|\;\text{location-independent}}\,\Big|\;\text{cultural scene}}$$

Form equation 1.4.5.a: The analytical strategy of this study as the unity of the differences in observing operational events in the context of them being located, yet location-independent, in the specific realm of a cultural scene.

1.5 Distinguishing Styles and Scenes

If communication about art does indeed have a basic code separating works of art that do not fit with their cultural context from those that do (Luhmann 2000: pp.

118), the narratives of such cultural contexts need to be developed and maintained as well. With a great plurality of cultural contexts in society, separations have to be made in order to determine which exact cultural context to apply when judging a work of art on the basis that it either does or does not fit its context. Being part of judgments, distinctions are a basic necessity allowing for communication about art. They make it possible for communication to discriminate between cultural contexts, artistic styles, consecutive performances, and individual works of art. By separating, they also order them into the same overarching category: For example, by underlining how different techno music is from 1960s folk music, both would be placed together in the category of forms of music. Again, the duality of medium and form (Ibid.: pp. 102) can be applied here: By distinguishing forms, communication continuously calls their medium as well. This becomes even more apparent when individual works of art are distinguished: Certain traits are used to make them separable, yet the fact that entities are distinguished on the basis of such details automatically places them into the same category. Clearly, this is an important mechanism in establishing the notion of a coherent selection of works of art that make up a distinct style. At the same time, this mechanism can also be used by artists or their agents attempting to become active in such a style by trying to place references to works of art in the decisive processes of discourse.

1.5.1 The Mechanism of Comparison

The mechanism of separating, yet keeping together lays the ground for one of the most important techniques of cultural practice: comparison. Various styles and scenes may be quite different and they may strive to be distinguishable, but they remain comparable as they all are styles of music and scenes of music-cultural practice. Every two things that can be directly distinguished, i.e. that share one medium to both forms, are also comparable. This is the case with individual works of art, such as record releases by a band, which share this trait – being releases of one and the same band – yet differ in their release date, which embeds them into the biographical narrative of the band. Also, they will vary in their musical features, potentially bringing them individually closer to different musical styles. An earlier album may be more rock-oriented while later albums included more synthetic, techno-style sounds.

In this function, the method of comparison is a social algorithm based on the oscillation between at least two perspectives, i.e. states of observation. If we take for example an artist A and an artist B, who are similar in some way known to us, we can compare them and in the comparison offer an evaluation. The comparison works by observing one artist in the context of the other, and vice versa. This is expressed in equations 1.5.1.a and 1.5.1.b.

$$\text{comparison}_{\text{artists A\&B step 1}} = \underline{\overline{\overline{\overline{\text{artist A}}\Big|\ \text{artist B}}\Big|\ \text{cultural context}}\Big|}$$

Form equation 1.5.1.a: Step 1 of the comparison between artists A and B as the unity of the difference between a cultural context and a reference to artist B, which in turn serves as context for a reference to the operational realm of artist A.

$$\text{comparison}_{\text{artists A\&B step 2}} = \underline{\overline{\overline{\overline{\text{artist B}}\Big|\ \text{artist A}}\Big|\ \text{cultural context}}\Big|}$$

Form equation 1.5.1.b: Step 2 of the comparison between artists A and B as the unity of the difference between a cultural context and a reference to artist A, which in turn serves as context for a reference to the operational realm of artist B.

These oscillating perspectives are operationally coupled in the communicational entity we refer to as comparison. Only in their coupling can we integrate the two perspectives and rationalize an evaluation in the form of a preference for one of the artists. However, when we observe the two perspectives as being coupled, we can only do so in a new perspective, taking all aspects of the previous perspectives into account. This is expressed in equation 1.5.1.c:

$$\text{comparison}_{\text{artists A\&B}} = \underline{\overline{\overline{\underline{\overline{\overline{\overline{\text{artist A}}\Big|\ \text{artist B}}\Big|\ \text{cultural context}}\Big|}\ \underline{\overline{\overline{\overline{\text{artist B}}\Big|\ \text{artist A}}\Big|\ \text{cultural context}}\Big|}}\Big|\ \text{preference A / B}}\Big|}$$

Form equation 1.5.1.c: The comparison between artists A and B as the preference for one of the artists in observation of the unified differentiation of a cultural context from which references to both artists are separated, with these references in turn serving as contexts for references to the operational realms of the respective other artist.

Another famous example from music history is the distinction between Bob Dylan's acoustic and electric works, publicly introduced at the Newport folk festival in 1965 (Marqusee 2002). For purposes of comparison, it does not matter whether the comparable differences are based on temporal developments or aesthetic features.

One important aspect of making distinctions and using them, for example in comparisons, is that they are necessarily the outcome of an observation, i.e. they can be attributed to an address in communication (see section 1.4.4), for example a person. A distinction, to put it bluntly, has to be drawn by somebody, and that somebody will be inextricably linked to that distinction. In the case of different musical styles, this may be a fan of one of the styles, or a music journalist, or someone who has just read about one or even both styles and is now drawing a distinction between them. In the case of Bob Dylan switching to an electric guitar, his shocked fans were most prominent examples of such observers drawing a distinction – and several of them immediately switching to a negative evaluation on the side of the new style. This is how commenting or critique, for example on comparisons, becomes possible. Observers of the second order can check out a comparison between two musicians that has been published on a website. The observation that led to this comparison is attributed to the website owner, for example. The second-order observers can now leave a comment dismissing this comparison, stating that, in their view, the difference between these two musicians is quite different. Also, they can dismiss the entire website as a place where such bad comparisons are being published. This is part of the risk a first-order observer has to cope with, drawing his distinction without the ability to foresee future judgments of it.

In the very act of making the distinction between good and bad comparisons, second-order observers operate in the mode of first-order observation themselves. This is inevitable, as there is simply no way to communicate without drawing a distinction: A form in the medium of meaning has to be offered as information; only then can it be encapsulated inside a message and can possibly be processed as understood in communication.

1.5.2 Differentiation

The idea of differentiation has a long tradition in sociological theory. One of its early advocates was Georg Simmel (1888 / 1983: pp. 53-60), who propagated the idea that the building up and repeating of differences is the driving mechanism behind the phenomenon of social complexity. Differentiation can happen when second-order observers build their own distinctions on the basis of other distinctions they observed. If similar distinctions are used over and over again, they can consolidate as social structures. Looking at musical differentiation, we can see how distinctive styles evolve. The style that dominated in the musical works by the artists in the field could be described as a mixture between electronic, technology-focused sound and mainstream popular music.

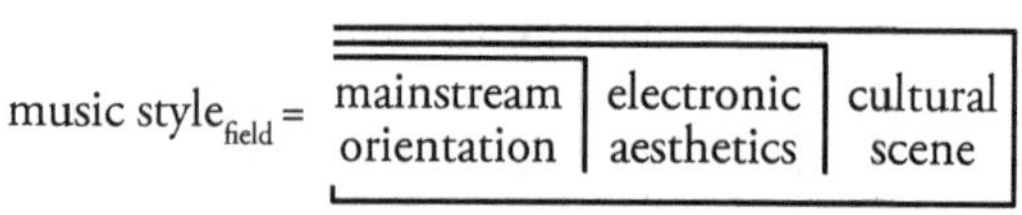

Form equation 1.5.2.a: The music style of the field as the unity of the difference between a cultural scene, from which is separated a realm of electronic aesthetics, from which is separated the operational realm of a mainstream orientation.

The cultural scene of the field can then be specified further:

Form equation 1.5.2.b: The cultural scene of the field as the unity of the difference between the operation of comparison and its context, including technology awareness, media art, and electronic music.

The notion of electronic aesthetics mentioned in equation 1.5.2.a refers back to the technological knowledge in the field, as I have described it in section 1.2.3.

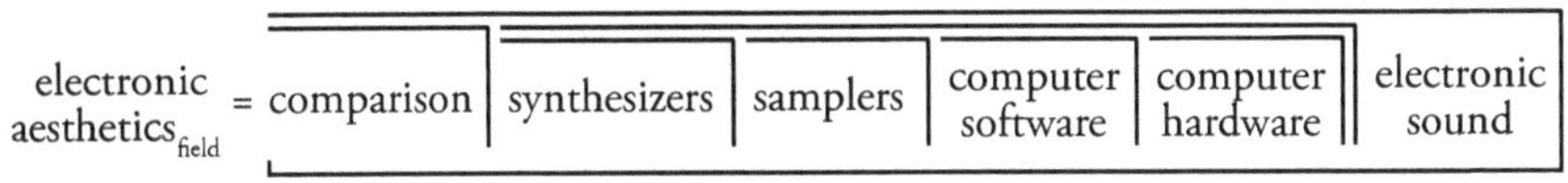

Form equation 1.5.2.c: The electronic aesthetics of the field as the unity of the difference between the operation of comparison and its context, electronic sound, which itself includes discourses on synthesizers, samplers, computer software, and computer hardware.

And the mainstream orientation of the field can be modeled as follows:

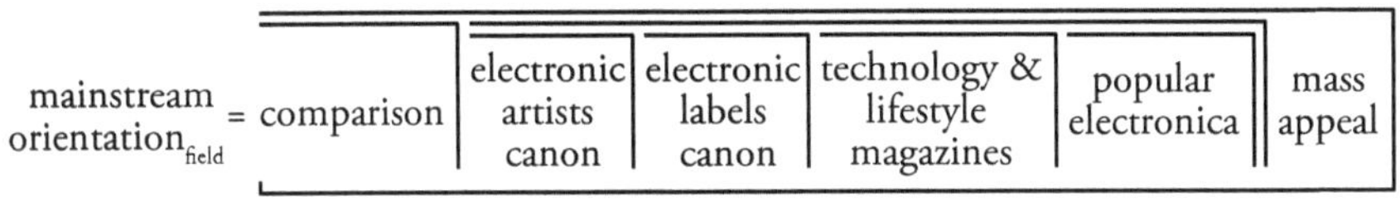

Form equation 1.5.2.d: The mainstream orientation of the field as the unity of the difference between the operation of comparison and its context, mass appeal, specifically including canons of electronic artists and labels, as well as technology and lifestyle magazines and popular electronica music.

In the cases observed here, comparisons serve as the operational basis for differentiation. They make it possible to decide whether or not an observed artifact fits the relevant contexts. However, as these equations make clear, comparisons in the field referenced different levels of contexts. Since communication in the field operated under the condition of a complex society, contexts were combined and influenced each other all the time. For example, if we look further into the application of the distinction of electronic-sounding versus not electronic-sounding music, we will find that both sides of this distinction have their own target groups and use different semantics in comparisons. At the same time, the nexus of these two distinctions partly defines the musical style. Notably, though, only the insides of the distinctions are well defined, the outsides are left undefined and leave room for further distinctions. If we stay with our example, the distinction of electronic-sounding versus not electronic-sounding music, the outside of that definition, the realm of not electronic-sounding music, incorporates everything from acoustic guitar to vocal to philharmonic music, and an endless field of further possibilities. Through recombinations of distinctions, new styles can emerge. Electronic-sounding music can be combined with acoustic guitar music, for example, forming a new style. However, it may not make sense to keep adding names for new categories to build internal differentiation. We would soon end up with names for categories too long to be used in everyday communication. What happens instead is that new names are generated by condensing the internal differentiation so that it is not immediately recognizable any more. Although this may appear to be primarily a mechanism for practicability, it also serves as a function, a social algorithm allowing society to forget how some of the definitions it uses in everyday communication were originally constructed. For this reason, we need not look for coherent usage of definitions, i.e. expect them to be logically determined by the differentiation they stem from. Rather, the condensation of meaning in differentiation processes makes it possible for distinctions to be rearranged in new and unpredictable ways. Although I did not observe one coherent self description among all actors in the network, there was a common notion of an overarching genre into which most musical works produced by these artists could fall. This genre was usually called "electronica". The name electronica already suggests the stylistic grounding in electronic music. Another name that was sometimes used to further define a style was the acronym "IDM", short for "Intelligent Dance Music". The acronym IDM was used commonly for categorizations of music releases by the artists in our field, for example on the website Allmusic.com (P757). Since this website is a good example of a differentiation process, we will analyze it in more detail.

Allmusic.com took the approach of becoming a full encyclopedia of recorded music, ranging from published recordings of old and classical music to all contemporary artists' works (P3179). The editorial parts, like the album reviews, were contributed by paid writers. The business model of this website was to license the metadata it created for publication to other companies, so that they could use it in commercial products. On the website itself, Allmusic.com used a dual approach to categorization, separating a genre as overarching category from a style as subcategory. All albums by an artist or artist group were collected on one page, and here, at least one genre category was attributed to the artist. This corresponded with the main categories on the website, and so the artists I observed were all subsumed in the category "Electronic". Other categories were, for example, "R&B", "Blues", "Jazz", "Pop/Rock", "Jazz", and "Classical" (P3180). In addition to the genre category, style categories were sometimes attributed with a finer resolution of descriptions. For example, one group was categorized as falling into both the Electronic and the Pop/Rock genre, while the additional stylistic descriptions categorized them as "Post-Rock", "Alternative/Indie Rock", and "Indie Electronic" (P3181). The form of the differentiation represented in the information structure on AllMusic.com can be expressed as follows:

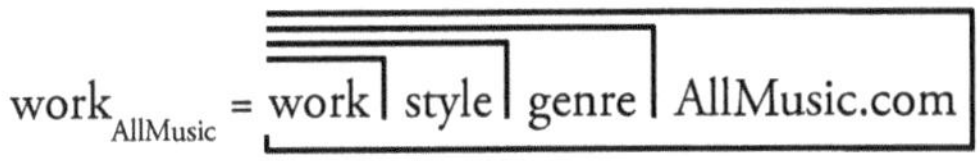

Form equation 1.5.2.e: A work on AllMusic.com as the unity of the difference between AllMusic.com, a genre definition in the context of AllMusic.com, separated from this a style definition, which is context for the operational realm of the presentation of the work.

Form equation 1.5.2.f: The work presented on AllMusic, observed in P3181, as the unity of the difference between the presentation of the work and the platform AllMusic.com with its definitions of the genres Electronic and Pop/Rock, as well as the styles Post-Rock, Alternative/Indie Rock, and Indie Electronic.

The website Discogs.com was very similar to Allmusic.com, as it also aimed to provide a comprehensive, all-encompassing directory of music recordings (P2939). The main difference was that Discogs.com did not pay its contributors, but rather relied on them to voluntarily create the metadata for the recordings. The website described itself as a service to its community (P3183), and did not sell or license the metadata in its database to third parties. The approach to categorization on Discogs.com was very similar to that on Allmusic.com. The same duality of overarching genre and fine-grained stylistic categories was employed here as well (P3184):

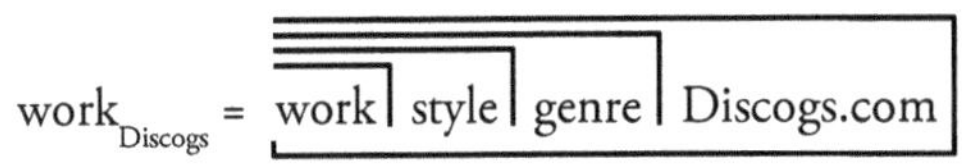

Form equation 1.5.2.g: A work on Discogs.com as the unity of the difference between Discogs.com, a genre definition in the context of Discogs.com, separated from this a style definition, which is context for the operational realm of the presentation of the work.

One difference was that only actual recordings were categorized, not the artist names themselves. As on Allmusic.com, every release had its own page, and was attributed at least one genre category. In the case of the group mentioned above, their latest release dating from September 2010 was categorized as belonging to the genres "Electronic", "Jazz", "Rock", as well as the styles "Downtempo" and "Contemporary Jazz" (P2621).

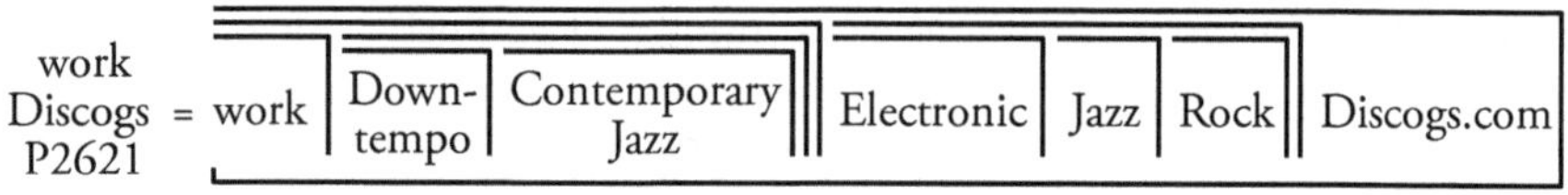

Form equation 1.5.2.h: The work presented on Discogs, observed in P2621, as the unity of the difference between the presentation of the work and the platform Discogs.com with its definitions of the genres Electronic, Jazz, and Rock, as well as the styles Downtempo and Contemporary Jazz.

Each of these categorizations states that from the perspective of Discogs.com, the presented work at hand is similar to other works in the same category. Such statements serve as an invitation for the observer to undertake his own comparisons, and to find his own preferences. The operation of such a comparison, for example in the style "Downtempo", can be modeled as follows:

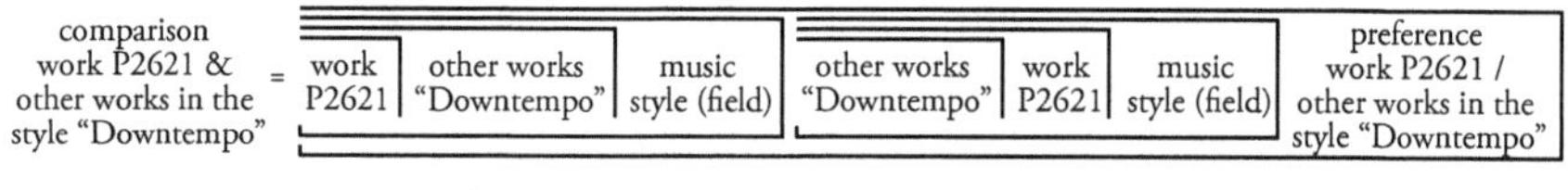

Form equation 1.5.2.i: The comparison between the work observed in P2621 and other works in the style "Downtempo" as the preference for one of the sides in observation of the unified differentiation of the music style of the field from which references to both sides are separated, with these references in turn serving as contexts for references to the operational realms of the respective other side.

Interestingly, the logic behind the semantic categorizations seems to differ between Allmusic.com and Discogs.com. While Allmusic.com used the names of the main genre categories in the subcategories, adding further definitions to them, Discogs.com did not use such a coherent semantic model. The naming of the subcategories on Allmusic.com made them exclusive to the main genre categories – "Post-Rock" clearly had to belong in the "Rock", and "Indie Electronic" in the "Electronic" genre. Such exclusivity was not given on Discogs.com at first sight. While the stylistic definition of the release as "Future Jazz" clearly placed this in the main genre category of "Jazz", the choice was not as clear with the term "Abstract". Abstract music could be conceivable in all three genres that had been attributed to this release. While it may seem as if Discogs.com would allow their contributors to simply select whatever styles they saw fit regardless of which genre choices they had made, this was not actually the case. In fact, Discogs.com had in place a very strict hierarchy of genres with styles as subcategories, and a mechanism on the site ensured that only styles that belonged to genres that had already been attributed to a recording could be selected. Of course, this did not help the visitor who could not know which genre the style "Abstract" was a subcategory of. In order to elaborate the genre/style relations, Discogs.com published (P3185) a comprehensive list of genres and their related styles in a wiki, and invited further suggestions of styles from their contributors. The cases of Allmusic.com and Discogs.com show how differentiation is being observed from similar, but different perspectives. Thus, it should not come as a surprise that the genre and style characterizations used by participants inside the field were all but consistent.

Within the field, explicit narratives could be made out separating themselves from other styles of popular electronic music which they observed being present in their direct vicinity in both cultural style as well as spatial arrangement within the city of Berlin. The most prominent music style during the period of my research was a distinct form of minimal techno music, which thrived mainly in Berlin, while being less popular elsewhere. With a strong notion of locality embedded into the style definition of this certain form of techno music, coupled with its actual dominance in mass media public perception, other styles of electronic music that also claimed to be rooted in local production contexts in Berlin could feel required to separate themselves from this dominant style. This was mostly achieved through the choice of venues for performances. The mainstream events were aimed at large crowds and thus had to take place in large venues, such as Berghain, Watergate, or Weekend (see Haaksmann 2007; Geisenhanslüke 2007). These clubs could easily hold around 1,000 people (1,500 in the case of Berghain, DJMag 2009), and were regularly filled up entirely on weekends. As the pop culture journalist Tobias Rapp has described (Rapp 2009: pp. 78), a large portion of the crowds at these clubs were tourists, not only from other parts of the country, but from all over Europe, as well as the Americas and Asia. With low-fare airlines offering direct connections into Berlin especially for the weekends, the public appeal of Berlin's famous techno clubs and parties reached most of the major cities in Europe at the time of research.

The venues for the label events I observed were usually much smaller, with the crowds attending rarely exceeding 120 people. These performance events were not frequented by tourists, which, however, did not mean that most of the visitors were Germans. Many of the visitors, but also of the artists, whether visiting or performing, were in fact non-Germans. Because of the differences in crowd sizes, the mainstream events and the label's electronica events had to take place in different venues. Clubs like the Berghain were huge operations (see Süddeutsche Magazin Online 2009), with a staff size of approximately 20 people there on weekends, working the door, cloakroom, bars, sound and lighting systems, and security, as well as additional office personnel who during the week looked after the booking of artists and other necessities such as accounting. The venues in which the electronica performances I observed took place were usually run by one or two tenants of the space and one to three bartenders.

There was usually no staff at the door, and the sound and lighting system was set up by the tenants and the artists themselves.

Although the selection of venues could be used to observe differentiation between the styles of electronic music, there were also notable exceptions to the apparent rules. Large clubs like the Berghain and the Weekend hosted special events at their venues that targeted smaller, more specialized crowds, and some of the artists from the label C's roster performed at such events. On the other hand, one of the label's artists was actually active in the mainstream style of techno music. This artist regularly performed in the larger clubs, in front of crowds of several hundred people.

1.6 Economics or Art – Lots of Music, Nearly no Sales

I have already mentioned the fundamental change that music-cultural practice was going through on the verge of the Next Society: Marketing recorded music as a commodity was no longer a widely successful business model (see Kusek / Leonhard 2005). Even at the height of economic success in the music industry, profitable album releases were the exception rather than the rule (Ibid.: pp. 108). The music industry built around the commodity model of recorded music was home to a variety of companies. Historically, a small set of companies that had been formed as part of larger industrial conglomerates with a focus broader than music had pioneered the market and continued to act as the major players in its development. These were the companies that marketed the superstars and that maintained huge production budgets (Millard 1995: pp. 158). On the other hand, a large number of smaller labels formed from the 1940s on, with the focus on releasing and promoting musical styles and artists that would not have been supported by the major labels, which had a strong focus on the mainstream of the market and no business models for the fringes, for niche developments with smaller sales volumes. This is where the smaller labels came in. They were not affiliated with the big industrial conglomerates, and thus were being referred to as "independent" labels (Ibid.: pp. 226).

Around the time of the research period, album releases that reached the same level of economic success that the major record labels had known in the 1970s and 1980s were even more scarce than before (Anderson 2006: pp. 33). The ratio of one successful album supporting the production and promotion of several unsuccessful albums dropped significantly to the point where the old subsidy model did not work any longer (Kusek / Leonhard 2005: pp. 84, pp. 108).

The economical strategy followed in our field did not count on a successful album subsidizing other productions, but rather treated each release as individually self-sustaining. In this business model, each album was expected to earn its own production and promotion cost, plus an additional share of the general operational cost of the label, and, in a best-case scenario, a little extra. In an interview (P1165), the owner of the label C stated:

> "We started with a small run, we're doing 1.000 CDs and 500 LPs, but we sent out 900 CDs immediately the day we got the shipment. You know, to the distributors. Of course, that cannot be directly translated into sales, but at least it is a pretty good sign. Yes, and I hope, that maybe around spring or so, I can start another pressing. In that sense, you could say this was a pretty promising restart. We'll see, if it all pans out like that. And I don't get back 300 pieces in February, you know. That could be as well. But I think, at 900 pieces, that should be doable. In that sense, this was pretty good. Where it's going to get interesting is with vinyl, but you know, we've had that topic before, that is my passion, so I'm not really bothered by it." (P1165: 22, transl. FG)

This business model of sustainable planning had been practiced by the independent labels since the 1940s and 1950s (Kusek / Leonhard: pp. 111). It was also the dominant model used for the releases I observed in the field during my research period. Albums were regarded as successes if they earned just a little more than their cost (P1216). Although the label owners probably would not have turned down earning more money with one of their releases, they did not aim at a high return on their investments, and did not expect it, either.

Sales of music as digital files were another important distribution channel. Online music stores such as iTunes generated a considerable share of the total revenue of an album or a single release (P1165: 197). Another important function of this channel was that it could be used to offer the entire back catalog of a label, i.e. older releases for which retail stores could not justify shelf space. These releases could now be made available even if their physical formats had been sold out before.

Online music stores added convenience to the buying experience of music shoppers. Recordings could be prelistened directly from the shoppers' own computers, and items they bought were delivered as downloads almost instantly. Releases did not sell out, and their presentations were usually accompanied by editorial reviews (e.g. P84). Nevertheless, the sales numbers achieved in online stores did not make up for the overall decline in sales since computers had taken over as primary listening devices (P47: 55). In our field, the physical products – CDs and vinyl records – still generated the main part of the releases. The label owner touched on the topic in one of our interviews (P47):

> "[...] I'm sure that the physical medium, regardless of its form, is not dead yet. I wouldn't mind if the CD disappeared soon, but I, it will stick around for a while, just like the vinyl record. And what's more, is that, now that the big hype around digital sales has cooled down and everybody started to look at the actual numbers, they're realizing, what has been said over and over again,

> in the past, somehow, that the digital sales just do not compensate for the decrease in physical sales, you know, it is a nice additional source of income, but it's not enough, it's simply not a one-to-one trade. So, you just have to continue, you just have to offer the people something physical." (P47: 55, transl. FG)

The sales problems of record labels did, however, not correlate with either a decreasing interest in music or with a drop in the number of music productions. Indeed, the amount of music available to the public had increased dramatically especially with the growth of the internet (Richter 1997). There, music was treated primarily as information, for example on the stylistic identity of an artist. As I have described in section 1.1.3, it was the notion of music as a commodity and the business models surrounding it that lost public support in the face of the broad availability of music of all genres and styles.

From competition of commodities, cultural practice had largely shifted to a competition of information. In order to succeed in this competition, music had to be made available for free, so that the public could access it and include the artist in its discussions. Providing music for free was a necessary prerequisite in order for an artist to be a part of the discourses on music (Leonhard / Kusek 2005: pp. 158). The free music was mostly provided on the online platforms the artists or their agents used for their identity representation. At the beginning of my research period, the platform MySpace was the internet offering most commonly used by the artists in the scene I observed. During the research, the preference changed over to the so-called social network Facebook. I will go into details of the platforms' respective features and social functions in sections 3.1 and 3.2.

We can, therefore, assume different definitions of success for the major labels on one side and the independent labels on the other side. Niklas Luhmann has identified several different success media, which he defines as symbolically generalized communication media (Luhmann 1997a, pp. 316). These can be very different in varying situations. For example, Luhmann includes power, affection, and money among the success media. One essential element of the success media is the presence of a code that defines success in each respective medium: To have or not to have power, to enjoy affection or not, and being able or not being able to make a payment (Ibid.). In the case of the major labels, success could be defined as gaining a monetary profit from an investment in a release. All marketing and distribution activities surrounding a major release were geared towards large-scale profitability of the product. With the independent labels, the situation was different: The initial production numbers of physical representations of the release – CDs and vinyl records – were much lower than that of any major release, which shows that high-scaled profitability of the release was not expected. The marketing and distribution of the release primarily targeted the existing fan base, or base of public interest, for this particular artist and release. The potential for sales was, therefore, maintained rather than expanded.

What, then, defined success for an independent release? First of all, economic factors were not left unconsidered by independent labels. Although their background and corporate affiliations might have set them apart from the majors, they were still part of the same, ultimately capitalist, economy. As companies, the labels still had to be profitable. Some of the most well-known independent labels of the 1970s and 1980s were even bought by major companies and continued to operate with the artists that had been signed to them before. An example would be Mute Records, the label that had signed the British synth pop act Depeche Mode and accompanied their worldwide success from the early 1980s on. The label owner of Mute Records later sold his company to the major label EMI, but continued to work with the Mute artist roster, including Depeche Mode, in his new executive position at EMI (Brown 2002). Although the electronica labels in the field were still being run by their owners as true independent labels, they were not run as money-losing operations.

For the independent labels, the important factors of success included their ability to continue to release music of their own liking freely and independently, and be an active part of a certain cultural scene. This was seen as an important value in itself (P1175: 66). Choices made on which recordings to release could be made without consultations with larger corporations or investors. The label owners essentially did not have to report to anybody. They decided on marketing and promotion issues together with their distributors and the artists. Budgets and thereby economic risks were kept on relatively low levels, compared to major productions and marketing campaigns. A higher risk lay on the creative choices made by the label and its artists: The release had to meet the expectations of the label's base of public interest, or the base would shrink. Again, this was more a matter of launching the right informational product, with economic considerations being of less importance.

1.7 Berlin: The "Center of the Universe" for Electronic Music

During the research period, the notion of Berlin's international role in the electronic music scenes took hold in the realm of the mass media. Descriptions of the Berlin nightlife appeared in several major newspapers. The center of gravity for this hype was the club Berghain.

1.7.1 Techno Music and the Berghain Mania

The following section contains accounts of a visit to Berghain on the occasion of the 10th anniversary of the record label Dial from Hamburg on March 21, 2010. Since I knew the owner of the record label, my name was on the guest list for the night (for the communication, see P1519), but I still had to wait in line to get in.

Front view of Berghain (P3184).

Modular construction fences made of steel created a small corridor in the waste-yard in front of the massive, tall gray building. With its dominance of vertical lines that run the entire height of the building, it looked like the setting of an early expressionist movie. The dull thumping sound of a four-to-the-floor bass drum beat could be heard even from the far end of the fenced-in corridor. The surrounding area was vast and empty at this time, shortly after midnight. On the other side of the street was the deserted parking lot of a home improvement superstore. Behind a tall metal fence, a wholesale megastore could be seen, with its wide parking lot holding only a handful of cars.

The vast emptiness of the surroundings was contrasted with the bustling activity in front of the old gray stone building. This was Berghain on a Saturday night. The proclaimed center of the universe (Waltz 2009), at least for the minimal techno following. The doors had opened just about twenty minutes ago, but a long line had already formed in the fenced-in corridor. The last ten meters, directly in front of the door, were dominated by massive steel crowd control barriers, and the people standing in line had to move in a slow motion zigzag through them. Here, they were already scrutinized by the bouncers, openly watching their every move and discussing their judgment on whether to let them in.

Crowd control barriers at the Berghain entrance (P3182).

Presiding over the door was Sven Marquardt, Berlin's most famous bouncer. He was a renown photographer of the old GDR, with a number of high-profile exhibitions in the reunified Berlin to his name (for a portrait see Hünniger 2009). Continuing his artistic work during the days while at night fulfilling his role as head of the bouncer team at the city's most famous nightclub, he was regularly portrayed in both scene and general-interest city publications, and even national newspapers. Those who were not let in by the bouncers were told to leave via the side of the crowd control barriers. The others were ushered inside in batches of four to six people at a time. Perhaps some 30-40% of those in line did not make it in, but no pattern could be made out as to which features the bouncers were looking for that assured one would get in. Some of those who were denied entrance tried to argue, only to be told to step aside in unambiguous terms.

I have already mentioned the dominance of the distinctive minimal style of techno music in Berlin during the time of my research. This musical style dominated in most inner-city clubs that catered to the publics interested in electronic music (see also Rapp 2009: pp. 27). Other scenes were present in Berlin during this period as well, but their venues were usually located in the outer districts of Berlin, and they did not take hold in the inner-city districts of Mitte and Friedrichshain-Kreuzberg. There were exceptions to this rule, with clubs like Magnet, Lido, or SO36 offering a selection of high-profile rock concerts (see Magnet Club 2012, Lido Berlin 2012, SO36 2012). With these few exceptions, most clubs in the central districts of Berlin were focused on techno music. The larger ones among the most popular Berlin clubs regularly showed up in international rankings of scene publications, such as DJ Magazine and Resident Advisor from the United Kingdom, or Groove and De:Bug from Germany. The most famous Berlin clubs in this scene during the period of research were Weekend, Watergate, Bar25, and, the most prominent of them all, Berghain. These clubs were the weekend destinations not only of the Berlin party crowds, but of large numbers of tourists from all over Europe and the Americas.

The music journalist Tobias Rapp (2009) coined the term "Easyjetset" to describe this particular form of tourism. The term refers to the low-fare airline Easyjet, and Rapp describes how the discount flight prices that became highly popular in Europe in the early 2000s facilitated the stream of tourists pouring into Berlin just for the weekend. Cheap flights made this possible, as traveling by car or train from Spain, Sweden or the south of Italy would have taken days. With return tickets starting at prices around 15 Euro in the early days of the low-fare airlines, spending the weekend in Berlin after a work week in Madrid, London, or Stockholm became feasible. In Berlin, this created a positive environment for investments in low-price accommodations. Between 2006 and 2011, more than 60 new hostels were added to the city's accommodation offerings (Frey 2011). Many of the hostels were placed in residential areas in the vicinity of the clubs, so that tourists could reach them by walking.

An extraordinary hype had been built around the Berghain. The club topped the DJ Magazine reader charts of favorite clubs in Europe in 2009 (DJMag 2009). National newspapers published stories on the club and the myths surrounding it (for example Süddeutsche Magazin Online 2009; Hünniger 2009; Spinola 2009). The Berghain story includes its predecessor, which was called Ostgut (Waltz 2009, pp. 124). This club opened in the late 1990s, and it was located exactly where Berlin's largest multi-functional arena, the O2 World, operated by the US-based entertainment corporation AEG, was to be built. Ostgut already established the stylistic focus on minimal techno, which was a very new development at the time. On the other hand, the club was embedded in the local gay party scene, and in the beginning allegedly attracted mostly visitors from a neighboring gay sex club. The club's impact in the larger music scene grew over the years, until construction work for the O2 World forced the club to close in 2003. The owners moved the club to an empty building nearby, a former heating plant that had been abandoned for decades.

This is where the Berghain opened its doors in the fall of 2004. In a parallel development, the club owners also co-founded their own record label, called Ostgut Ton (Discogs 2011a). This label released music that fit the stylistic focus of the Ostgut and Berghain clubs, and the roster was populated mainly by resident DJs of Berghain, and by several regular guest DJs (Ibid.). The background in the gay scene was maintained by the Berghain. Set away from the dancefloors, but still located inside the main building, the Lab.Oratory operated a darkroom where gay sex parties were held (Lab. Oratory 2011). The same crowd also populated the main club, mixing with the local techno music scene and the party tourists. On a regular weekend, about 25 % of the visitors inside the Berghain openly exhibited and celebrated their homosexuality.

As a club, Berghain had two dancefloors, the main Berghain floor and the Panoramabar (for a stylistic analysis, see also Waltz 2009). While the main floor was located centrally in the building and had no windows at all, the Panoramabar was one level higher than the main floor and featured a large panoramic window front overlooking the area in front of the club with a view reaching as far as the S-Bahn line behind the home-improvement superstore.

1.7.2 In the Shadow of Berghain

Looking to the left from the line in the crowd control barriers in front of the Berghain door, dim lights could be made out in the shadow behind the corner of the huge building. The metal construction fence creating the corridor opened a passage along the front of the building, but there were no extra lights, and a few trees kept most of the light away from this dark corner. Past the corner, secluded by another metal fence with a gate towards the entrance corridor, a gravel yard opened with tables, chairs, and small trees in it. Here, tucked away on the side of the tall main Berghain building, was a separate complex, low and flat, only one story high, but spread out along one side of the yard. This was Berghain Kantine, or Bierhof Rüdersdorf, as it called itself officially (Bierhof Rüdersdorf 2012), a venue that operated as a café during the days in the summer and as a separate club on certain nights all around the year. The building used to be the cafeteria for the workers of the heating plant, but now it had been converted to house a dancefloor with an elevated stage section, and a long bar. The outside area included an open fireplace with stone benches and several tables and chairs in the yard as well as on a deck on top of the flat roof of the building. The fireplace, located close to the door leading to the inside of the venue, was enclosed with a wooden construction during the research period, changing its appeal to a semi-indoors atmosphere. A cloakroom was constructed in this area as well.

View from the Berghain entrance towards Berghain Kantine (P3183).

The Berghain Kantine was sort of the off-venue next to the famous, Berlin-mainstream flagship techno club. Unrecognized by most tourists, the venue hosted small-scale label nights and concerts by artists with a more moderately sized fan base, compared to the artists performing at Berghain itself. While Berghain had an official capacity of 1,500 people (DJMag 2009), and likely had twice as many visitors over the course of a regular weekend, the Berghain Kantine was full with only about 200 people. This made it a much more suitable and manageable venue for events in the electronica scene, while still retaining the famous Berghain name in the title for event announcements. Unlike the main club, the Berghain Kantine was also open on certain week nights, with an event series called Killekill taking place every Wednesday during the research period (P839).

1.7.3 Music Technology Manufacturers

Berlin was home to a broad variety of organizations attached to the electronic music scene. This included clubs and performance event organizers as well as music labels and their artists, together with other agents, such as the bookers matching artists and performance events and promoters matching artists and publications. In addition, several manufacturers of technology used in these scenes of artistic and cultural practice had their headquarters in Berlin and maintained close relations with them. Some of these companies were well-established internationally, and the use of their products reached far beyond the scenes they were embedded into in their home city of Berlin. Companies such as Ableton, Magix, and Native Instruments, where I worked during the time of research, sold their products worldwide and, especially in the case of Ableton and Native Instruments, had a clear focus on the US markets, where they generated a large part of their revenue (for Native Instruments, see Haver / Galic 2009).

Despite this international focus, Ableton and Native Instruments were active in the local Berlin scenes, sponsoring performance events and organizing parties celebrating company events with the involvement of relevant actors in the Berlin electronic music scenes (e.g. P1415). In the early 2000s, Ableton was a regular sponsor of Club Transmediale, the nightlife-oriented part of the renown annual Berlin media art festival Transmediale (Ableton 2004). Native Instruments, on the other hand, was involved with the All2GetherNow conference, which was held in parallel with the Popkomm trade show and the Berlin Music Week, conceptualized as an independent alternative to what was perceived in the local scene as performance showcases of the major record labels at Popkomm (All2GetherNow 2010).

Both Ableton and Native Instruments were well established as manufacturers of professional music software products. Native Instruments had been formed in 1996, and the company's first product was a technological innovation. The software, called "Generator", was among the first to offer high-quality sound synthesis on standard computer hardware (Walker 1998a). As I have mentioned in section 1.2.1, expensive dedicated hardware components had been required for this task before. With Generator, musicians could use relatively cheap computers designed for office use to synthesize sounds inspired by the well-known analog synthesizers of the 1960s and 1970s. Generator was modeled after the modular incarnations of these synthesizers, where the users could create their own sound-generating structures using virtual wires on the screen. This approach allowed for great flexibility, yet required deep knowledge about synthesizer technology on the part of the users. As a remedy, pre-fabricated structures were offered directly by the company, and structures created by varsity users were compiled on the company's website. At the same time, Native Instruments expanded its portfolio, offering dedicated software instruments with a pre-set structure that could not be altered by the users, but which were conceived to allow them to focus on sound creation within certain limits. Over the years, the company created a variety of instruments, which were used in several different musical genres. With the software sampler "Kontakt", the company also marketed an instrument that became a studio standard for the playback and the management of sampled sounds.

Ableton was founded when a group of employees at Native Instruments started to collect ideas on how to create an innovative sequencer, a software to arrange musical parts, i.e. notes, samples, and sounds, into larger compositions. After they could not convince the company's management to divert resources towards the development of their concept, they decided to leave Native Instruments and start their own company. This they did together with the musician Robert Henke, known as Monolake (see Future Music 2011). The software sequencer they had conceived came to market in 2001 and was called "Live" (Ibid., see also section 1.2.2), and it was designed mainly to make live performances of electronic music easier.

While both Native Instruments and Ableton were originally focused on musicians producing and performing their own music with the help of computers, both companies started to cater to DJs as a new target group in the mid 2000s (see for the business growth implications Haver / Galic 2010). This paid off during the research period as more and more DJs switched their performance rigs to computer-based setups. Native Instruments and Ableton both managed to become key players in this market segment, getting access to entirely new target groups, such as hip hop or wedding DJs.

1.7.4 Hired Guns With Record Deals

As big music technology manufacturers, Ableton and Native Instruments were active in Berlin's electronic music scene. As I have mentioned, they sponsored several local festivals and events and also organized their own festivities with the involvement of the local scene (P1415). However, their embeddedness into the local scenes went much deeper as employers. A large number of employees at these two companies were active in the local electronic music scenes, both as recording and performing musicians and as organizers of events (see Hoffmann 2010, Ableton 2011). The companies were usually not involved in these activities, and they were not mentioned in the announcements of events or the metadata on releases.

Both Native Instruments and Ableton had a preference for active members of electronic music scenes. This could include musicians and organizers who had been active in Berlin before, but the international scope of hiring efforts among the companies actually brought many musicians to Berlin. Many of them joined their colleagues and became active in the local scenes (Hoffmann 2010). At the same time, print and online publications were important as employers of members of the local scenes as well. However, their organizations were much smaller (see for the case of De:Bug Magazine Magdanz / Hillmann 2008), and therefore fewer members of the scenes could depend on them for their economic subsistence. Nevertheless, some of their employees were in key positions in the field during the research period, and in addition to their involvement with the cultural practices of local scenes, they usually also had business ties with both Native Instruments and Ableton as manufacturers, and some of their employees were present at events. This included myself, as I was employed by Native Instruments as Public Relations Manager at the time and thus had professional relations with some of the members of local scenes, who were present at the events I observed. I was, however, not directly involved with the cultural practice I observed, i.e. I did not organize performance events or release music during the research period.

In the following chapters, I will look at some of the details of the relationship between musicians and organizers on one hand and publications and manufacturing organizations on the other hand.

Chapter 2: Observing a Scene of Electronic Music Culture

From the general descriptions of music scenes and their participants especially in Berlin, as I have laid them out in the first chapter, I will now shift the focus to a detailed analysis of a particular cultural scene and its activities. This chapter starts with an overview of the collected data types, and the methods used for their collection and analysis. Following this, the field is introduced in detail.

2.1 Methods of Data Collection and Analysis

The analysis is based on data collected in research that began with preliminary work and initial data collection starting in early 2007, followed by a period of structured data collection beginning in April 2009, and ended, at least in its structured form, in late 2010. I have continued to follow the relevant activities after this period, and will include additional data sporadically, whenever it fits and helps to further develop the argumentation.

The data collection includes a few different formats. During the research period, I traced the activities in the scene mainly through their online representations. My starting point was the website of the label C, where most of the live performances of artists releasing on the label were announced. My personal acquaintance with one of the artists helped me to get in contact with the label owner, who then referred me to further artists. My job at a music technology manufacturer served as an additional door opener, as all of the artists knew the company and several of them were interested in how it worked and how they might get involved with it themselves. However, it was important to me that I did not exploit this position and the interest the artists had in it, and whenever I saw the necessity, I made it clear that I was in no position to hire anybody or to get them onto the list of artists sponsored with free products.

2.1.1 Web Pages

The website of the label C (P515) had dedicated sub pages for all the artists on its roster, containing a photo and a short informational text (e.g. P517). If the artist or artist group had a website, the link could be found here. Not all of the artists or groups had their own websites, though, and of those referenced from the label's website, several were outdated and had not seen updates in months or even years. In the first half of the research period, most of the artists had MySpace pages that were active and up to date. The features and social functions of MySpace are analyzed in detail in section 3.1. During the research period, Facebook took over from MySpace as the most active platform hosting representations of artist identities (Quantcast 2011), and many of the artists followed this trend and created a representation for their artistic work on this platform. The features and social functions of Facebook use are analyzed in a dedicated section, 3.2. In addition, there were also representations of artistic work that were not maintained by the artists or their agents, but by interested members of the public who followed an artist's discography and performances and kept the profiles up to date. The most important and most active of these platforms compiling information that was primarily user-generated were Discogs.com and Last.fm.

Screenshots were recorded of all relevant web pages containing information on activities in the field. This method ensured that the exact rendition of the web pages could be conserved, as the browser had displayed them upon access at the time the screenshots were taken. Saving the web pages as HTML documents together with the individual images they referenced, a feature offered by all standard web browsers at the time of research, would not have ensured adequate conservation, as large parts of the content especially on platforms like MySpace, Facebook, and Last.fm was generated on demand by databases. This means that the HTML code a web browser could save only contained links to entries in databases stored on the platform's servers, which were called upon accessing the page, and which delivered their content in up to date form to be rendered by the browser. The database entries themselves, however, could not be saved as raw data by the web browser on the client side, which is why the rendered form of data representation was chosen for data collection. The software Screengrab (http://www.screengrab.org/) was used to take the screenshots, acting as an extension of the web browser Firefox. Screengrab allowed the user to save an exact screenshot in either the JPG or the PNG format. As the JPG format introduced heavy compression artifacts, the PNG format, which applied lossless compression, was chosen for the screenshots. In the beginning of the research period, the Screengrab software managed to capture all elements of a web page except for elements in the Adobe Flash format. These elements were not included in the screenshots, and simple single-color rectangles were saved in their place. Later versions of the Screengrab software also captured Flash content.

In order to cover changes on the web pages occurring during the research period, screenshots were taken repeatedly. If a web page was involved in any direct activities I observed, screenshots were taken according to the temporal structure of the activity. Web pages relating to the inner circle of artists and organizations of the research scope (see section 2.2) were conserved roughly on a monthly basis. Web pages that were newly created during the research period were added as they entered the scope of observation, and in most cases, it was not possible to determine exactly when they had been introduced. This applies especially to Facebook pages and personal profiles, which were added in great numbers in the course of the platform's enormous gain in popularity during that time (Quantcast 2011).

The screenshots of web pages were then assembled in a research database. As all data was either collected in digital form directly or transferred to a digital file format, the database was handled entirely in software. An advantage of this procedure was that all primary data assets were accessible directly from within the database. The software package used for database management, as well as for further stages of analysis, was Scientific Software's ATLAS.ti (http://www.atlasti.com/). Inside ATLAS.ti, individual items of collected data are called primary documents, and each of these documents was assigned a unique ID number. This unique ID number is used throughout this study to reference items in the data collection.

The ATLAS.ti software package was designed to facilitate both quantitative and qualitative methods of data analysis, with a clear focus on the qualitative side (Scientific Software / Friese 2011; Lewins / Silver 2007). Primary documents of a variety of formats can be accessed directly from within the program. The screenshots of organizations' and artists' web pages were stored in part in the JPG format, applying destructive compression, and in part in the lossless PNG format. The reason for this was that the version 5 of ATLAS.ti, which was current when I started with the analysis, could not import and display files in the PNG format. Therefore, the stored PNG files were converted to JPG files with the batch conversion feature of Apple's Automator software, a part of Mac OS X (Apple 2011c). During the analysis period, Scientific Software released version 6 of ATLAS.ti, which added the functionality to import and display PNG files (undocumented by the manufacturer). Therefore, files that were created after the incorporation of this new version were directly imported in the qualitatively superior PNG file format. However, the batch converted JPG files were still of better quality than JPG files directly stored with Screengrab, and have proven fully sufficient for the purposes of analysis in this study.

2.1.2 Interviews

Another important set of data contains the 18 interviews conducted with persons active in the cultural network around the label C. The interviews were conducted as half-structured ethnographic interviews (Schlehe 2003: pp. 78). The interviewees were selected on the basis of their belonging to an inner circle, a densely connected group of artists, most of which had releases during the research period (see section

2.2). In addition, I interviewed the label owner, a label assistant, and the owners of a record store. The interviews were conducted on the basis of a prepared guide covering fields of research interest. The guide was constructed in the form of a mind map using the software Freemind (http://freemind.sourceforge.net), and already contained pre-formulated questions. During the interviews, I used this guide in printed form to steer the conversation, but did not go through the questions in an ordered way. Rather, I attempted to touch all fields of research interest and used the pre-formulated questions only to get the interview started and if one of the topics did not come up automatically.

The interviews started with questions about the interviewee's most recent cultural or artistic activity. For example, if an artist had just released an album, the first question could be how long he had been working on the production. From this outset, different aspects of the practice were explored, such as the technological setup used for production and how the artist collaborated with other artists and organizations such as the releasing label during that process. The questions also touched aspects of marketing a release, such as who the artist saw as target group of the release and what he was going to do to promote it. From there on, some of the interviews covered the communication with the releasing label, the distribution organizations, and fellow artists on the label's roster as topics. Another route through the conversation first put a stronger focus on a self description of the artists, including questions regarding other jobs or activities they might be involved in besides music and how they saw their own involvement with the local scenes. A separate set of questions touched the artist's own view on events where he had performed, sometimes asking about a specific event and sometimes staying on a general level, depending on whether I had recently observed a performance by this artist. The artist was asked to describe the performance situation, the audience, and whether he knew a larger part of the audience personally. Finally, if it had not been covered before, questions were raised concerning the artist's interaction with the interested public, and which communication media were of relevance in these processes. This field of interest also included questions about the artist's involvement with online representations – did he create and maintain his own MySpace and Facebook profiles? – as well as his approach to react to comments on profile pages. If the interviewee was part of an organization and not active as an artist himself, the questions concerning the performances stayed on a general level, while the questions about the organizational setup went into more detail than with the artists.

The interviews were recorded with a portable digital recorder, and are included in the research database as MP3 files. The ATLAS.ti software package allows for direct playback of these files, and in version 6, audio files could be linked to text files, including anchor points relating positions in the text and the audio (Scientific Software 2011: pp. 20). This way, transcriptions could be produced with links in the text making the transcribed part of the audio recording immediately accessible. In the transcriptions, no words were omitted from the recording, but incomplete words were completed to achieve better readability. Also, fillers such as "ah" and "mh" were omitted whenever, in my observation, they served no purpose of utterance. Every interview has two entries in the research database, one for the original audio file and one for the transcribed text. The relation between the two is directly visible from the text for most interviews, where the links to the audio passages show up as small red dots above the text.

2.1.3 Participatory Observation

During the research period, I visited as many performance events organized in the field as possible. This amounted to 50 accounts of participatory observation. I got to know more field participants at these performance events through the acquaintances with artists and organizers I had established through the interviews. My interviewees regularly introduced me to other visitors and suggested new interviews. In addition, I knew some of the other visitors through the business relations I had working at a music technology company. Several of the visitors were either colleagues of mine or business partners I had dealt with before. Any observations I could make at these performance events were, therefore, not objective or distanced from the interactions taking place there. Rather, I was part of the same social mesh I was observing from a research perspective, albeit in a distanced position that allowed me to retain a role of an outsider when it came to questions of artistic and cultural practice.

I then produced written records of my observations at the performance events. They covered the timespan from getting to the performance event to the next activity after the performance event. After experimenting with taking notes directly at the performance events, I discarded this method as it proved too invasive. Firstly, it provoked reactions among the other visitors, and secondly it distracted my own attention away from the interactions and performances at hand. Therefore, I decided to postpone the writing of the records to either directly after the performance event, or the next day. In any case, the records were produced within a time-frame of 48 hours after the performance event. In some cases, addenda were enclosed at a later time.

The written records were guided by Clifford Geertz' approach to "thick description" (Geertz 1987). Inspired by his approach, I tried to make my own observed subjective assessments of situations or statements as clear as possible, and attempted to specify assessments I observed among the other visitors, artists, and organizers. Also, I tried to reduce presuppositions in my descriptions, i.e. being careful with guesses as to what was meant by something as opposed to what was observably said or done. Of course, none of these distinctions could be followed through perfectly.

2.1.4 MySpace Survey

At least in the first half of the research period, the MySpace platform was still the most important social network where most of the artists and organizations involved in the scene I observed hosted their own representations. As I mentioned, Facebook gradually took over this social function over the course of the second half of the research period.

Using a software package called MyFriendsManager (http://www.myfriendsmanager.com, now offline), I was able to collect information provided by other MySpace members who had registered as "friends" of a given MySpace profile. The information these members had entered in their own profile could be read out and saved into a table in the Microsoft Excel format using MyFriendsManager. The data was used in aggregated form only, so that anonymity of the members was secured. The information gathered via this method included the type of membership, whether the member was registered as an individual person or as a band, as well as data on the sex, age, religious and sexual orientations, and even yearly income of the member. Most of these fields were not mandatory, though, and so the number of entries in these fields varied greatly. Also, probably more importantly, there were no measures implemented to verify the information given by the members. They could enter any numbers they wanted or select an arbitrary account of religious orientation, for example. Indeed, data on the members' yearly incomes, for example, appear way off balance when compared with real income distributions (for Germany, see Bundeszentrale für politische Bildung 2009). Therefore, the data collected via this method cannot be read as quantitative data referring to any reality beyond their presentation in the context of the MySpace platform itself. Instead, it provides valuable information on how members present themselves in this social surrounding.

For the survey, I collected this information for all the "friends" of the label C's MySpace profile. From the 2,917 member profiles included in this collection effort, a random set of 159 members was selected for a survey. These members were then contacted via the messaging feature available on the MySpace platform. This feature was designed similar to email communication, where members had an inbox and could send messages to other members. For this, only the recipient's member name had to be known, and the sender and recipient did not have to be related as "friends" on the platform in order to exchange messages. I had set up a member account (P3169) for my research work, which only contained information regarding my location in Berlin. The set of members to be included in the survey was enlarged several times, as 26 members who had been selected randomly could not be included. The reasons for this were either that they had ended their membership in the meantime, that they were too close to the label C to give an independent statement, or that I was already in contact with them through my own participatory observations or the interviews I conducted, which also would have prevented independent statements.

The questions I sent to the "friends" of the label's MySpace profile differed depending on whether or not they had provided Berlin as their current location. If they had entered a different home city, I asked them about a possible relation to Berlin. If Berlin was set as their location, I sent them questions about possible preferences they might have for certain cultural activities in the city. The different versions of the questionnaire were sent out in both English and German versions, depending on the language spoken by a member, if it could be made out. In total, I received 22 replies, which is a response rate of 13.8%. The answers and the analysis report can be found in Appendix 3. The findings are mainly provided in section 3.1.

2.1.5 Coding

The research database contains primary documents in image, text, and audio formats. The web pages, interviews, participatory observation records, and the survey answers in the research database were then subjected to different stages of coding in iterations of the analysis process. Coding is a method to reduce complexity in large datasets so that certain factors become easily accessible. Thereby, it generates an overview of the content of the elements in a research database. Originally based in the methodology of grounded theory (see for example Strauss 1998: pp. 56), coding is an approach in the semantic analysis of empirical data. There, coding is used to select parts of a primary document that have a certain, coherent meaning, and assign to them a term, the code, under which this meaning can be subsumed. Other parts of the same or other primary documents that have the same meaning are assigned the same code, and sets of codes are then grouped in categories. In grounded theory, all codes and categories have to be generated from within the data; the methodology is understood as a means to get the data to speak for itself (Ibid.: pp. 29). One problem with the data-centric approach of grounded theory is that it does not take the observer serious enough. This can be problematic, as it potentially keeps the most important decisions in the research process, the selection of which data to collect and which codes to assign to which parts of primary documents, out of the focus. The data is seen as an entity existing largely separate from any presuppositions the researcher might already have. Grounded theory thus employs a claim of objectivity, while the dataset subjected to the analysis was forged by the very subjective decisions of an observer, in most cases the researcher him- or herself.

I did not follow this approach, but rather tried to lay open the relations of codes to certain theory-induced questions which guided the collection of data. The first set of these questions targeted the understanding of operational processes in the network. For this, the operational involvement of observed process parts was coded. The first theoretical assumption here was that momentary observations of actions can be attributed to larger, overarching constructions of processes. Niklas Luhmann has described such processes as structuring society in a top-down perspective (Luhmann 1997b: pp. 743). The modern society as observed by Luhmann was differentiated in functional subsystems, such as economy, science, and religion. Each of these functional subsystems has a code, a core distinction separating its communicative actions. In the economic subsystem, for example, communication was structured by the core separation between payment and non-payment, while in the case of the scientific subsystem, the core distinction separated truth from not-truth. Luhmann also described organizations as social systems that are able to negotiate between communication in different functional subsystems, i.e. that could, for example, arrange for a trade-off between truth and payment (Ibid.: pp. 826). Art as a social system is described by Luhmann as a mechanism applying and negotiating criteria for how society can deal with works of art. Part of this process is determining whether or not the works fit and fulfill expectations held towards them (Luhmann 2000: pp. 118). Artists anticipate this evaluation and, at least partially, take the criteria and expectations held towards their works into account. In the case of electronic music, such strategies can be observed in the selective use of certain sounds or strategies of arrangement that are aligned with a certain musical style and that fit a specific situation.

Organizations in the realm of cultural and artistic practice have the ability to mediate between the cultural and stylistic embeddedness of works of art on the one hand and economic considerations on the other hand (Luhmann 1997b: pp. 826). Thereby, they can try to establish and, to a degree, manage what amounts to market valuations of works of art. This does not only refer to paintings being auctioned off or sold in galleries, but also includes the willingness of visitors at a venue to pay for a performance, or of an interested public to buy a music release either physically as CD or vinyl record or as a download from a website or via iTunes. Mediating between the different interests in economic and artistic considerations was the domain of organizations in this field. On the side, they also took over mediations in other directions, such as the legal system, negotiating agreements on questions of copyright and right of exploitation.

Mediating in the field between cultural and artistic practice as well as the broader economy, operational categories such as marketing and distribution were predetermined in the analysis. These basic operational processes of the organizations were used as the first set of codes. With them framing other activities, further codes were introduced, getting into the details of the processes. At the same time, the core set of identities, the densely connected inner circle of participants in the field I was observing, were added as codes as well. This way, operational processes, their footings in performance events and on the web, as well as the participating identities became traceable. For the full set of codes deduced from the research interest in the operational structure of the network, please see Appendix 2.

The other area of research interest related directly to sociological theory. Coding was used here to attribute data fragments to modes of communication as described in the theories I have introduced so far, especially sociological systems theory (Luhmann) and network theory (White). The categorizations brought forth here were not in any way exclusive; rather, via coding, I attempted an ordering of observations into fuzzy sets of communicational modes. This included dominant themes, e.g. when identities or the relations among them were discussed, as well as functional aspects, such as the communication of expectations towards a performance or towards a certain role in an organization. The full set of theory-induced codes including short descriptions is also provided in Appendix 2.

2.1.6 Networks from Codes

Inside the ATLAS.ti software, codes can be arranged in freely definable relations. The relations used in the analysis for this study mostly defined containment, e.g. "Code A is a part of Code B" or "Code A is a function of Code B". This way, another layer of insight could be gained especially with regard to the connectivity among operational processes in the network. In Appendix 2, the network view of operational codes is given. Similarly, the theory-induced codes were structured in network views representing the coherent theoretical interpretations as used for analysis. Network views for the theoretical interpretations, which will be detailed further in the following chapters, can also be found in Appendix 2.

Coding is inherently a qualitative method of data sorting, as the decisions on which codes to apply to which segments of data are arbitrarily taken by the researcher, and can only be rationalized after the fact by taking a coherent theoretical framework into account. However, once this qualitative method is accepted, the codes themselves can be subjected to quantitative analysis. For example, ATLAS.ti automatically counts how many times a code was applied. More sophisticated queries could be constructed and run across the coded research database, for example how many times a specific code followed another specific code, or how many times it was enclosed by another. Of course, the results of such queries were more a quantitative account of the qualitative method of coding, but when used inside one individual or one homogeneous class of primary documents, it could indeed provide additional insights.

2.2 Tracing a Music Scene: The Label and its Artists

All references to phenomena are anonymized in this study. The reasoning behind this is that, although I started out with interviews where the interviewees gave their consent to have their names appear in the study, I soon encountered situations where field participants gave me information on the condition of anonymity. It could be argued that such information should be excluded from the study, but that would not have been a realistic account of my observer position in the field. I soon realized that I could only gain access to some of the more risky discussions, where personal opinions were brought to the table, if the participants trusted me in keeping their opinions anonymous. Therefore, I will use codes for the participants and other entities, and all explicit references in images have been made unrecognizable. As I have already mentioned, the starting point for the data collection was an electronica record label in Berlin, which I simply call "C". The choice to start here was motivated by previous observations of the scene, where this label stood out as one of the few labels that connected very different aspects of the culture it was embedded in. First of all, the label had been founded in the 1990s, under economical circumstances which I expected to differ dramatically from those at the time of data collection (see Kusek / Leonhard 2005 and section 1.6). Secondly, the label offered a connection between electronic music styles that pioneered in the 1990s and their evolutionary descendants contemporary to the research period. In addition, the scope of the label was clearly global, with its two founders located in Manchester and Berlin, and artists scattered in various places ranging from the US to Europe and Japan. At the same time, though, the label's activities were deeply embedded in the local Berlin scenes, and it appeared to help draw some of its artists into the city. In addition, the label founder in Berlin also worked as an editor at one of the most influential magazines in technology-aware electronic culture in general. This combination of aspects promised a broad range of multi-faceted phenomena, linked together by one coherent identity. In the vicinity of the label, I observed a total of 30 artists actively involved in producing and performing music.

2.2.1 Observing Differences and Relations

The selection of artists on a label's roster can be stylistically diverse. As the artists used the label name together with their own in their communication, they fostered the establishment of a relation with the label and thereby, indirectly, also with the other artists on the roster. At the same time, these artists also signaled their uniqueness by expressing differences separating them from the references they related themselves to (see for example the self descriptions in P466; P1423, and sections 3.1.2 and 3.2.1). Therefore, there was no typical artist embodying the average traits found in the label's roster. Instead, each artist had a field of specialty, which was used to point out his or her uniqueness. This principle is expressed in the following two equations:

$$\text{profile}_{\text{artist A}} = \boxed{\boxed{\text{work}_{\text{artist A}}}\ \text{differentiation}_{\text{artist A}}}$$

Form equation 2.2.1.a: The profile of an artist A as the work of artist A observed in the context of the differentiation constructing the identity of artist A.

$$\text{profile}_{\text{label C}} = \boxed{\boxed{\text{work}_{\text{label C}}}\ \text{differentiation}_{\text{roster label C}}}$$

Form equation 2.2.1.b: The profile of the label C as the work of label C observed in the context of the differentiation constructing the identity of the roster of label C.

The differentiation among the artists on the roster had an influence on the stylistic profile of the label. At the same time, the vast majority of artists had releases on other labels as well, either before or after their releases on the label C, sometimes both. Also, most of the artists did not significantly vary their stylistic orientation between releases on this or other labels. There was, therefore, no stylistic exclusivity to be claimed by the label. Similar music was released by artists from the label's roster, as well as other artists, who had nothing to do with the label, on various other labels all over the world. In some cases, there were collaborations (e.g. P1205) with other labels releasing similar music, but I did not observe a notion of coherence among labels with a stylistically similar profile.

Some level of coherence could however be observed in the distribution chains in which the labels were embedded (see P1165: 37). Physical representations of releases were usually only sold in specialist record stores, but they did not show up in the music release shelves of the huge electronics retailers, such as Mediamarkt or Saturn for Germany during the time of research (P47: 51), which accounted for the major share of the in-store retail sales of physical releases. The situation was very different at the smaller specialist stores. As these stores catered to very specific musical interests, the selection of releases by certain labels and artists to be sold there were an important part of the stores' identities. As some of these stores, such as Hardwax or Dense Records, both in Berlin, gained attention in their own right (see online search results for HardWax P2364), their selections of records to sell could be observed as a determining part of their identity in the public perception, not unlike that of a record label.

The mechanism of specialization for specific interests worked in a similar manner among the wholesale retailers of physical releases. While the major labels usually had their own distribution branches targeting the general-interest electronics megastores (Kusek / Leonhard 2005: pp. 86), the small independent labels signed contracts with mid-sized specialist distributors in different geographical regions or countries who then represented the sales interests of the label in their territory and delivered the physical releases directly to the record stores.[9] At the same time, the distributors also took over much of the responsibility to promote the releases among magazines, radio stations, and other mass media outlets of importance in their territory. The label C had distribution contracts with two companies in Germany (P1166: 12), one big wholesale distributor in the US, and specialists for the electronica genre in various other countries, among them the UK, Japan, Australia, and France (P588). Many of these distributors had a focus on a specific selection of genres, partly because they were labels themselves.[10] In addition to working with distributors in different market territories, the label C, one of their cooperation partners, another record label, and a clothing label had started a web shop together, where physical products could be ordered (P1165: 163; P88).

The website of the joint web shop (P2708).

While physical representations of releases remained an aspect that was regarded highly in the field and celebrated with release parties (for example P1192), a large proportion of actual sales was accomplished via downloads of releases (P1165: 197). The distribution setup for downloadable releases differed significantly from that for CDs and vinyl records. The labels provided the product in the form of digital music files,

9 For the label perspective, see for example P1165, and for the record store perspective P1187: 88.
10 This distributor, for example, had an extensive discography of its own (P2326).

and specialist online stores offered them for paid download, managing the logistics of secure payment and delivery. In the field of this study, Apple's iTunes and Boomkat (P2342; P598; P599) were the most important online stores. While Boomkat had a browser-based store, iTunes was only accessible through its desktop software or clients on Apple's mobile devices. Also, Boomkat was highly specialized in that it only sold releases from a few genres of electronic music, mostly in the field of electronica or experimental music. iTunes, on the other hand, was the undisputed leader in the overall market for music downloads, covering a broad variety of styles and genres ranging from the mainstream to special interests. Both Boomkat and iTunes provided reviews of releases. Boomkat commissioned reviews directly from its own writers (P1165: 215). These reviews were not only used in its own store, but they also appeared in the iTunes store as well as other places.

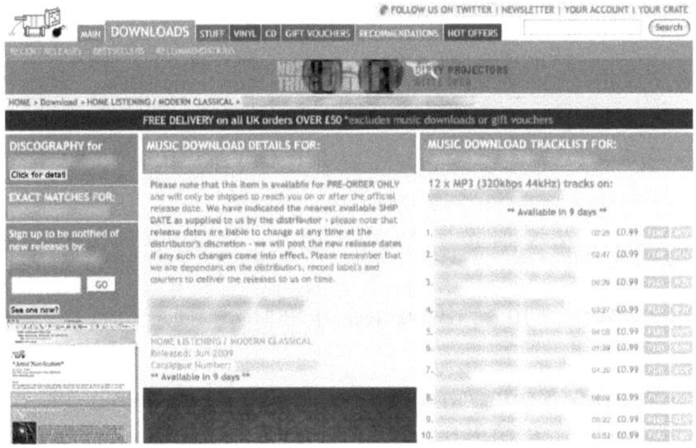

Boomkat website (P3307).

For the label C, the main difference between the distribution of physical releases and the sales of music downloads was that the label owner dealt directly with the online stores, without the intermediary distributors in the case of the physical releases. This included not only the negotiation of business terms for the conditions under which the music was to be sold, but also, for example, the manual upload of digital music files onto iTunes' servers and the entering of relevant metadata into the system's product database (P1216).

Some of the artists who released music on the label C owned labels themselves. Although they could have released their music on their own labels – which most of them had done previously – they chose to release on the label C instead. In one interview, an artist (artist O, see section 2.2.2) offered credibility as rationalization of his decision to release his second album on the label C instead of the label he co-owned and partly managed (P1175: 77). This rationale hints at a notion of independently verified quality of music that could not be attained without going through the selection process of a label and the different cultural contexts surrounding it, which was not yet associated with the artist in any way. Also, the label owner used to release his own music on the label C and other labels as well.

Artists who ran a label themselves necessarily had to fulfill several tasks similar or identical to those which the label C's owner had to engage in. They, too, dealt directly with distributors, sometimes even the same companies, as well as the different download stores. The same artist/label owner referenced above mentioned that the label C's owner had shared templates for contracts with him and offered detailed advice on several occasions (P1175: 104).

Aside from tasks involving cooperations in the distribution chain, there was other organizational work that most of the artists on the label's roster took on themselves. This mainly involved tasks in the process of organizing for live performances of any sort. The artists usually dealt directly with either the venue owners where they played or the organizers of events that hosted performances. The label C usually did not take part in this organization process (P47: 67). Notable exceptions were the performance events organized and branded by the label itself (see section 4.1).

2.2.2 Persons

The notion of personhood will be discussed in section 2.3. Here, persons are described as phenomena in the field.

The first person I am going to describe is the label owner H. The label C was co-founded by H, an artist and music journalist from Berlin, and the owner of a record store from Manchester. During the research period, the co-owner from Manchester was not present in the label operations. An artist told me in an interview that this had not always been the case, and that indeed this co-owner used to be his primary contact at the label (P1167: 202). The co-owner H in Berlin told me (P1165: 206) that his partner had withdrawn from operations gradually over time because his workload with other tasks had left him no time for the label. Besides running the brick-and-mortar record store, this co-owner had opened an online store for music, which had become a success, but which also demanded the partner's full attention in management.

The label owner H was from Berlin originally, and had already worked there as an artist and journalist in the early 1990s (P1222; P1216; P47: 91). His roots were in radio journalism, but he had started to work in print in the 1990s (P47: 3; Ibid.: 107). He joined one of the primary German technology-aware lifestyle magazines as editor shortly after it was founded. The magazine had been started by several former editors of a legendary German techno music magazine that had entered bankruptcy and seized publication in 1997. The label owner still worked at the magazine during the research period, with a work schedule of four full days a week. This left him enough time for label work (P1165: 136; P47: 15). Also, he used some of the magazine's infrastructure for the label. He had a separate room at the magazine's offices where he kept the server with the label's website and email services as well as boxes with CDs and vinyl records of releases that had not yet been shipped to a distributor or dealer (P47: 95-99).

Communication between the label owner H and the artists was done mostly via email. Artists told me that it was sometimes hard to communicate with him because his email replies were sometimes scarce and usually very brief (P1175: 101-104; P1212; P1442). Also, the label owner attended only very few of the performance events I observed. Communication between him and the artists usually peaked just before a release, when they discussed the material to put on the record and, in some cases, also the sequence of tracks on a release (P1163: 68; P1175: 80). One of the artists releasing on the label C described the collaboration as follows:

> "I might have an idea of an album, but he is a little bit the selector, you know, who says, hm, this track, well, maybe better leave out, but these two are good, and then also the order, it's like, when, for example, you really don't know, with such an album, where it is better, when someone else finds the dramaturgy. He pretty much did that with the last one, and with this one it really worked very well. Or I just trusted him, I just told him, you do the order [...]." (Artist M, P1163: 68, transl. FG)

The final sonic mastering of a release, a studio process where the sound of the mixes to be released was finalized, was usually done in Berlin (P1167: 85). If the artists lived elsewhere, the label owner arranged for them to come to Berlin for this process, and he attended the studio session himself as well (P1165: 130). I was present at such a session for one of the releases by the artist O, before entering the research phase for this study. Most of the label's releases were mastered by the same engineer, who was known as an expert in mastering for releases on vinyl records, but who also had an exquisite track record of high-profile releases in digital formats (P1550). The mastering process seemed to be an important aspect of the relation between the artists and the label owner. I did not observe similar occasions of focused collaboration between him and any of the label's artists in other situations.

The next person to introduce is the artist T. This artist had moved to Berlin after he had already released five records on the label C as part of a duo he formed together with a US-based techno producer and DJ (P1162: 59). Of Japanese origin, this artist had lived in Los Angeles before, where he had studied guitar and played in various formations as well as solo (P357). In Berlin, he established himself in the live music scene, focusing on his guitar playing with added electronics. This allowed him to cater to publics outside of the realm of electronic music in addition to the label's typical scene. I engaged in participatory observation at 23 of his performances. He had released a solo record on the label C, with only his acoustic guitar playing. He told me in an interview that the idea for this actually came from the label owner C:

> "[...] the one reason I'm doing this classical guitar part again is that [the label owner H, FG] really wanted to continue the idea. So that was kind of his idea first. I kind of, first I was against the idea, but now I kind of, I understood, and then, I'm very happy that I am going to try to write some classical solo guitar material." (P1162: 39)

T was also part of a trio together with the artist M (see below), also from the label's roster, and an external musician (P485; P486). In this group, his guitar playing added an acoustic part to the computer-based parts played by the other two musicians. The trio had formed after the artist T had played a couple of guest appearances with a larger group of computer musicians, sharply contrasting their distinctively digital sound with his guitar playing. The two other members of the trio had been part of this larger group and decided to continue to work with the artist T (P1162: 13; P1517; P1208). In another musical engagement, the artist T played together with a clarinetist, who, as a member of yet another group, had also released music on the label previously (P1219). In addition, T was active in at least one more music project together with another techno producer and DJ (P1443). The descriptions of these activities show the artist T's focus on collaborative music making and performance. He had a vast network of musical acquaintances, which he had gathered through collaborations in Japan, the US, and Germany.

For practice and recording, T had a dedicated music room at his apartment, with a semi-professional computer-based recording setup and several electronic sound devices (P3178). A large part of this setup was owned by his wife at the time, who was also from Japan and an active musician herself (P1206). They both used this music room, and played some performances together as well. As T's specialty was the seven-string guitar (adding a baritone string to the regular six-string guitar concept), his unique guitars were his most important pieces of equipment (P1162: 43). He had one electric seven-string guitar that was industrially made in a neck-only design – omitting the resonance body – and another electric that was custom-made for him by a guitar luthier in New York City (Ibid.). Another essential aspect of his setup was that he almost always combined his guitar with a loop pedal, a separate device he could operate while playing the guitar by stepping on it, and that would sample entire parts of his playing and then repeat them continuously (as observed in P1201). That way, he could build layer upon layer of his own playing and create complex musical patterns. This technological addition to the guitar considerably expanded his musical expressiveness in a solo performance situation. He did not use a computer on stage himself, which means that in his solo performances, no external sound material was used in addition to his guitar. Nevertheless, he could create complex rhythmic and harmonic pieces via his layering method.

During the time of research, T also started to work for a Berlin-based music software manufacturer. First, he started out as freelance writer for website texts in Japanese, but soon moved on to become a support agent in customer care, serving Japanese-speaking customers on the phone and via email. In addition, he helped out in the support team serving the US market (P1213; P1439; P1443; P1192).

After his solo record, T released two more records together with his duo partner, the techno producer and DJ in Los Angeles. The first of these albums was released on his duo partner's own label, while the second record appeared on the label C (P2980). In our interviews and conversations, T mentioned repeatedly that he was working on another solo album, but this was not released during the time of research.

The next artist I want to introduce is the artist O. This artist had been my point of entry into the field of this study. I already knew him from university, where we worked together as undergraduate students on a project researching aesthetical strategies in computer-based music production. As I mentioned, O was also the co-owner of another record label, which he founded together with other undergraduate students from our university, three of which were also working on the same project team (P1175: 62-74). He released his first full-length album on his own label, but then moved to the label C for his second full album. I have mentioned the rationalization he gave, that he believed it would be better if he didn't release his music on his own label, at least not exclusively (P1175: 77):

> "[...] to somehow reach other regions, both regions as well as classes of people, to just be perceived differently. Always this [label name, FG], and [artist name, FG], sounds even almost the same, and that is somehow, this Lüneburg thing. [FG:] So a bit to get out of this Lüneburg context? [O:] Yes exactly. Well, not get out, I do like to get back in, and I am still in, but I didn't want, I don't know, it's silly to always release on your own label, then it's like, for me that would've felt like a compromise, maybe." (P1175: 77, transl. FG)

He described how he got in touch with the label owner H through a mutual friend, and how his release on the label C came about:

> "[...] one time when we went with [the friend, FG] for a beer in Berlin, then [the friend, FG] negotiated a bit and said, the next album, who knows, if this will still be released on [the label co-owned by O, FG], and [the label owner H, FG] was very interested to hear it, but I also knew, that he listens to a lot of albums and doesn't, I wasn't counting on it. And by that time I had already

> sent out like 20 demos for the next album and I thought, it will be released on [the label co-owned by O, FG] again, but it would've been nice to not just stew in one's own juices, but to be somewhere else for once." (P1175: 74, transl. FG)

> "And no word from [the label owner H, FG], nothing, not even a simple mail saying, I'm going to have a listen soon or something, just nothing. And then I was back in Berlin and we met, I think, at NBI briefly, but just waving across the bar, and I had played with [name of mutual artist friend, FG], and I didn't have much time, and I was in Berlin for this and not to meet [the label owner H, FG] or something. And then I get a text the next day, let's meet today about your album, or like, to talk about your album. Yeah, and that sounded pretty positive somehow. Then we met and it was like, well, we won't make it this year, but that was in September, but we could make it next year in March, and it was like, to him it was totally clear that it hadn't been accepted anywhere else, so somehow, yeah, let's just do it. But before that, he never said that he liked it, or if I couldn't perhaps move this or this song towards the end or take it out or something, it was only like, yeah, let's just do it." (P1175: 80, transl. FG)

The artist O was trained in playing the cello and the drums, and especially the cello was featured widely in his music. All production work was done on a computer, though. I had also collaborated with this artist, working on an interface technology connecting his cello and computer. For this, we were granted a residency at an art institute in Amsterdam, which offered studio space and technical support for artists and engineers who worked on experimental instrument concepts. After the residency, we established and maintained an institutional cooperation between the institute and our project team at our home university.

During the time of research, O lived in Hamburg. Two of his label co-owners also lived there. Together with them, he organized a monthly label night in a small bar, where the label owners and selected guest DJs played vinyl records for the guests. Also, O regularly played performances together with a techno DJ who was based in Hamburg, as well. In this duo, O used a computer setup together with his cello (P1175: 8; P1177: 26). This system had originally been inspired by the work we had been doing together in Amsterdam, but later it was changed and then realized with different technological means. With this setup, O also played with other musicians or as solo performer. The cello retained its status as the main instrument in these performances, but the computer interface and the software behind it augmented the instrumental paradigm by allowing O to sample short pieces of his cello playing and play them back by performing gestures with his bow. He had added a motion sensor to his bow that was connected to his computer. This method differed from the approach used by the artist T in that O only sampled short sounds of either individual notes or clusters of notes, or one melodic pattern at a time, but he did not build multiple layers of repeating patterns. Instead, sampled sounds were played back as individual voices of his setup, their pitch, length, and tonality being transformed in realtime via the gestures of the bow hand and commands from an additional floorboard offering an array of switches the artist could access while playing.

In the beginning of the research period, O had still been active in a duo with a guitar player in Hamburg, playing live scoring performances at screenings of silent movies (P445). When he came to Berlin to perform at one of the regular performance events hosted by the label C, he brought this guitar player as his duo partner to perform live versions of the tracks from his second album (see section 4.1.4; P1224).

In terms of production, O did much of his work at home, where he had a semi-professional setup that was good for production, but not optimized for recording. For recording and longer production sessions, the artist regularly scheduled periods either at the art institute in Amsterdam, where he had access to a dedicated room and sometimes even a full-sized professional recording studio, or retreated to a former water mill and inn in the black forest, which was owned by his family (P1175; P1513). At either of these locations, he would spend anywhere from one to several weeks working on new material or his performance setup. Although he had mentioned producing material for another album on the label C (P1175: 2), this did not materialize until 2013, when it was released on the label he co-owned.

The third artist from the label C's roster who played a major role at the outset of my research was a German artist who lived in Berlin, although this was not his home city. I am mentioning his nationality because there were observable differences between him and the Japanese artist in terms of their embeddedness in the local scene. The Japanese artist could take advantage of organizations dedicated to promoting artists from his national background in Germany, or even Berlin (see section 4.2.1; P1204; P1219; P1443). The apparent advantage of the native language could not necessarily be utilized by the German artist M, as English was spoken widely at the performance events I observed. This, of course, would have to be accredited to the specific situation in the culturally thriving unified Berlin.

The artist M had released one EP and one full album on the label C prior to the research period (P654). During the time of research, he released his second full-length album there. Differing from the two artists I have described before, M did not have a primary acoustic instrument to feature prominently in his electronic productions. In a way, aesthetically, his productions were the most electronic-sounding out of all the productions by these three artists. At the same time, his music appeared to be guided by the mainstream of popular electronic music of the 1980s, while the other two artists mainly referenced techno, hip hop, and jazz styles. He described his music production background as follows:

> "[... FG:] so you're coming from the guitar, and then started to make music with the computer? [M:] Yes, basically yes. Although, my very first instrument was keyboards. As a kid, you know, I played home organ, keyboards. You know, really well behaved, really organ school, home organ school. At some point, that really started to annoy me, and I somehow bought an electric guitar. That was the liberation, somehow. But at some point I realized, that it is somewhat limited, well for me, there are other people, all they want is to play the guitar. For me it was rather, I wanted to have a four-track recorder, and with other instruments and so on, and then it became really obvious for me to start arranging with the computer. That is really a continuation from the four-track recorder. I believe, when I do pieces like that, it is a little bit like a tape simulation. You know, it is of course all abstract and virtual, but somehow I imagine that as a band, like, and now the bass line and like, now the drums [...]." (P1163: 49, transl. FG)

M performed his music mostly as a soloist, strongly focusing on his laptop while playing (see P1192; P1222). The other two musicians often put their acoustic instruments in the foreground at their performances, in the case of the artist O also utilizing the instruments' established paradigm for controlling parameters in the software he used during the performance. Although M, as a solo act, played his music without additional performers on stage, he regularly collaborated with a duo of visual artists. During his performances, they would be placed away from the stage, and produce visuals in realtime that were projected behind the artist on stage (see P1460). Besides pursuing his solo work, M was also active in groups, two of which he had together with T (see above). M was one of the musicians in the larger group of laptop performers where T was brought in to add his guitar playing as a separate element (P1476; P1304; P1308). Also, the two played together in the trio that formed as a spin-off of this larger group.

M also worked as a producer for other artists, and maintained a dedicated studio in a downtown business building during the time of research (P1207). He did, however, also keep several devices at home and produced some of his music there (P1163: 138). In terms of professional involvement, M was in touch with the music software manufacturer where I was employed at the time, and tried to get a commission for the production of sound material to distribute with their products. For the software manufacturers, having enough high-quality sound material to accompany their products was crucial, as the motivation among the users to create their own sounds was generally not high. At least, they expected to get some inspiration from factory-provided sounds. The software manufacturers had some internal resources that produced this material, but they also worked with a large number of additional freelancers. M had pitched some of his work at the manufacturer where I worked, but no commission followed from this. A few months later, towards the end of the research period, he started to work as a freelance writer of website texts for the music software manufacturer where the artist T worked (P1443). As a writer, he also held a position very similar to that in which T started his career at this company.

Finally, I will introduce the label assistant L. L was a journalist by profession, just like the label owner H. They had worked together at the magazine where H was editor, and L had been commissioned to write articles on a regular basis. He did not, however, write exclusively for this magazine. He told me that he was also editor for another, smaller lifestyle magazine.

> "I always wanted to do something in journalism and really write cultural journalism, but I never found the right channel. And that was like, this internship was the possibility to finally do this. But before that I basically had always, always followed that, read the music magazines and so on, but that was like, the initialization for the journalistic writing for me, and also, to broaden that from there on. Well, and I studied cultural journalism here in Berlin, did my masters, and have, and now work as editor at a magazine, that's named [name of another magazine, FG]. Well, also as music editor, really." (P1160: 7, transl. FG)

On another occasion, L mentioned that writing was very important for him, and that he would take almost any job as long as it allowed him to keep on writing. For the label C, he took over the responsibility of organizing the label's "Allnighter" events at the venues. The planning was mostly done by the label owner H, but L was present at the venues to organize the sound check with the artists and the venue staff, and also to moderate performance times between the artists and the venue owners (P1160: 25). In addition, he took over the role of DJ regularly in between the sets of the guest DJs and the artist performances (e.g. P1202).

Additionally, L was also involved in setting up and maintaining the label C's MySpace presence (P1160: 4). However, his role with the label was not made official by the label owner, and his name did not appear on the label C's homepage or in any official communication surrounding the label events.

2.3 Persons in Networks

In the previous section, I have described how a few persons were engaged in the cultural practice of running a label, releasing music on it, and in pursuing the artistic practice of producing music and performing at concerts. These persons were related in various different ways: The label owner H received music for potential releases and commented on it, while the artists were connected through collaborations. In addition, two of the artists also became co-workers at a music software company, and the artist M used to write record reviews for the magazine where the label owner worked as editor. Even these few persons whose activities I have started to describe were connected in various ways. This can be visualized as a densely connected network of hubs with ties.

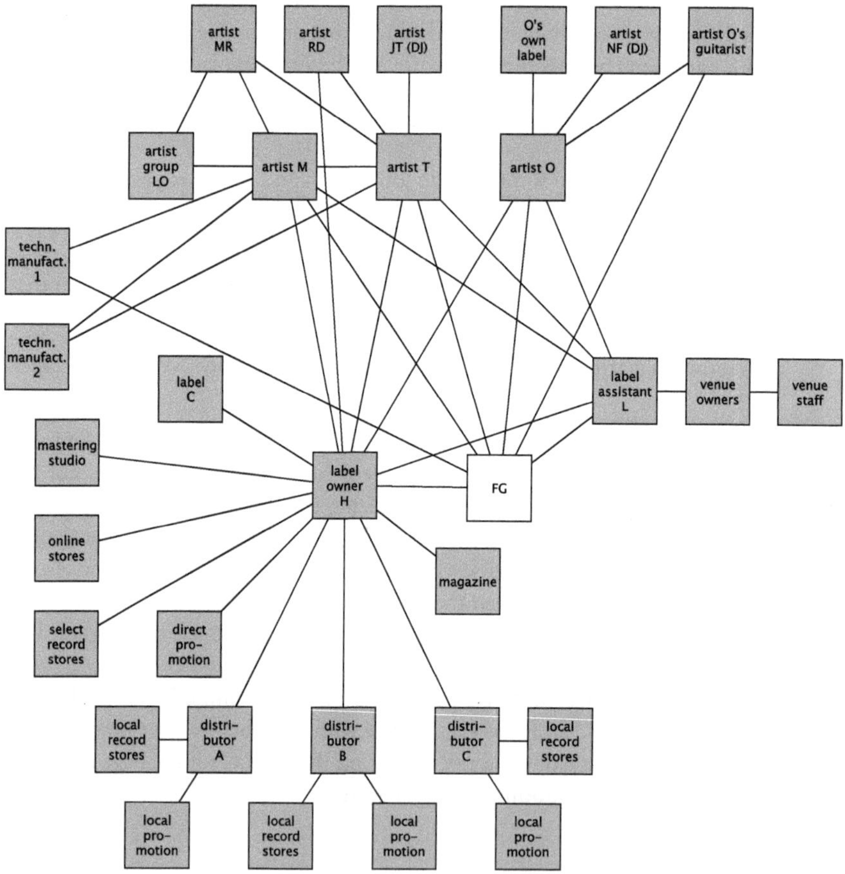

A network visualization of relations in the core part of the field, including my own position.

A visualization like the one shown above is only partially helpful, as it draws an entirely static image of the connectivity in the network. Looking closer at the activities, it becomes clear that not all of these connections were active at any one time. Rather, most of these connections were inactive most of the time. They were explicitly activated on an event base, when they were needed to fulfill a certain function or make a reference, for example upon being asked for in an interview with me. This is not to say that they were irrelevant, or only relevant in certain situations. The knowledge of their latent existence can be expected to play an important role in the planning and carrying out of social activity, for example among the persons whose actions I have started to describe. The connections were, however, not fixed and always activated in a technological sense. Activating a connection between e.g. the label owner and an artist was a social endeavor, subject to various influences on both sides of the connection. Artists, for example, mentioned a few times that the label owner was too busy in his job as editor at a music magazine to look after their needs as artists releasing records on his label. Him being busy was a circumstance of this connection, but one they could not do anything about, as they had no way of influencing the distribution of tasks at the magazine. If, for example, we reconstruct the perspective of the artist O in this situation, we can model the following equation:

$$\text{label owner } H_{\text{perspective artist O}} = \text{identity H} \mid \text{operation}_{\text{label C}} \mid \text{roster}_{\text{label C}} \mid \text{magazine}$$

Form equation 2.3.a: The label owner H seen from the perspective of artist O as the notion of H's identity in the network contexts of operational work for the label C, communication about artistic topics with the label's roster, and work at the magazine.

Therefore, the technological paradigm of network connections has to be used with caution, and with the knowledge that connections in the realm of social activity are much more involved than the connections in technological systems. Nevertheless, it can teach us caution when using the notion of personhood, as it shows how individuality is constructed out of the referencing of identities from a certain perspective.

2.3.1 Network Domains

Within the identity/control networks he described, Harrison C. White (2008) has identified clusters, inside which control efforts are structured in largely similar ways. He refers to the specific way in which control efforts are operationalized as culture, and to the clusters that form out of these operations as network domains. This is compatible with Luhmann's notion of culture, where meaning as the medium of all communication is knowledge, and where society has the capacity to find different ways of applying knowledge in different areas of social action, comparing and evaluating them against each other, and thus forming cultures.

However, the specific ways of applying knowledge and operating control efforts is not static. Together with meaning, they evolve as social processes adapt and renew the underlying semantic categorizations. We can see this in changing processes of cultural and artistic practice, when, for example, a certain style of clothing or of playing a musical instrument gets out of fashion. The fashion industry itself is a good example of a huge social institution that is built around these very changes in cultural processes. We can make out similar changes in the field observations we are analyzing: Not only do musical styles change, but the waves of cultural fashion also influence how the venues that host instantiations of cultural practice are being viewed.

The choices that are being made to apply knowledge in a particular way are functionally equivalent to the implementation of specific control efforts in the network. For example, knowing how to produce a drum loop is basic technological knowledge that is fundamental to artistic practice. Applying this knowledge to create a specific drum loop that fits the expectations held in a particular network part means building a bridge between artistic and cultural practice. It is, however, also a control effort, in that it marks a) the identity of the artist producing the drum loop, b) the identity of an artistic realm, i.e. a style, where such drum loops are produced, and c) the identity of a public in which an interest for this production can be expected. Of course, the production of a particular drum loop is usually only a small fraction contributing to such an effort, which involves not only directly talking about works of art, but also an entire set of metadata (data about data) involving several aspects of an artist's work and its reception. The differentiation of the control effort described above is expressed in the following equation:

$$\text{loop} = \overline{\left.\overline{\left.\overline{\left.\overline{\text{loop}}\right| \begin{matrix}\text{artist}\\ \text{identity}\end{matrix}}\right| \text{style}_{\text{loop}}}\right| \text{public}_{\text{style}}}$$

Form equation 2.3.1.a: A musical loop observed as a loop that is attributed to an artist identity, in the context of a certain style the loop fits, and a public interested in that style. This arrangement is bridging the operative realms of artistic and cultural practice, between the loop as a production and as an observed artifact.

The artists' attempts to adapt to expectations they anticipate is at the same time an effort to control how they as artists and their works will be viewed by others in the future. It is, therefore, a genuine network process in the theoretical sense that White has established. Their attempt at adaptation is not directed towards an individual's expectation, but towards a more generalized understanding of a set of expectations that govern the evaluation of art. On the other hand, artists are not alone in trying to fulfill such a set of expectations; usually, a similar set is being catered to by an entire group of artists. Through this process, different artists may find out that they produce similar music and collaborate, or look for ways to differentiate themselves from this similarity. At the same time, visitors at a concert may lead a discussion about how works of art fulfilled or failed to meet their expectations, and whether these expectations may need to be changed. All the while, artists can themselves become part of audiences, and they can also communicate expectations towards works of art. Audience members can become artists because they have such intimate knowledge of how artists try to fulfill a certain set of expectations.

The notion of culture does not only incorporate the production and reception of works of art, but includes every occasion where selections on specific ways of applying knowledge are made. This means that organizations can have a culture, or even a variety of cultures. Markets have cultures (see White 2001), as well as, for example, families, cliques, and religious groups. Because of this internal structural similarity, these conglomerates can be observed as network domains. In our field, we can make out several network domains in addition to the inner circle of music production and performance described above. For example, the functions enacted in order to organize releases acted as a network domain, establishing or activating connections on the basis of the event at hand, e.g. the common theme of getting a music release out and into the hands of the public. This governed not only what was to be communicated, but also who could participate in the communication. In addition, manufacturing organizations, observed both as individual companies and together as a culture of professionalism, and, in a similar way, the venue organizations with the owners, technicians, bartenders, and sometimes security staff, consisted of structured network parts that included roles with a certain functional focus.

For example, the network domain shown below visualizes the relations with focus on artistic topics among the artists in the inner circle of the field and the label C, including some further artists who were involved in collaborations. Notably, the entities in this visualization do not show persons, but rather roles as parts of identities. The notion of persons can possibly be constructed out of the observation of roles, with the construction becoming more detailed as the number of observed roles increases.

The label owner H had an exclusive relation with the identity of the label C, in that only he could make official statements on its behalf. That is not to say that no other perspective on the label was possible. Indeed, many perspectives could be observed, and they did have an influence on how the label was perceived. Rather, this should indicate that – at least within the scene – the label could not be observed without also observing the label owner. The artists M and T were linked together in a densely connected network part that included many more identities – artists, artist groups, and other collaborators – than are shown here. On the other hand, the artist O was rather separated in his relation with the label C.

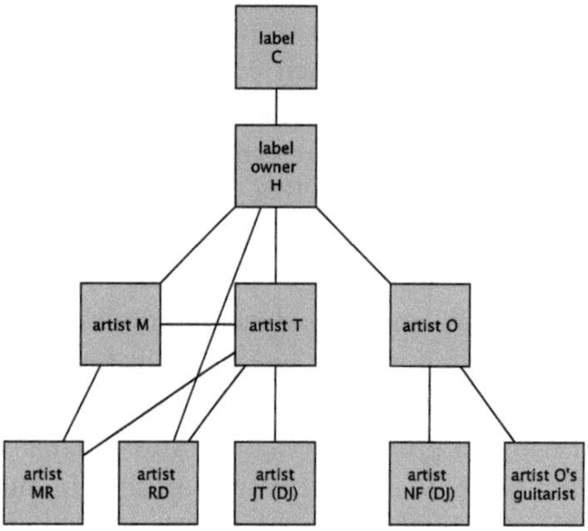

Network domain: Artists' relations with the label C.

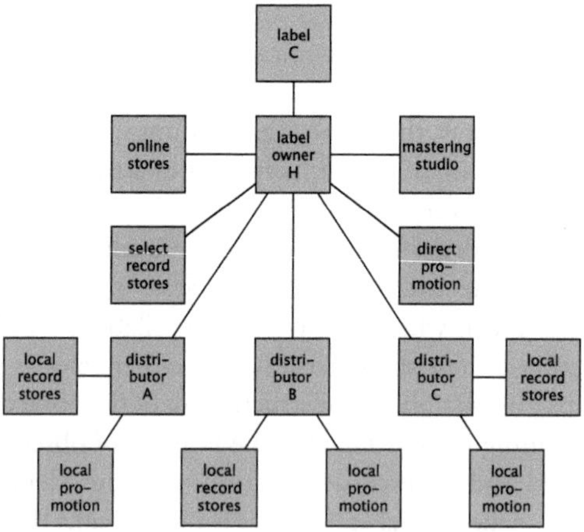

Network domain: Operative business relations of the label C.

In the image directly above, the label owner H again takes on a central role as the only entity directly connected to the identity of the label C. In this role, he handled all operational matters involved with the production and distribution of physical and downloadable releases of recorded music. He communicated directly with the mastering studio, the online stores, and certain promoters and record stores. All other communication regarding promotion and the placement of the physical releases in record stores was handled by distributors with a specific focus on locality. These distributors mainly served individual countries, some of them entire regions of the world.

At the "Allnighter" events organized by the label C (see section 4.1), the label assistant L fulfilled an important role as the organizer in charge of the concrete setup of the schedule and the spatial layout of the performance events, in the context of what was possible at the selected venues. He was also the primary contact to the venue owner and his staff.

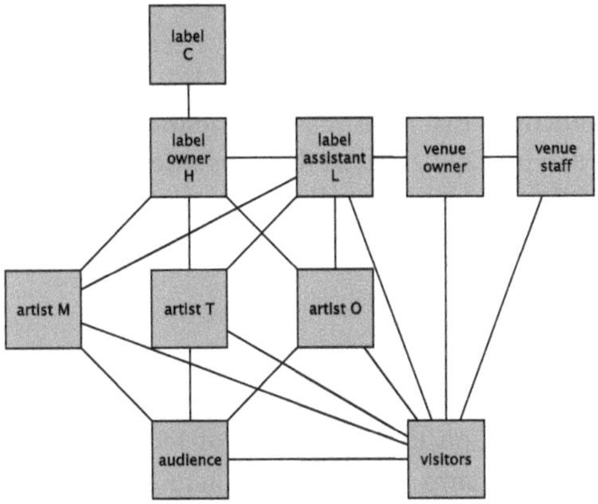

Network domain: Operational arrangement at the label C's "Allnighter" events.

It is important to note again that network domains include roles, not persons (White 2008, pp. 7). Artists' involvements with labels were never mutually exclusive, i.e. other artists released on the same label, and the artists also worked with other labels to release their music. Similarly, employment at a music software manufacturer or a venue for music events was separable from artistic work or other involvements. Identities encompassed roles, integrating them into framework stories, which served as narratives in attempts at anticipating and influencing the public's response to an artistic offering, for example. We will come back to this.

Organizations such as music software manufacturers, venue operators, record stores, journalistic publications, etc., had established structures and their own functional focus, yet the perspective on the production and publication of music was essential to their existence. In that sense, them being so close to the process of artistic practice that took place involving the persons I have begun to describe made them stakeholders in the field. They relied on artistic productivity for their own work, because this is where they drew their information from as to what to produce and offer, and this is where they saw their markets as well.

2.4 Publics and Audiences

Publics and audiences fulfill different social functions, and they take part in forming distinct sociocultural niches. This distinction is similar to the separation between publics and crowds, as Gabriel Tarde has described it (see Tarde 1969). Crowds gather mainly for one topic only, while publics are open to many different topics. Habermas (in Habermas 1990) has expanded the notion of the public as a function of civility, where any member of the civic class has access and can raise any topic. In her study on Japanese culture, Eiko Ikegami (in Ikegami 2005) has argued that publics can rather be seen as network functions that emerge around aesthetical topics. I observed similar functions in the field, while audiences as the remainders of crowds were also present and played a much valued role. In the following section, we will look at how publics and audiences operated in our field.

2.4.1 Baiting Publics

Artists, label operators, and distributors worked together in a conglomerate of network domains that focused on the production of recorded and performed music. However, the work did not stop there. The products that came out of the production-oriented network domains' operation had to find or build an audience for themselves, an audience that would be interested enough to listen to the music and watch the performances in the forms that had been conceived for them during their production.

Even though technological advances may have made production potentially much easier and cheaper, as I have laid out in section 1.2, the artists, labels, distributors, and music stores still had to face the very realistic risk that nobody would be interested in their work, and therefore no audience would form. The key to building an audience was to get relevant publics interested. The label could not expect to sell any number of records automatically. The label owner stated with reference to the label's presence at the "Allnighter" events:

> "Well, it is nice to be present, but mainly for the band, not so much for the label, because this, this cultic following of certain labels, as we know it from the nineties, that doesn't exist any more. That is over." (P47: 59, transl. FG)

Audiences were the consumers of the products, whether in the form of releases or of performances. Niklas Luhmann (in Luhmann 1995b) has described the mode of reception as part of the communication surrounding and dealing with art. Audiences engaged with the network parts focused on production, although these connections were extremely volatile in comparison with the internal structure of the production network domains. Audiences were not tied to artists or labels in any way; they could disappear as quickly as they formed. The artists in our field did not have much of a dependable audience, either. The audiences therefore had to be built almost entirely by generating public interest, i.e. by getting people who would not automatically listen to the recordings or attend the performances to check out the information about them, and eventually give them a try, thus becoming at least a temporary part of the audience. In order to build this interest, information about the offerings of the production network domains had to become accessible in places where potential future members of the audiences were likely to find it. Looking at network processes, both the product and the target groups as potential audiences were engaged in different domains of the same overarching network that is the society. The matching of production domain and audience was then accomplished by a part of the target group making the more or less probable switch and becoming part of an artist's audience. In order to make this switch, the necessary information about the offers had to be available to the target groups in a public situation.

The function of the public situation was that it brought together concrete offers and potential audience members. A public in our field can be described as a specific network configuration in which potential listeners and artists offering references to their work could participate, so that eventually, the potential listeners could make a selection and follow an offer, i.e. start listening to a recording or watch a performance. With Harrison C. White (1995), such an event can be described as a switch from belonging to the group of the merely interested potential listeners or spectators to becoming actual listeners or spectators. Technically, potential listeners could thus be seen as potentials for switchings. Online platforms like the ones used in our field facilitated such situations, as did performance events in which all participants could engage in direct interaction, taken out of their respective network domains. In such a situation, where a public had formed, involvement in particular network domains was not in the focus, or, as Harrison C. White put it, the network domains were "suppressed" (White 1995: p. 1045). Potential connections were not hindered by having to form within the realms of specific network domains; rather, the situation of a public established the theoretical possibility of full connectivity, where all participants were potentially connected with each other (Ibid.). This had practical benefits: The visitors to an artist's profile page on MySpace or Facebook did not need to know the configuration of the network domains in which the artifacts on offer on these pages had been produced or where the presentation on the profile page had been organized. From the artist's perspective, it was impossible to know in which situations the offers made on a profile page would be evaluated by a potential listener. The matching between potentials for switchings and offers was, however, not entirely random, either. Artists, labels, distributors, and stores all enhanced their offerings with metadata, i.e. data about the concrete offers, which effectively served as an attempt to create a narrative embedding the offer into the overarching framework of cultural differentiation, as explicated in section 1.5.2. Potential listeners navigated through this framework of differentiation, guided by their interest. This phenomenon of narrative embedding is captured in the following equation:

$$\text{narrative embedding}_{\text{offer}} = \overline{\overline{\text{offer}\,\Big|\, \begin{matrix}\text{cultural}\\ \text{differentiation}\end{matrix}}\,\Big|\, \begin{matrix}\text{offering}\\ \text{identity}\end{matrix}\Big|}$$

Form equation 2.4.1.a: The phenomenon of narrative embedding adds a context of explicit cultural differentiation between the identity of the offering party and the offer itself.

This narrative embedding opens up a network domain surrounding the offers, while also presenting several different topics and concrete offers, often in the form of music or video players, to let a new public emerge in situ, e.g. on an artist's profile page. In this public, it becomes possible to switch between topics and audiences of the material or the works on offer.

2.4.2 Offers for Switching Generate Interest

In the field of cultural practice we are analyzing, interest was more a notion of anticipation than an observable phenomenon. The concept on the side of the artists and labels was simple enough: Establish and maintain a placement in the framework of cultural differentiation, in our case in the segmentation of genres and differentiation of styles (see section 1.5), and then offer a link to an artifact with a narration of novelty, in the hope that potential audience members will follow the offer. Examples in the field were the offers and categorizations by the artists or other participants acting on their behalf, with consecutive selections by an audience. All these phenomena instantiated combinations of redundancy and novelty in a process of mutual recursivity: They had to offer something perceivably new in order to be distinguishable from what was already there, yet they also had to largely remain redundant in light of existing offers, so they could be recognized as belonging to the same cultural niche.

The metadata provided in order to attempt a categorization of the offers referenced redundant information, e.g. well-known music styles and their protagonists. At the same time, novelty at least in some details was claimed for the works of art on offer, proactively rationalizing a selection out of interest that could occur if the offer was to be recognized in the public discussion.

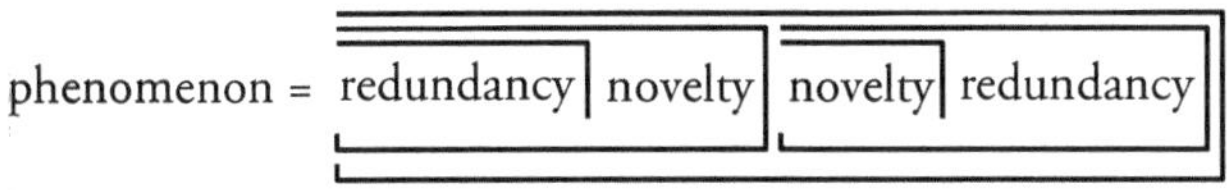

Form equation 2.4.2.a: A phenomenon observed as a process combining redundant elements in a context of novelty with novel elements in a context of redundancy.

2.4.3 Operating Publics

Publics relied on indications from within the network domains for guidance in the process of switching. They could not generate the necessary information themselves, but rather had to select from what was on offer and then follow the directions provided. In the case of the artist profiles, mentions of and links to other artists were such indications, offering starting points for switchings. Via evaluation of observations, it could then be decided whether or not these comparisons did indeed fit the expectations in the cultural context in which they were situated. The artists, or whoever made these offers to the public, could anticipate possible judgments in the public opinion, and thereby select which comparison offers to make. The offer as phenomenon can be modeled as follows:

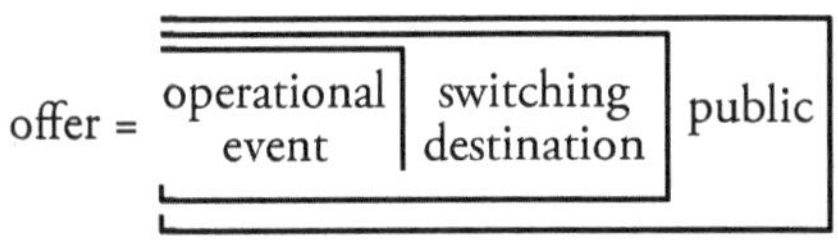

Form equation 2.4.3.a: The offer as an operational event in a context of a switching destination, embedded into a situation of a public.

The public can then be described as a situation integrating different offers for switchings. It can, therefore, make network domains observable for each other.[11] The precondition for this is that all network domains known to the participants can potentially become topics in the public communication, allowing members of the public to make the switch and engage in communication specific to a certain network domain. The principle of the public situation is modeled in the following equation:

11 Dirk Baecker (2007c: pp. 85) has described a similar function of the public (although the German word "Öffentlichkeit" does not seem to translate to "public" entirely). Baecker defines one function of the public as the marking of boundaries between social systems, i.e. providing an independent secondary version of otherwise determining boundaries that can be discussed as an observation.

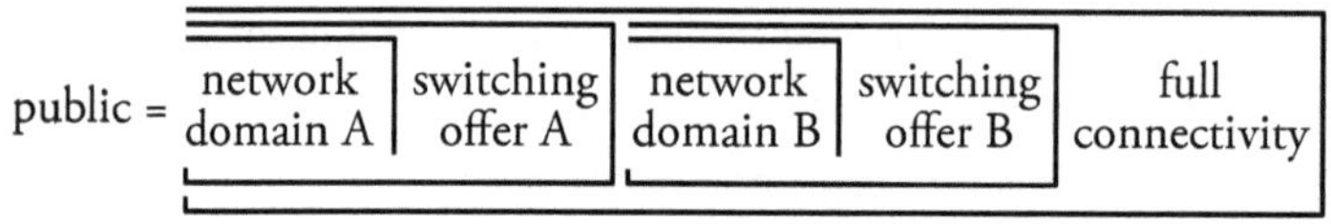

Form equation 2.4.3.b: The situation of the public as observations of network domains A and B, embedded in the context of switching offers referencing them, respectively, all in the context of full connectivity among the different switching offers.

The public opinion can be seen as a conglomerate of different assessments of switching offers. In our example of artists comparing themselves among other artists, such communication could be observed in written comments on MySpace or Facebook profiles, in journalistic writing, on blogs, and as themes in situations of interaction. For example, if an artist named a certain well-known musician as an influence to his work, this mention could be taken up and discussed in online forums or in an article in a music magazine. The public opinion forming there could agree that indeed such an influence was credible and that the artist's work was somehow comparable to his influencer's work. This would then have been a publicly made positive evaluation of the artist's profile, and it could help deepen the embedding of the profile in the domain of cultural practice. As the basis of this principle, I have already introduced the notion of comparison (see section 1.5.1):

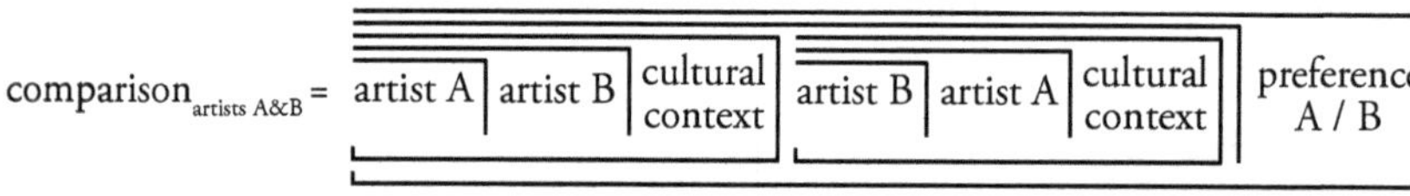

Form equation 2.4.3.c: The comparison between artists A and B as the preference for one of the artists in observation of the unified differentiation of a cultural context from which references to both artists are separated, with these references in turn serving as contexts for references to the operational realms of the respective other artist.

The preference could then be communicated separately, in a form I have been referring to as evaluation. In an evaluation, the preference is connected to an identity communicating it. By triggering this identity, other network domains this identity is involved in become accessible. Therefore, evaluations in public communication can themselves serve as switching offers.

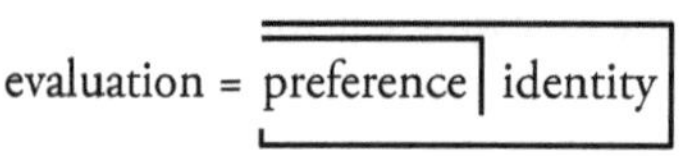

Form equation 2.4.3.d: Evaluation as a preference observed in the context of an identity.

Another option besides observing explicit evaluations, which always required indicating the observer expressing the evaluation, was to simply not select a potential relationship at all. In fact, the vast majority of comparison offers made on artist websites and profile pages were never evaluated in the sense that they would have been talked about in interaction or mentioned in online comments. Such switching offers may still have left an impression with visitors to the website, or even triggered a switching, but their failure to directly establish themselves as themes in public communication meant that they could not have an immediate and explicit positive influence on the public image of the artist.

What is especially notable about the offers we are analyzing is that the largest proportion of indications that led to switchings was provided directly by the protagonists in the field: the artists, the label owner H, and his assistant L. This information was not processed by any intermediate party, such as expert journalists at music magazines, for example. It had been selected for public presentation directly by those who had to be concerned about their public image.

The online publics were in a situation where its members had broad access to original material in terms of audio and video recordings of the artists' work that was provided by the artists themselves. The public as a switching device between network domains (White 1995) operated with information that it received directly out of those network domains, without intermediate buffering layers of expert selection – which material to discuss –, or judgment. Such expert opinion would have been available in evaluations that could be more successful in public communication simply because of them originating from a privileged network position in broadcast media, such as print magazines, radio, and television. These media of communication, and with them their experts, still played an important role in the public reception of the works produced in the field, but the information they provided in terms of offers for switchings amounted to only a minority of all information available.

Because it could not rely on experts for the preselection of switchings that would be worth pursuing, any public situation where interest in the artistic practice of our field was present could potentially process a vast amount of primary material and subsequently come up with evaluations. So, while the situation could certainly be described as one where the experts lost influence, another valid perspective is that indeed the public took over many of the social functions that were otherwise performed by the experts. In this view, we see the evolution of publics into expert publics (see Hutter 2007, pp. 36). Such expert publics had to engage in a complex distributed process of creating valuation orders, forming public opinions. They were not necessarily new phenomena, as predecessors can be found e.g. in fan clubs[12] or fanzines[13]. However, these predecessors typically did not have to deal with the same load of primary material accessible to them, provided directly by the protagonists of the field of practice they were interested in.

The notion that the public situations forced the artists to engage in the process of directly providing information that the publics could use for switchings became prevalent in the field. The artist O mentioned that the label owner H had asked all artists on the label C's roster to create their own MySpace profile page, if they hadn't already done so (P1513). The reason the label owner gave for this request was that he feared other MySpace users, who were unrelated to the label, could create profile pages in the artists' names, effectively hijacking their identities on this platform. He warned that it would be hard to take control of such profiles once they were created. Therefore, the best remedy was to prevent this from happening altogether by creating official profile pages for each artist in time. Notably, the label owner saw this as the responsibility of the artists themselves and did not, at least not openly, consider making this a centralized task for the label. No similar call to action by the label owner was issued regarding the creation of Facebook pages.

2.4.4 Different Public Situations

Social situations facilitating publics could be observed in different instantiations in the field. In his definition of the public, Harrison C. White (1995) pointed out the full, all-inclusive connectivity of a public, which seems to suggest that such situations would foster interaction systems as Luhmann described them (Luhmann 1995a: pp. 405). However, the situations in which switchings between different network domains took place did not all involve interaction systems. In fact, the cases in which instantiations of publics also rendered interaction systems were only a minority in the field.

One of the cases in which a public situation did contain interaction systems was at an event with a performance. The performances took place in front of audiences, but not everybody inside the venue was part of the audience. In fact, the decision whether or not to make the switch – e.g. from interacting with peers – to engaging in the audience was often made only after the performance had started. The details of these situations are analyzed in Chapter 4.

Other public situations were not based on face-to-face communication. An operation where someone read about an artist in a music magazine, then entered the

12 For a study on fan clubs of the TV series Star Trek, see Wenger 2006.

13 Renner and Renner (2011: pp. 40) describe how fanzines, music magazines produced by fans, could be distributed because photocopy machines became available at the end of the 1970s.

artist's name in an online search, visited the artist's website or MySpace profile page, and listened to the music offered there, also took place in a situation of a public. Of course, this is not limited to computer technology, as the printed magazine has allowed for similar actions for much longer than the computer has been around. The difference, however, is that with the possibilities available to the artists in the field, the printed magazines – or, for that matter, their online counterparts – were not exclusive grounds for publics any more. Searches for interesting artifacts with an appreciated novelty value did not have to rely on information gathered and channeled by professional music journalists. Rather, they could come directly from the artists themselves. Whereas before, the announcement of a new release or a concert would have been sent to magazines and similar outlets by the artists or their agents, the availability of the so-called social networks made it much more probable that the text in which an interested member of the public read about an upcoming release for the first time had actually been written by the artist himself, and would be continuously updated as the release neared publication.

This had various implications in our field. Music magazines and similar publications still existed, but they took on new, diversified roles, extending beyond the information channels that had been the basis for their operation before. During the research period, the magazine where the label owner H worked tried to establish its own monthly party event, with relatively prominent guest DJs and live acts (P1203; P1217; P1396). The party was originally conceptualized as a celebration of the publication of the monthly print issues, and, as part of the concept, each paying guest could grab a free copy of the new issue at the entrance. The party event was announced in the magazine, but the email newsletter sent out by the editors was at least as important to get the word out and draw the interest of potential visitors. Towards the end of the research period, the party events were discontinued, despite a good number of guests at the instances I attended (P1203; P1217).

At the same time, the artists also had to assume new roles. The advent of the social networks had drawn in artists of all categories and genres, united by the understanding that the production and distribution of works of art could benefit from direct involvement with the processes of reception. Audiences formed right there within MySpace, Facebook, and sometimes Last.fm, and their members appreciated the channels of direct communication with the artists; channels that had been facilitated by the technology of the internet. For the artists, this involvement brought the opportunity of being able to express their own opinions and views on their own music in the context of the broader cultural practice. They could address at least a part of their target groups, without the intermediate stages of professional promotion, including giving interviews and inside stories. These had been introduced as structural processes of the cultural industries (Kusek / Leonhard 2005: pp. 57), and as such, they were based on the concepts of broadcasting, one-to-many network configurations and the notion of opinion leaders as influential hubs in relevant network parts. Notably, these processes did not disappear: Releases were still professionally promoted (see P1166), and artists still had interviews with music journalists (P1188). Via their online profiles, however, they could be a part of their target group's regular processing of information, partly by setting themes themselves, but more often by assuming the role of commenters in the continuous flow of themes occupying their cultural scene.

Artists acted as members of the public most of the time, and they used this role in building and maintaining their artist identity. This was especially visible on Facebook, where almost every new piece of information that entered the platform via a member was added to that member's "wall" and could be commented on either by the member's "friends" or by all members of the platform, depending on the respective member's privacy settings (see section 3.2 for more details on the technology of Facebook). For the artists, this socio-technological possibility brought about a potential to place themselves in relation to relevant cultural processes, i.e. announcements of releases and concerts by other artists, but also television shows, popular online videos, etc. This new potential could utilize a much larger amount of sources of novelty for the artists' work on their identity than what would have been possible with only the artists' own output of releases and other news as material. The artists' comments on material from other sources were themselves offers to the public, as they added new information, if only a relation or perspective, to the original material.

This directness of being involved in a continuous flow of themes also posed a risk for the artists. In the structures that the cultural industries had professionalized, possible misinterpretations or other unfavorable outcomes of information provided by or on behalf of an artist were carefully examined and could be reviewed and discussed before publication, if necessary. With the artists' direct involvement on the so-called social networks, this corrective was not available. Comments came from the artists themselves, and since the comments were read by many who knew the artists personally, any ghostwriting would have been identified quickly.

On MySpace, the use of anonymous agents keeping the artists' profiles up to date was a little more accepted. MySpace had different uses than Facebook, though, since the focus was much more on the presentation of information and less on taking a stance on information presented by someone else. It was more a replacement for an artist's website than a place for personal involvement by the artists themselves. Facebook, on the other hand, allowed the artists to get involved on a much broader basis.

2.4.5 Audiences out of Publics

An audience in the field can be defined as the group of members of the public who engage in the reception of a piece, a song, or an entire performance. Niklas Luhmann has described this mode of communication for the reception of art as a mode that is focused primarily on perception (Luhmann 1995b, pp. 39). This part of art reception is non-functional, and only the mere act of perception can be observed by a second-order observer. There is no understanding of the work of art as such to be observed. After decoupling from listening to or looking at a work of art, the act of focusing on perception can itself become a theme of communication and thereby serve a function, e.g. to indicate the listener's knowledge of aesthetic categories. All this happens in successive communication decoupled from the actual reception of a work of art. An audience is a precondition for the observation of art and artists, for if any given entity cannot be imagined as being perceived as art, it cannot be described as such. Of course, this does not rule out the possibility that the artists themselves make up their own exclusive audience, or that indeed the observer giving the account is the only member of the audience. Also, an audience may falsely be observed by others, without any reception actually taking place – think of the thin line between deep listening and sleep, for example.

With the exception of interviews and direct personal communication, all the data we are analyzing was originally published for public situations. In these situations of potential full connectivity (White 1995), messages containing information on the artists, labels, distributors, and other participants in our field faced competition for attention from a vast number of more or less similar offerings from other artists, labels, and distributors. In order to increase the chance that members of the public would switch their attention to their offerings, the participants in our field created distinct profiles in which they embedded their messages. In marketing, this process is known as target group marketing (Kotler / Armstrong / Saunders / Wong: pp. 441), where the presence of a specific interest in a public is assumed, and the offerings are then tailored to accommodate this assumed interest.

Perhaps the most obvious method of target group marketing I observed in the field was the splitting up of an artist's or organization's identity representation into separate sub-identities targeting separate interests. One example is the separation between the label C and its two sublabels. While the main label was known for releases in the broader realm of popular electronica music, one of the sublabels hosted music by bands or instrumentalists with a sound that was distinctively guitar-oriented, yet was situated in the same broader cultural context as the musical style of the main label (P76). The other sublabel focused on vinyl-only releases, so any music released on this sublabel could not be bought on CD or as MP3, at least not initially at the time of its release (P1216). Thereby, this sublabel was targeted towards purist aficionados of the vinyl medium. The differentiation, the notion of distinctness in the context of the main label, was established through aesthetic classification in the case of the first sublabel, while in the second case being based on a preference for a specific technological medium. By addressing different publics, both sublabels could also have been the exclusive contact for audiences that did not consume the offerings made by the main label C. Similar cases can be observed among the artists: If an artist's work deviated enough in musical style, the artist would usually create separate areas of publication for each area of artistic work. In some cases, these areas were so strongly separated that distinctive identities with different artist names emerged in each area.

On the other hand, even a targeted publication by an artist or label could still gain attention from members of the public with different interests. One member of the public might be interested in the acoustic part of an electro-acoustic performance, while another could be interested mainly in techno music and therefore focus on the electronic part. If they made the switch and became part of the audience, each of these two members of the public would contextualize the performance differently, as each would use the performance as a starting point to reference comparable experiences and areas of knowledge within their particular background.

Thus, offers from participants in our field and the attention they received cannot be linked by any overarching rationalization or causal relation. Areas of interest could be targeted, and this was done in various forms, yet it was impossible to foresee any switchings. It was, however, possible to observe which mechanisms did not play a major role in channeling attention. For all the artists, their releases, and performances, I did not observe a single instance of paid-for advertisement; neither in print magazines nor in online publications. Also, no paid-for placements of search results appeared openly on Google (e.g. P1008; P1015; P1030; P2580). Therefore, we can almost rule out the possibility that any visitor to a website or profile page belonging to the field found his or her way to an artist or a label from an otherwise unrelated site through traditional advertising. When conducting searches myself, the artist and label profiles on MySpace, as well as the official websites showed up high in the ranking of search results on Google (Ibid.). Therefore, the label and its artists could easily be found if their names were already known in the public domain. Another way for members of the public to find the label and the artists was through related sites offering links, either on the open web, or within MySpace or Facebook. Most of the artists on the label C's roster had the label as a "top friend" on their MySpace profile, and were themselves featured on the label's profile page. The artists were also referenced by other artists outside of the label's inner circle, often because they belonged to more than one label's roster (e.g. P32; P445; P447; P676), or because they had collaborated with these other artists in the past (P78; P548). Public interest in one of the artists' profiles could then lead to a fraction of the members of the public actively switching over to the other artist's profile. Each artist added more and more such references to the profile over time, thereby gradually building the potential for attention from the public.

The "top friends" section on the profile page of the label run by artist O (P32).

Participants in the field offered metadata to the publics not just hoping that members of the publics would read through them, but with the actual goal of building audiences. An audience would not just know of an artist, but would actually listen to his music, attend performances, and likely take part in discussions of works or of the artist himself. Therefore, the offerings by the artists and the label C often included direct invitations to listen to works or watch videos. This included interviews in print magazines and online publications as well as websites and profile pages on social network sites such as MySpace, Facebook, Last.fm, and others (for Last.fm, see for example P2; P373).

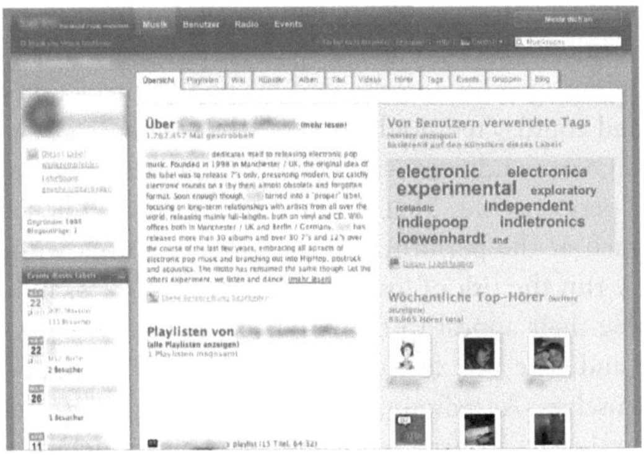

The Last.fm page dedicated to the label C (P2).

None of this could have been achieved without social embedding: Statements about the quality of an artist's own creative output were usually backed up by mentions of references to other artists, claiming similarity to their work – while retaining the claim of originality for the artist's own work –, and sometimes naming collaboration projects with them, or quoting from their assessment.

The claim of artistic originality could be found primarily in the combination of references. Each reference was directed towards certain expected interests among members of the public, and by combining indications towards existing knowledge with references to areas that were new, the artist could eventually hope to shape an original profile. White (1998: pp. 9) has described this process of building identities as a sequence of mismatches between expectations and outcomes, where the specifics of the mismatch are then attributed to the identity, which thereby gains informational value. Baecker (2005a: p. 229) has expressed the process of maintaining an identity in the following equation:

$$\text{identity} = \overline{\overline{\text{deviation}}\rceil\,\text{norm}}\rceil$$

Form equation 2.4.5.a: An identity as the process of deviation from an established norm (Baecker 2005a: p. 229, transl. FG).

With such a combination of references as the basis for an original profile, an artist could try to build an audience out of the different participants in the public situation who observed the profile. However, the sum of the people present at any of the performance events I observed was not identical with the audience for the performances happening there. Indeed, in several cases only a very small audience formed inside a venue full of people. The rest of the people present remained engaged in a situation of public interaction, which the audience had decoupled from in order to engage in perception of the work of art. Decoupling in order to enjoy the work or artistic performance and coupling again in order to join the public interaction could happen in quick succession and could often not be observed as separate states of engagement.

The observation of an audience was a necessary precursor for the observation of a work or artistic performance. That is why control over audience formation was sought after so much at the performances I observed. Artists without an audience would immediately run the risk of losing their status as artists, and with this status, they would also lose their appeal to the public. Therefore, any decrease or increase in the size of the audience was carefully observed both by members of the public and the artists themselves. As tedious as it may have been, the artists had to take the approach of attempting to attract the interest of as many members of the targeted publics as possible in order to build the potential for winning over at least a significant part of them as their audience. The presence of interested members of the public at a performance event was already an improbable phenomenon in the light of all the different options on offer at any given night in a city like Berlin. The next step of convincing the members of the public present at a performance event to actually engage in listening to the music and following the performance was also hard to take, as the possibilities to remain engaged in public interaction with other visitors at the performance event were many.

All efforts at getting members of the public interested in artistic work could only create the potential for an audience to form at a performance event. The potential then had to be seized, either by attempts to change the social situation so thoroughly that interaction neglecting the presence of the performance was forced to break up (see section 4.2), or by creating a strict, enforceable schedule for the performance event.

Not all communicational offers were directly related to the forming of an audience for an artist's work. Via the public, other important wins for the artists could be gained as well. For example, an artist could get a commission to work on a score for a television feature, just because the director of the feature had read about the artist in a newspaper article.

Taking on and enacting the roles of performers was in part an attempt to get action from the public present at a performance event. A performance was still a situation of mutual recursive observation, not unlike the situation within an interaction (for a detailed analysis of such a situation, see section 4.1.5). Since the performance was temporary, the audience always dissolved into the public again.

2.4.6 Audiences as Performers

Audiences were important network domains in the cultural practice in the field. The artists, labels, and organizers of performance events all constructed a large part of their actions focusing on their respective potential audiences. Yet, the desirable act of participants in a public situation switching in, engaging with an offer, e.g. starting to listen to an embedded music file on a MySpace profile page, or watching a performance, was not observable directly. If we take communication to be the unity of an uttered information being understood (see section 1.4.3), then we can observe the uttering of information in any public situation, but we cannot take its being understood for granted. Although a large number of people might have been present in front of the stage where an artist was performing, their sheer presence did not necessarily lead them towards uttering signs of understanding, which might be observable as reception. We have to look carefully for signs of understanding being uttered as fresh information, so we can indirectly come to conclusions about participants that included themselves in the audience. Online, this can only be achieved by the traces an audience left behind, e.g. in counters or other web statistics tools.

Understanding was signaled mostly through comments on the music. Of course, such comments could only be given while the commenter was not listening, so it required a decoupling from the audience to signal the engagement in the audience. Decoupling from the audience, the commenter became a participant in the public situation again, which was where the comment was placed and could itself be observed and understood. The most ritualized form of commenting was applause, which was given either in between songs or tracks, if there were noticeable breaks or even moments of silence between them, or after longer parts of the performance. Some performances went on without any breaks leaving room for applause, so it could only be given at the very end of the performance.

I have described a few basic mechanisms how audiences can form from publics. Both areas are thus not separate operations, but rather deeply interwoven. In the next two chapters, we will look at case studies where these processes can be analyzed in detail.

Chapter 3: Online Publics and Practices

With the decline of the mass media's role in providing information on artist activities to the publics, the artists and labels started to rely primarily on themselves for getting their messages across. They utilized internet-based platforms to publish information on their own works, their releases, concerts, tours, additional material such as photos and videos, or to simply voice their opinion on topics in their general cultural realm. The internet platforms allowed the artists to reach a large part of their relevant target groups directly, as they had exhibited a social dynamic drawing in many, if not most of the groups interested in the various electronic music scenes (Vincent 2006).[14]

I propose to look at the situation thus created as a new form of public. The social operation within these internet platforms, or so-called social networks, was running in a context of full inclusion, where every communicational offer could be accessed by any member of the platform at any time, and the platforms themselves were open to large parts of society. There was no temporal, social, or factual decoupling hindering accessibility. Therefore, the situations we will analyze in this part of the study fulfill the major requirement – full inclusion – set forth by Harrison C. White as the basis of a public (White 1995). Publics have a history as long as that of communication. In the evolution of first the different societies and then, eventually, the world society, publics were the means by which information could be processed among different contexts.

As the relevance of so-called social networks has become more and more apparent, it has also become a research focus in social sciences. Although the field of research is still in its infancy at the time of writing, some studies are already available. Danah Boyd is a pioneer in the field, having conducted early research on the role social networks have played for American teenagers (Boyd 2008). In this context, she developed the notion of networked publics as "the space constructed through network technologies" (Boyd 2011: p. 39) and an "imagined collective" (Ibid.) integrating people, technology, and practice. She describes phenomena I encountered in my field as well, such as the "invisible audiences" (Boyd 2011: pp. 49) or the updates of rela-

14 The popularity of tutorials in music publications explaining to musicians how they can set up their own MySpace profile page (such as Vincent 2006) hints at the function of the platform in getting artist representations online for the first time.

tively low news value, which nevertheless amount to an important reactualization of the network structure (Boyd 2011: pp. 45). Thomas Wanhoff (2011) gives a descriptive account of the use of Facebook across different social realms, with an empirical focus on Germany. His book provides a good overview of different strategies in the usage of Facebook, as well as some other, more specialized social network websites.

In the introduction to their book "Generation Facebook", Oliver Leistert and Theo Röhle (2011: pp. 7) collect different research approaches in the study of phenomena related to Facebook. In the same book, Dirk Baecker (2011: pp. 123) hints at the ambiguity of expressions as the most prominent – and often misunderstood – feature of communication on Facebook. Geert Lovink (2011: pp. 183) sketches out strategies to break out of the communicational patterns suggested by Facebook. One of his findings (Ibid.: p. 196) is also very obvious in our field: Online and offline activities were rarely synchronized, although the technological means for doing so would have been available. Two of Facebook's core features are also investigated in Generation Facebook: Ralf Adelmann (2011: pp. 127) takes a look at the characteristics and politics of "friendships" on Facebook, while Carolin Gerlitz (2011: pp. 101) describes how Facebook "likes" become a measure of success not just for activity on Facebook itself, but across the entire internet, as more and more websites make use of Facebook's integration features.

Daniel Miller (2012) has conducted ethnographic research on the use of Facebook on Trinidad. In his qualitative analysis, he comes to the conclusion that Facebook has transformed the communicational habits in his field profoundly, and has enabled new forms of social activity, e.g. through games embedded into Facebook, but that power distribution remains largely intact. With a broader perspective, Mercedes Bunz (2012) investigates how mass media are transformed by the emergence of online publics. Journalism, but also political activism and other strategies in mass media are deeply influenced by the possibilities of new technologies, and are forced to adapt their operations or invent new ones.

In the following section, I will first lay out the functionalities offered by the social network platforms used in our field, and then look at specific cases. Both quantitative and qualitative data types will serve as basis for analysis and argumentation in the following discussion of the form of online publics.

3.1 MySpace

In the beginning of the research phase, MySpace was the single most important platform for the hosting of self-representations among the artists in our field. This changed, together with MySpace's overall role, around the year 2009.

3.1.1 *Platform*

MySpace was – and at the time of writing, still is – an internet platform that started out offering a combination of services that allowed users to connect with others and create profile pages (MySpace 2011c; MySpace 2011d). The platform operated internationally, with dedicated homepages and public relations teams for a number of countries. The member pages were in the focus right from the beginning, hence the name MySpace. The users could present personal information on their pages, much like they would on a personal website. MySpace made it easier for the users to create those pages by taking away from them most design decisions, and instead offering preset designs with only a small margin of adaptability available to the user. This resulted in great similarity between the pages, but it also provided easy orientation around the information presented, as the visitors knew where to expect which element.

Within the page concept, a focus was on multimedia material. MySpace offered embedded players for audio material, which worked on the basis of Adobe's Flash framework. This meant that audio material could be played back from the page, but the listeners could not download the original file. With this, the material was copy-protected in a light way. Visitors to the page could listen to the material whenever they liked, but they had to stay on the profile or else the music would stop. This meant that the music still had to be bought in order to be listened to in situations when no internet connected computer was available, e.g. on mobile players and in cars, or if the users wanted better audio quality than the streaming format offered. With some technical effort, the material being played back could be recorded, but the added complexity of recording, cutting the files, and naming them correctly effectively prohibited such methods from becoming popular among a majority of users. Nevertheless, most artists from the field who had a MySpace profile offered full songs or tracks to be played back on their profile pages. This was highly attractive for users on the lookout for new music, as it allowed them to make the switch and engage in listening directly on the page. For the artists, it was a convenient way to facilitate the forming of an audience for their music without the involvement and restrictions inherent to producing physical representations of music releases or playing live performances. Recall the model of the communicational principle of the offers observed in the field from section 2.4.3:

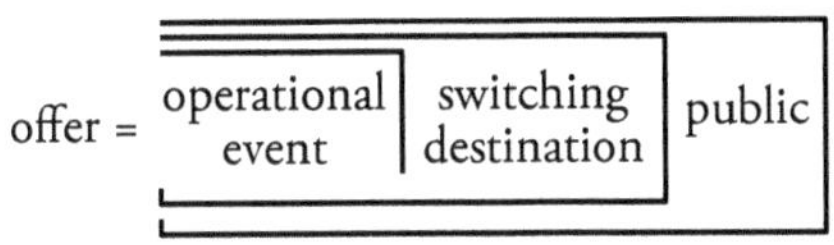

Form equation 3.1.1.a / 2.4.3.a: The offer as an operational event in the context of a switching destination, embedded in a situation of a public.

The principle of the layout of a MySpace page. The first comment by a visitor is at the very bottom (P682).

The survey conducted among the label C's MySpace "friends" shows that music and related material was the primary focus for page visitors. The categories provided below were established in the analysis of the survey, and any one answer could fall into more than one category. Promoting content and gathering information about music were the most important tasks on MySpace. Networking, i.e. a deliberately dialogic activity, was only in third place, and audience contact, i.e. a one-to-many communication, even less important. Notably, a relatively large proportion (7 out of 22, or 31.8%) answered that they used MySpace to stay connected with their local scene, e.g. find information about upcoming concerts or promote a local performance event.

Type of activity	Number of responses
promotion	12
information about music	10
networking	8
referencing local scene	7
audience contact	6

Use cases for the MySpace platform among a surveyed sample (n=22) of the label C's MySpace "friends".

Of the 30 artists observed in the field, 25 or 83.33% had an active profile on MySpace in the summer of 2009. All of the artists I asked about it answered that they maintained their own profile, without letting someone else or an organization deal with it. One artist mentioned that because of the amount of messages he received on MySpace, he could only superficially skim through them and direct any booking requests to his agent (P1185: 10, 12).

On a typical MySpace profile page, the information was organized in boxes. These boxes contained text, images, and interactive elements, and they were clearly visible against the background of the profile page, which could be a solid color, or filled with a tiled image. On the very top of every MySpace page, there was a banner advertisement that the owner of the page could not influence. This was a targeted advertisement operated by Google and selected on the basis of past preferences the user had exhibited when exposed to Google's tracking mechanisms (Brin / Page 1998). Below the banner advertisement, one could find the MySpace logo on the left side and a search bar operating on the MySpace platform on the right. This search feature was also operated by Google, and the search could be narrowed by categories, so that the results would only contain music acts, for example. By default, the search feature operated on the full text of the information entered by page owners. This, as well, could be narrowed down so that a search only returned names of members.

The header bar of a MySpace page (P682).

Below the MySpace logo and the search bar followed the main navigation elements for the platform. This included a button for the home page – directing the user to one of the main portals for the different languages MySpace supported – as well as links to music and other categories and subcategories, an area dedicated to finding other members with similar interests, and areas with direct access to original audio and video material. During the time of research, MySpace also experimented with its own download shop for music (MySpace 2009). This shop, however, was not successful, and it was not used by any of the artists I interviewed. On the very right of this navigation bar were buttons where members could log in and visitors who were not yet members could register. Below the navigation bar, there was another bar, indicating which section the currently open page belonged to. In the case of our field, all pages I included in the research belonged to the music category, which had its own logo derived from the corporate MySpace logo.

Navigation elements on a MySpace profile page (P1144).

The owners of the profile pages could not influence any of these elements placed on the very top of the page. The elements were included in all design templates, and they were framed by the same background as selected for the entire page.

The topmost part of the page containing user information consisted of one box on the left with the core information on the identity of the page owner and, typically, a player with original audio material on the right. The box on the top left once again featured the MySpace music logo and then, directly below it, the artist or label name. This was accompanied by information on the category of musical style that was selected by the user for this profile page. The possible selections were predefined by MySpace, and only three styles could be selected, e.g. "Alternative / Indie / Electronica" in the case of P1144. The naming of the styles was rather generic, keeping the range of results very broad when the style was selected in the criteria for a search in the music domain on MySpace.

Below the artist name and categorial information usually came a picture. Also on the left side, the artist could post names of other artists who he or she wanted to appear as influences. Naming one's influences also created points of reference for the visitor, hinting at where to place the artist in terms of stylistic categories as well as quality valuation within one or more categories.

Directly on the right, next to the picture, was the number of visits to the page, called "Profile Views" (e.g. P1403). This number did not count individual visitors, as they could be tracked with so-called cookies stored locally on the user's computer, but rather it simply counted the number of times the system had delivered the page to any receiver. This receiver could be a true visitor, with an interest in the information on the page, or it could be a software, e.g. an indexing agent for a search engine, or even a software designed for the sole task of increasing this very number (Jag 2007). Such software packages existed, but I did not observe any participant in our field talking about using them. Nevertheless, the label C's MySpace profile page did show an unusual jump in the number of visits, going from 29,601 (P443) to well over 500,000 in less than three months. Since the profile page had accumulated its 29,601 visits over a period of two years since its launch, this jump in the number of visits to the page cannot be explained with mere public interest, especially since the growth of the cumulative number of visits after the jump returned to the pace it had exhibited before (see below).

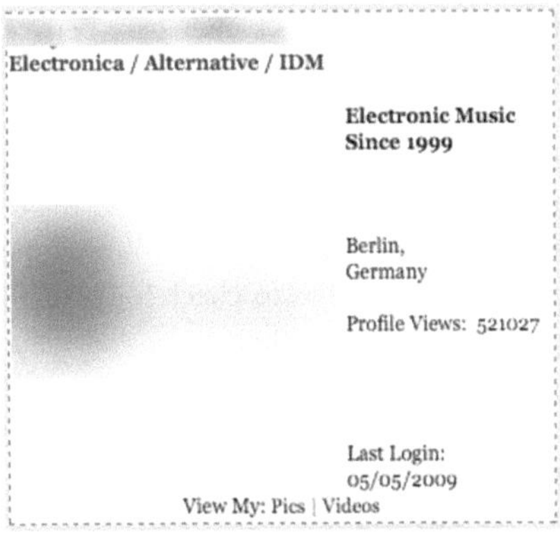

Information box on the top left of the label C's MySpace profile page (P1403).

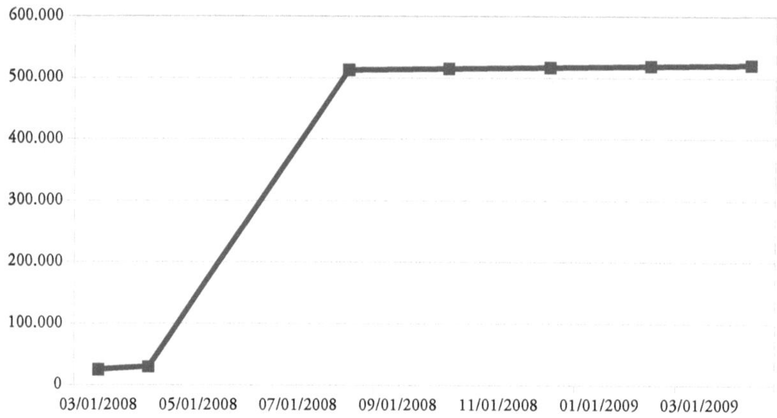

Page views on the label C's MySpace profile page between March 22, 2008 and June 10, 2009.

Despite such inconsistencies, the accumulated number of visits to a MySpace page was nevertheless observed as an important indicator of an artist's popularity. An artist relations manager working for a music technology manufacturer told me that he would not even consider an artist for the company's artist affiliation program if they had fewer than 10,000 visits to their MySpace profile page (P1199). This was in 2008, and the benchmark certainly had to evolve since the numbers on all MySpace profile pages could only stagnate or grow, but never decrease. A typical number of visits to the profile pages of artists in the field was somewhere between 10,000 and 20,000 during the time of research.

A first hint at an artist's activity on MySpace was given in the publicly shown last login date. This date was placed prominently directly underneath the number of page visits. The amount of time between their last login and the current date was a hint at how active this artist was on MySpace, and also how important it was for them to keep their profile up-to-date, as well as to check for possible messages from other MySpace users and to potentially reply to them.

In addition to the profile page, MySpace members could also host a blog on the platform. While the profile page itself was used to publish general information on the artist or the label in a way that more or less resembled a traditional website, the blog format was designed to hold information with a news value. All items published on the blog page were arranged in a list, with the most recent entry at the top. As older entries moved down the list, it was broken down into multiple pages.

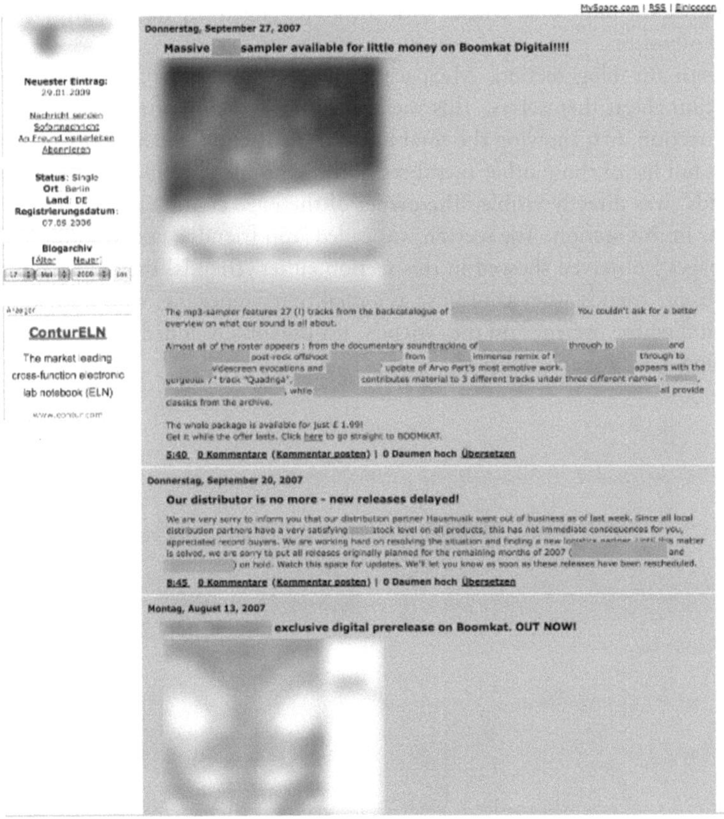

The label C's MySpace blog (P3329).

The MySpace members could choose to have new blog entries appear automatically on their profile page. The profile page was always the main page, while the blog pages were treated as sub pages. Some of the participants in our field made extensive use of the blog feature, others did not use it at all. Those who did have a blog all featured it on their profile page, and used it to publish information on current events, such as new releases or upcoming performances. Visitors to the blog site could comment on the individual entries, but this option was rarely used in the field. From a visitor's perspective, the blogs were rather hidden behind the profile pages. While the information that also appeared on the profile page was clearly visible, there was no further attraction offered to entice visitors to visit the dedicated blog site beneath. The comment feature for individual entries was, therefore, effectively hidden away from the majority of visitors.

Beneath the blog section, MySpace members could offer additional, detailed information about themselves. This was usually a paragraph of text. Next came the "friend" section, first showing the total number of "friends" the member had, with a link to a full list of those other members. On the profile page itself, only a selection of "friends" was directly visible. The owner of the page could select who he wanted to appear in this section. The section was called "top friends", and accordingly, most profile pages I observed showed in this section either "friends" they had a close relation with, or "friends" they could use as a quality reference, i.e. who were known to visitors and whose presence on the "friends" list potentially added value to the profile (see section 3.1.2 for an example).

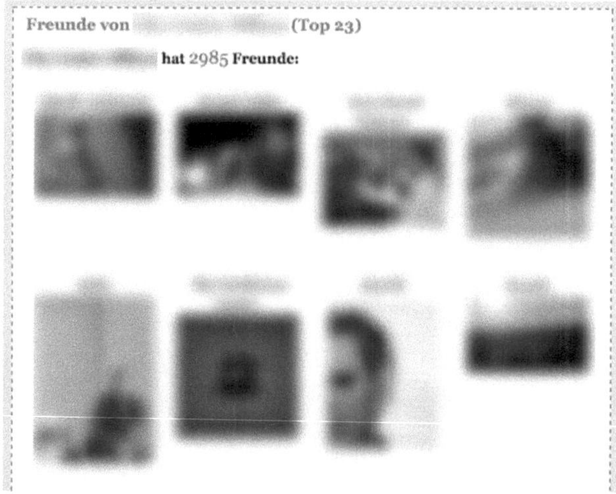

The label C's first eight entries in the "top friends" section on its MySpace page (P3357).

The comments on any MySpace profile page were placed beneath the information provided by the profile owner. Profile information and comments, i.e. information coming from other MySpace members, were therefore separated on the platform. It was not possible to comment directly on any item on the page, so in case they wanted to give their opinion on something on the page, members had to explicitly make the reference.

As they were placed so far down, comments were often not even visible to the visitor without scrolling down the page. In the comments section, the latest entries were placed at the top, with older entries moving down the list. The list of comments shown beneath the member information on a profile page could become very long, as more and more older entries accumulated. All in all, the comments were not integrated with the profile pages, but rather added at the bottom.

3.1.2 MySpace Case Study: Artist O

The artist O had a relatively active MySpace profile during the time of research (P445). The page design was customized within the limits of the MySpace platform: The background color was a bright orange, and on the left side, he had added a combination of two versions of his latest album cover, which automatically repeated themselves down the entire page, including the comments section. His profile picture showed him outside, in front of a green field and a paved track, yet with a steel gray sky and in overall rather cold colors.

Directly underneath the artist name at the very top of the user-configurable part of the page was the stylistic association with the genres electronica, ambient, and techno. These were direct references to overarching cultural categories, and their position at the top of the page effectively helped usher in visitors through the genre-based search function. At the same time, these references also created a differentiation structure, stating that this page was part of the cultural and artistic practice of these three genres, keeping everything else outside.

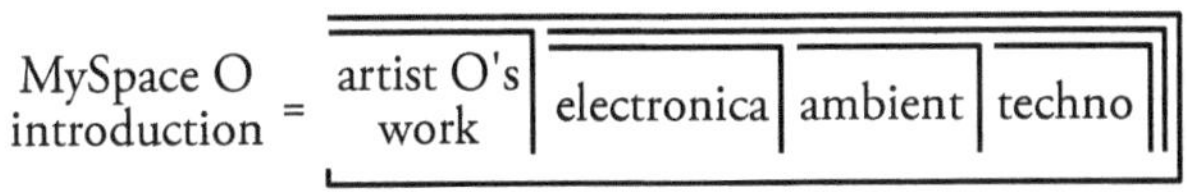

Form equation 3.1.2.a: The introduction of the artist O on his MySpace profile page as the placement of his work in the context of the genres electronica, ambient, and techno.

Next to the picture, there was a claim stating "'natural°syntax°dub'" (P445). Directly below this cryptic claim came the statement of the artist's location, for which he provided "Lüneburg / Amsterdam, Germany" (P445). Directly below this, MySpace's technological framework displayed the number of total visits to the artist's profile page. With well over 13,000, this number was in the middle range of all the artists I observed in the field. It was well above the numbers of visitors that hobbyist musicians had drawn (for example 4,556 in the case of P542), but far below the numbers shown on more mainstream artists' pages (for example 58,022 in the case of P442). The artist O's MySpace profile page had a constantly growing number of total page visits:

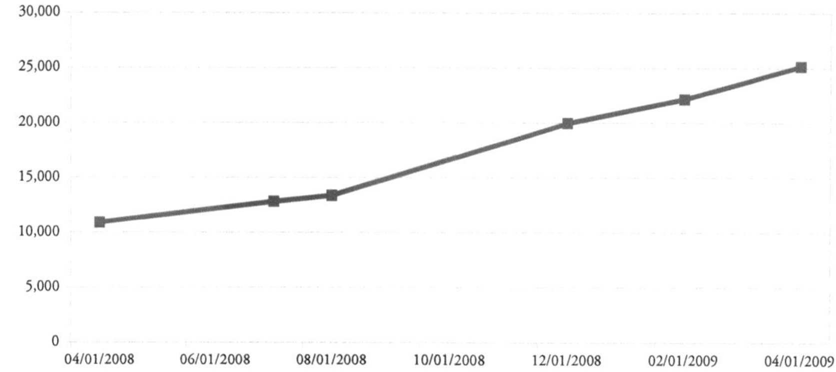

Accumulation of visits to the artist O's MySpace profile page between April 20, 2008 and April 15, 2009.

Again, this reference has to be observed with caution, as mentioned in section 3.1.1. Also, the artist's last login date was provided as being two days prior to my access to the page. Taken as a hint towards the artist's activity on MySpace, this two-day period – although just a one-off sampling at the time of access – also placed the artist in the middle range of the field. Many of the participants seemed to access their MySpace profiles every day, while some were only active once every one or two weeks.

To the right, the artist O offered some of his music productions in full length for streamed playback. The generic MySpace player application embedded here contained three tracks from two different albums O had released, plus a live recording.

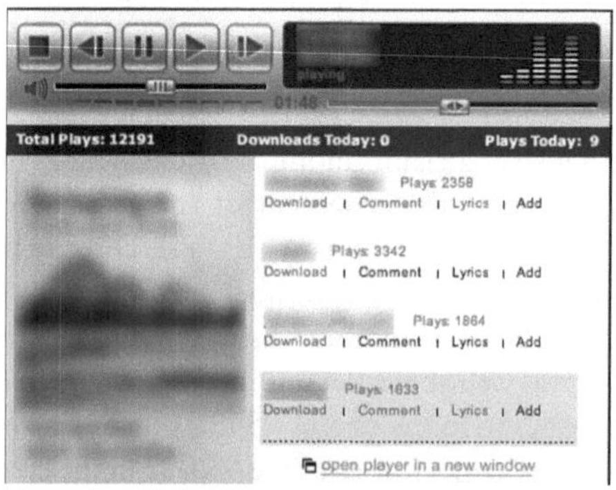

Music streams on offer on the artist O's MySpace profile page (P445).

The most popular track had been played back 3,342 times, while the least popular one had received 1,633 plays. Again, these numbers have to be observed with caution, as they could be manipulated easily as well (Jag 2007). The artist had also included the relevant album cover, its name, and year of publication with the respective tracks inside the player. The offer of a music stream, as seen in the image above, can be observed as a music track – e.g. the one selected in the image and loaded in the player – in the context of other music tracks, as well as further information on the work of the artist. This differentiation structure is modeled in the following equation:

$$\text{offer}_{\text{music stream}} = \overline{\overline{\overline{\text{music track}}|\ \text{other tracks}}|\ \text{artist information}}|$$

Form equation 3.1.2.b: The offer of a music stream as a music track embedded in the context of other tracks and the context of information on the recording artist.

This offer is attributed to the artist's identity:

$$\text{offer}_{\text{music stream}} = \overline{\overline{\overline{\overline{\text{music track}}|\ \text{other tracks}}|\ \text{artist information}}|\ \text{artist identity}}|$$

Form equation 3.1.2.c: The same differentiation structure as above, in the context of the artist's identity.

The offer has to follow the rules set by the MySpace platform, e.g. what can be placed where on the profile page:

$$\text{offer}_{\text{music stream}} = \overline{\overline{\overline{\overline{\overline{\text{music track}}|\ \text{other tracks}}|\ \text{artist information}}|\ \text{artist identity}}|\ \text{MySpace platform}}|$$

Form equation 3.1.2.d: The same differentiation structure as above, in the context of the MySpace platform.

The offered track and the information it was embedded in can be observed in situations of online publics, which are embedded in the publics of the network structure of the field. These are the publics addressed by the network domains of the field, some of which I have described in section 2.3.1.

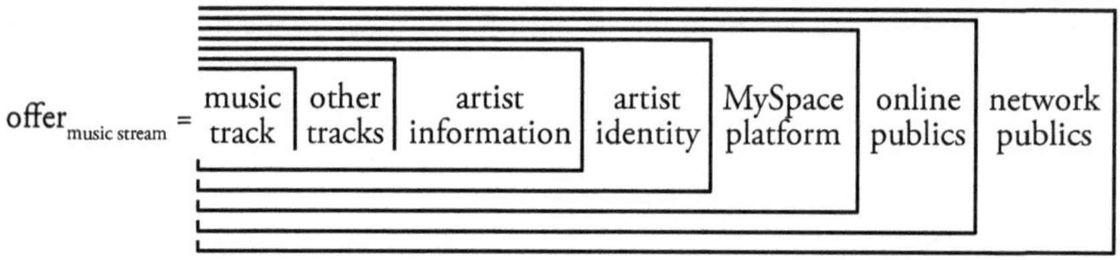

Form equation 3.1.2.e: The offer of a music stream as a music track embedded in the context of other tracks and the context of information on the recording artist, attributed to the artist's identity, following the rules set by the MySpace platform, observed in situations of online publics which are embedded in network publics of the field.

The music track selected in the image above was built on a sampled loop of O's cello playing. It was released on an album that strongly featured the cello, combining short samples and longer phrases with electronic sounds from other sources. The resulting tracks were ultimately pieces of electronic music, importing the sonic world of the cello into their own mixture of hip hop-inspired beats and techno-compatible sounds.

This specific piece was based on a scarce loop of a melodic riff played on the cello. It was played in the picked style, i.e. with the fingers picking the strings instead of using a bow. The riff was melodic in that it contained different notes of one musical scale, and also included harmonic intervals. In the track, it appeared in different variations, both harmonically and rhythmically. Nevertheless, the basic structure of the riff was always very similar and recognizable. It was, however, not used entirely throughout the track. Rather, a noisy clicking sound that was sometimes filtered lasted from beginning to end of the track, laying a foundation for the entire piece and also defining its tempo with clicks that played back as regular 1/16th notes almost until the very end. On top of this, other rhythmic elements were arranged, resulting in a rhythmic structure stylistically resembling a mixture of hip hop and techno elements. Except for a sampled ride bell that stood out as the element on the offbeat in the main part of the track, and a snare-like sound that resembled a drop of water, all other sounds used for rhythmic elements were sampled by O from his cello. The tempo was rather slow for the stylistic context of the rhythmic structure.

On top of the melodic and rhythmic foundation, O had recorded long cello notes played with a bow. These notes expanded upon the melodic fragments in the cuts from the picked cello riff. In addition, O had used a software I programmed in our collaborative project in Amsterdam, and included both long harmonic sections as well as individual notes quickly changing pitch in the track. Another element came from a hand-held synthesizer that derived its pitch from the skin capacity of the person holding it. Both these sounds as well as the individual notes from the software I programmed in collaboration with O exhibited erratic elements, where the synthesizer was not controllable to play specific notes, and the software was designed to produce glitches in certain situations as well. O combined these elements with quickly repeating – stuttering – rhythmic samples from his cello, which added a considerable amount of error aesthetics to the track. With its scarce arrangement and the mix of sampled cello and electronic sounds, the track brought together the sonic worlds of classical music and the electronic productions of hip hop and techno. It achieved this not in the mode of importing from one realm into the other, but rather as a composition by an artist who was equally at home in both areas.

The usual, MySpace-generic box of options for getting in touch with the owner of the profile page was also present on O's MySpace profile page, as was the direct URL one could use to link to this page. Following below this part was the member information. This showed that the artist had been a member since February 2006, which means that he joined around the time it became truly a mass platform, especially for music marketing (Dhar / Chang 2007). As external website, the artist provided a link to the label which he co-owned. At the time of research, this artist did not have his own dedicated website.

Below this, the artist named himself under his real name and a guitar player as members of his band. This is notable, as it marked an episode in which he opened his artist identity towards a collaborative project, whereas before and after, he had described it as his personal project only. This opening corresponded with the more detailed self-description given on the right side of the page. There, the soloist identity was mentioned as a period of the past, while the collaboration was described as the contemporary form of the project. Consequentially, the rest of the self-description was written in plural.

The artist also stated that they were working on an album as a duo. This album, however, did not materialize during the research period, nor did any recorded tracks beyond the existing working relationship of the two. In addition, they played regular live performances, which was also mentioned here, where they accompanied the screening of silent movies. The option to book them directly was mentioned on the profile page, together with a dedicated email address for such requests. In the general information section on the left side of the page, the artist went on by providing the influences for what he described as a duo band. Notably, all the names of influences mentioned here start with the letter m, which hints at a much longer list of influences that would have to be mentioned here, but that were omitted for an unknown reason.

As labels on which he released, O named both his own label and the label C. The latter was named first. As for the type of the label, the term "Indie" (P445) was used. To the right of this section follows a list of the artist's releases, with references to the labels that published them. Below this, the artist placed a reference to the art institute in Amsterdam that had funded our collaborative work. In this section, the artist also provided a reference of location by stating that his studio was placed "in a forest near Hamburg / Germany" (Ibid.). This statement combined a notion of remoteness with a sense of connectedness to the metropolitan city of Hamburg and its international role.

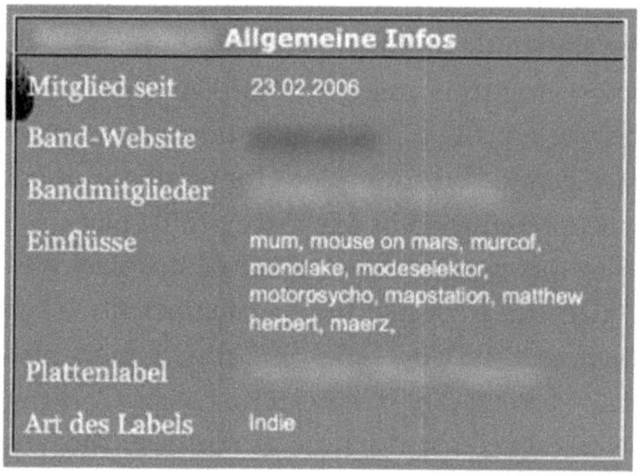

The general info section of the artist O's MySpace page (P445).

The next paragraph of the self-descriptive text on the page offered an explanation of the artist name this musician – or, in the description given here, this band – used. Directly below this, we can find the information about the artist's "friends" on MySpace. At the time this screenshot was taken in August 2008 (P445), the artist had 836 "friends", which was not a lot compared to the close to 3,000 "friends" of the label C, or the well over 1,500 "friends" in the network of the artist T. The artist O showed 16 of his "friends" as "top friends" directly on his page. These 16 "top friends" displayed on O's page were arranged in a 4x4 matrix. Eight of them had released music on O's own label before (see discography on Discogs.com, P2541). This label was also included among the "top friends", as was the label C. Six of the "top friends" had collaborated in music production with O before (partly documented on Discogs.com, P1917). In the first row was one other co-owner of O's label, who was also active as an artist in his own right. One other artist featured here was a close collaborator of O, but had not released music on his label. The first row was completed by two artists who had released albums on the artist's label recently. In the second row, the two labels were grouped together, and next to them came the collaborator who O claimed as a member of his band on this page. The other artists featured in the list of "top friends" were a mixture of personal friends and quality references, i.e. artists who were well known and had a good reputation in the scene. One very well-known group featured here was also mentioned as an influence in the self-descriptive part of the page. Having them in his list of "top friends" can be seen as a function to potentially increase the value of this representation by showing that the artists whose work was a great influence for him did indeed respect his work enough to have him as a "friend" on MySpace. Thereby, he offered a reference to a valuable identity, which valued him enough to reference him back. Of course, being featured among the "top friends" list of this reference group would have been even better for the artist O, but this was not the case (P721). Notably, other artists from the label C were absent from this list, although they were MySpace "friends" with O at the time.

Below the list of "top friends" came the comments by other members of MySpace. Within two months prior to the date of access in August 2008, four comments had been left on the page. Two of these comments did not include direct references to the offerings in terms of information and music material available on the page. Rather, they contained information about the commenter's own work, i.e. referenced away from the current page. One comment was simply a thank-you note for accepting the request to become MySpace "friends". To accept someone's "friend" request was referred to as an "add" (P445) on MySpace, and members commonly left these thank-you messages on new "friends'" pages, indicating that they had indeed visited their profiles and thereby had shown a minimum of interest in what they had to offer. Only a small fraction of the comments would usually reference the music offered on the page, but all of them made a positive judgment of its quality. I did not observe any negative comments directly on MySpace profile pages, which may of course have to do with the members' ability to choose which comments they wanted to appear on their profile pages, and which they wanted to withhold. Of the two comments referencing the commenter's own work, one promoted a music release, while the other promoted an upcoming concert the commenter organized. Only the fourth comment explicitly referenced the music on O's MySpace page, commenting with a very positive evaluation.

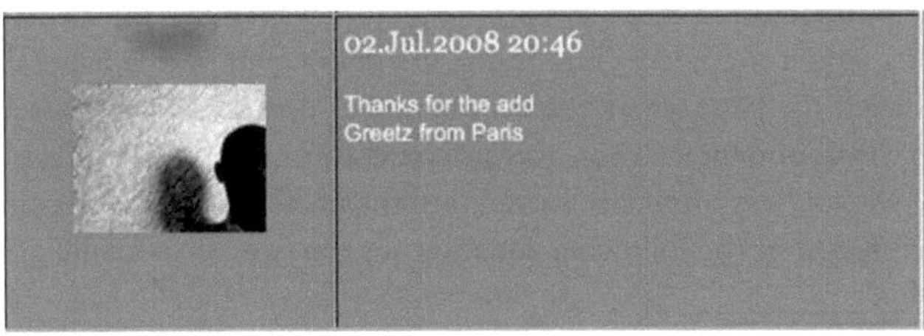

Thank-you note as comment on the artist O's MySpace page (P445).

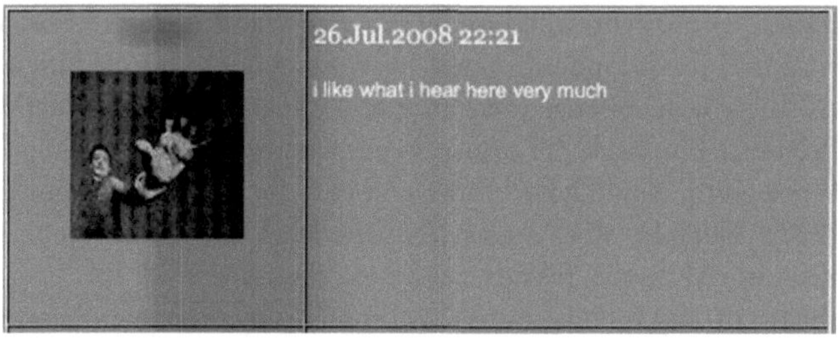

Explicit evaluation as comment (P445).

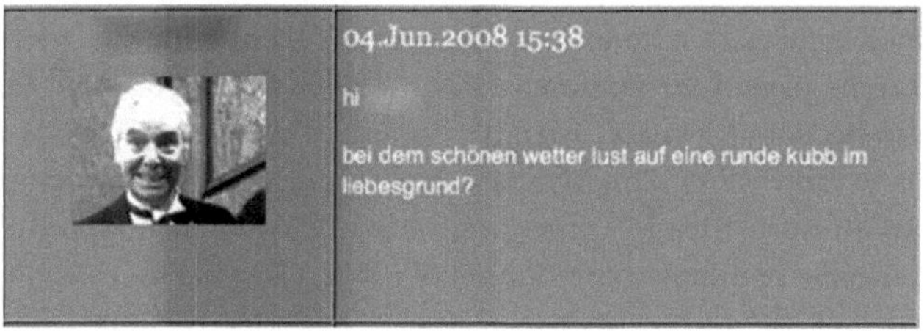

Personal message as comment (P445).

Personal messages such as the example given above were very rare on MySpace. I did not observe a case where a personal message received a reply directly on the page. A message such as the one shown above, contacting the owner of the profile page about a meeting on the same day seems out of place in the context of the other comments, which were not focused on getting an immediate reply.

In any case, reactions on a MySpace page referenced the identity of the member making the comment. The member's profile picture was shown on the left side of the comment box, and it included a link to the member's own profile page. Clicking this link, a visitor left the page where the comment was posted and was taken directly to the page of the commenter. Thus, the personal context of the commenter, as presented on MySpace, was implicitly woven into the profile page via the comment. This relation is expressed in the following equation for the case of an explicit evaluation:

$$\text{reaction}_X = \overline{\overline{\text{explicit evaluation}_X} \;\big|\; \text{personal context } X}\;\big|$$

Form equation 3.1.2.f: A reaction by member X as an explicit evaluation by X in the personal context of X.

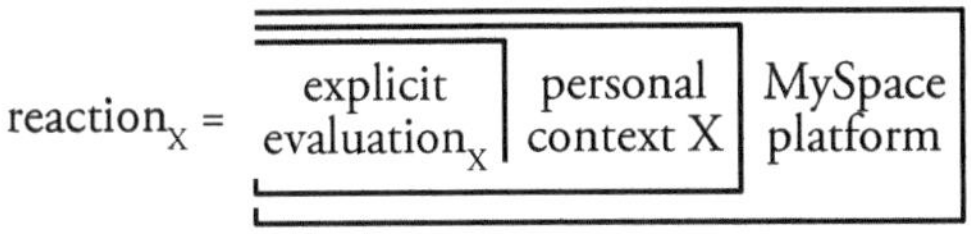

Form equation 3.1.2.g: The same differentiation structure as above, following the rules set by the MySpace platform.

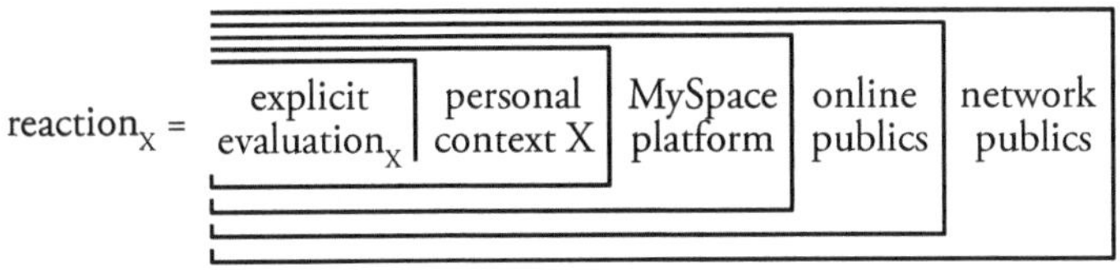

Form equation 3.1.2.h: A reaction by member X as an explicit evaluation by X in the personal context of X, following the rules set by the MySpace platform, in a situation of online public communication, which is embedded in the publics of the network structure of the field.

The comments left on O's MySpace page mostly had a marketing background, i.e. they tried to promote music releases or cultural events that did not relate to O's activities. I have counted these entries as external references. Furthermore, many comments also included references to certain localities, mostly when they promoted cultural events in a specific location, but also when the commenter specified his or her own location in the comment.

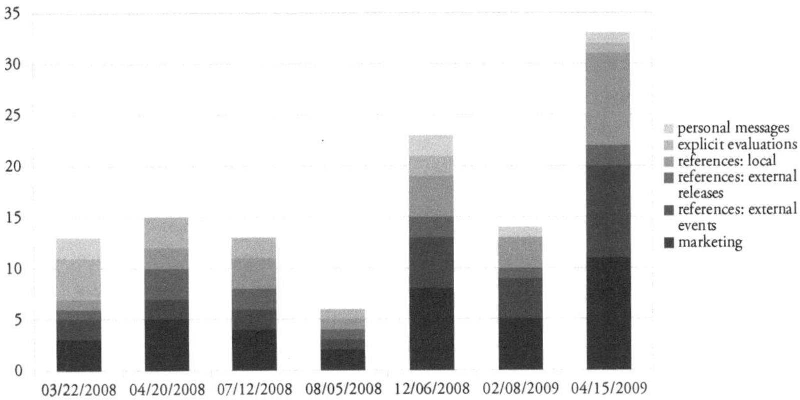

Types of comments on the artist O's MySpace profile page over a period of two months prior to the sampling date. Any one comment could fall into more than one category.

As the chart shows, the number of explicit evaluations, i.e. comments which directly referenced an offer made on the profile page and gave the commenter's opinion on it, was relatively small. While the total number of comments varied over time, the internal differentiation remained relatively similar.

The following table shows the ratio of explicit evaluations against comments, i.e. how many comments it took to get one explicit evaluation as reaction to the offers on the page:

Date	Comments per explicit evaluation
03/22/2008	2.75
04/20/2008	2.67
07/12/2008	5.00
08/05/2008	4.00
12/06/2008	7.00
04/15/2009	12.00

Average of the number of comments it took for one explicit evaluation to appear on the artist O's MySpace profile page. Note: There were no explicit evaluations in the two months prior to the sampling on February 8, 2009.

This analysis shows how difficult it was to get explicit reactions to the offers made on a MySpace profile page. Most comments tried to divert attention away from the page on which they appeared. Nevertheless, even such comments focusing on their function of external referencing still contributed activity to the MySpace profile page, thereby making it more attractive overall.

3.1.3 MySpace Case Study: Label C

Although MySpace was mostly aimed at musicians, many labels used the platform as well. For the label C, the label assistant looked after the representational profile page. The label was presented as a "band", and all of the artists on its roster were listed as band members. The label's logo was used as profile picture at the top left, and the genre definition was provided as "Electronica / Alternativ / IDM" (P443). This was both a narrow and a wide definition, as "Electronica" and "IDM" were relatively clear-cut genre names that were even sometimes used synonymously, while the definition of "Alternativ" was implicitly one side of a binary distinction that referenced the entire music scene. The additional individual description statement read "Electronic Music Since 1999" (Ibid.). This temporal and genre reference indicated that the label had been around for almost a decade by the time of access, and that it had not changed its genre focus, formulating the statement in a way typical of companies with a long history in their segment.

In the music player, the label presented single tracks from recent releases. Each of them was accompanied by its respective album cover. At the time of access in August 2008, the tracks had received between 2,162 and 3,543 plays (P443), which placed them in the middle range of plays on MySpace profiles in the field, although it has to be taken into account that the label added new tracks regularly, which was not necessarily the case with the individual artists. The offers thus made were similar to those on the artist O's MySpace profile page, with the only difference that the identity of the label C became an important context of the presentation:

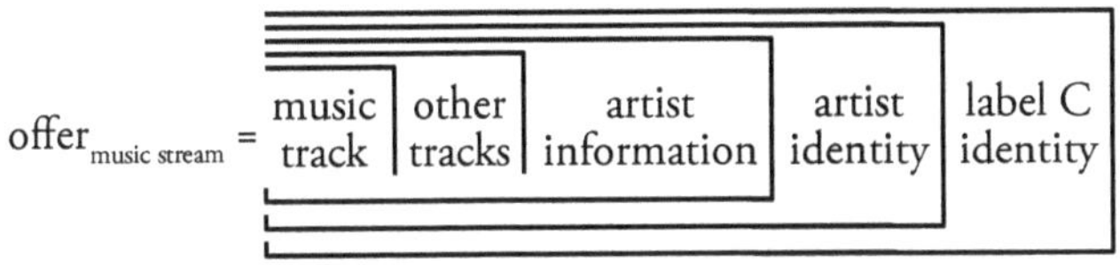

Form equation 3.1.3.a: The offer of a music stream as a music track in the context of other tracks and of information on the recording artists, embedded in a reference to the recording artist's identity, made in the context of the label C's identity.

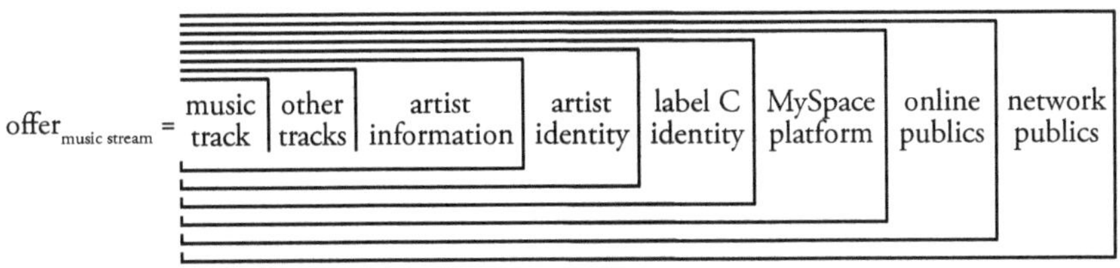

Form equation 3.1.3.b: The offer of a music stream as a music track in the context of other tracks and of information on the recording artists, embedded in a reference to the recording artist's identity, made in the context of the label C's identity, following the rules set by the MySpace platform, in a situation of online public communication which was embedded in the publics of the network structure of the field.

The label used the dedicated section for upcoming shows provided by the MySpace framework to announce performances by its artists. In August 2008, there was only one entry, but at other times, there were up to 14 entries in this section (P77). Another important section for the label to publish information was the blog linked to the profile page. This feature was used to publish news about upcoming releases as well as announcements of label events coming up. Corresponding with this, they placed the image of the flyer for the next label "Allnighter" event at the top of the "About" section, which followed directly underneath the blog.

Online version of a flyer for an "Allnighter" event on the label C's MySpace profile page (P443).

Below the flyer, the "About" sections contained large logos with links to the guitar-oriented sublabel's MySpace page, and the external webshop the label was a part of together with its collaboration partners. Interestingly, the link to the guitar-oriented sub label (P939) was titled "for anything indie", thus excluding the label C itself from being "indie". Nevertheless, the type of label was given as "Indie" in the "General Information" section. This contradiction might be based on a differing usage of the word "Indie", which could refer to both the organizational setup of a label and the guitar-oriented rock music published by the traditional independent labels since the 1940s (Millard 1995). Beneath these links, four of the label's recent releases were presented with their cover graphics and a direct link to the iTunes store (see one example below, from P443). Finally, down below the latest releases, the label had placed a self-describing text, with indications towards both a historical narrative for its development as well as a defined placement in both technological and genre contexts. The text begins and ends with the placement of the label's stylistic and cultural focus on the inside of a distinction separating "catchy" (Ibid.) and danceable electronic music from experimental styles, implying that these were less danceable and "catchy". Secondly, the original release format of the 7" vinyl record is indicated as an "almost forgotten" (Ibid.) format that was used by the label to release "modern" (Ibid.) electronic music. By using this specific format, the label separated itself technologically from the mainstream that was, by the time the label was founded at the end of the 1990s, almost entirely focused on the CD as the primary format of publication, with occasional releases on 12" vinyl records, although the latter were practically confined to the electronic music genre.

Links to the label C's sublabel and the joint-venture online shop (P443).

The label started out just releasing 7" vinyl records, but discarded this separation later, releasing music on CDs and 12" vinyl records as well. Altogether, as the text claims, the label had released more than 30 "full-lengths" (Ibid.), i.e. albums, and an equal number of vinyl singles in both 7" and 12" formats. Once again, the physical representation of the releases was used exclusively for their description, although almost all of the releases, both albums and singles, had been made available in download formats as well. In the way it is mentioned here, the number of releases indicates an achievement and, especially in conjunction with the timespan the label had been in operation, can be understood as an indication of professionalism.

Like the artist O's profile page (P445), the label C's page also included a "top friends" section. Here, 23 out of the 2,867 "friends" were shown (P443). However, while the artist O featured a mixture of collaborators, i.e. identities on the same level as himself, and influences, i.e. identities on a different level, the label only featured its own sublabel and artists from its own roster in its "top friends" section. There is no apparent order in the way they were arranged on the page; their placement resembled neither a discernible hierarchy of popularity nor a chronology of the latest releases on the label.

Announcement of a release (P443).

Notably, the entire self-description provided by the label on its MySpace profile page included relatively few explicit external references in terms of identities to be compared with. While the artist O named influences and collaborators as well as institutions he had a relation with and technologies he was using, the label restricted itself to its own roster and the technologies used for physical representations of its releases.

The comments left by other members on the label C's MySpace profile page again were focused on promotional efforts, often trying to divert attention away from the page. The following image shows a typical marketing comment, announcing the release of an album that was not linked to the activity of the label C:

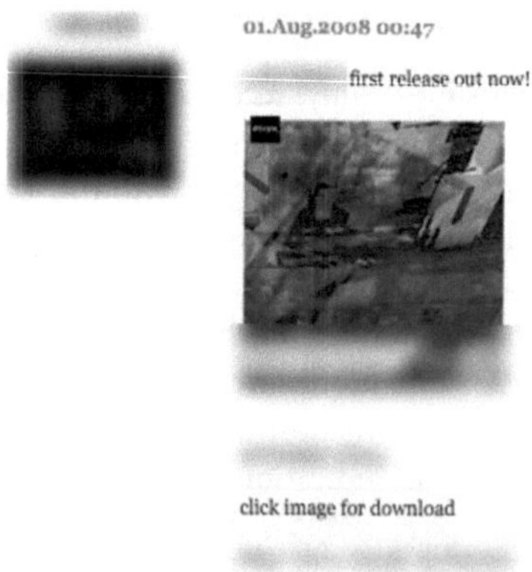

Release announcement in a comment on the label C's MySpace profile page (P443).

As a reaction to the label C's profile page, the comment above is both a post on the page, thus adding activity to it, and an explicit offer to switch away from this page. This principle is expressed in the following equation:

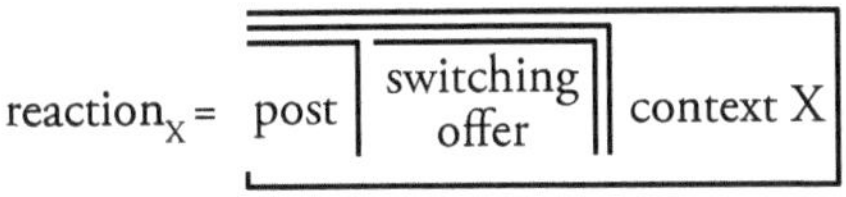

Form equation 3.1.3.c: The reaction by a member X as a post and a switching offer, in the context of the member X.

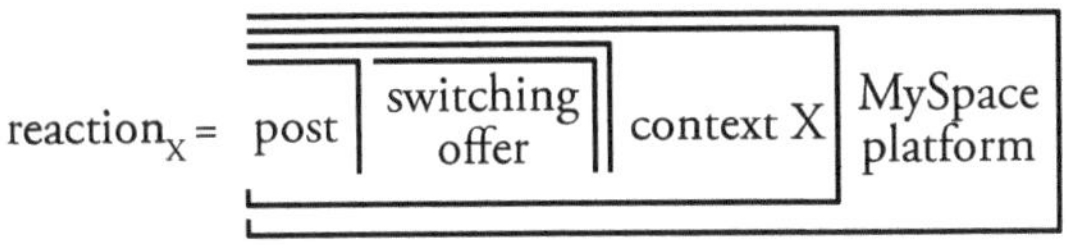

Form equation 3.1.3.d: The same differentiation structure as above, following the rules set by the MySpace platform.

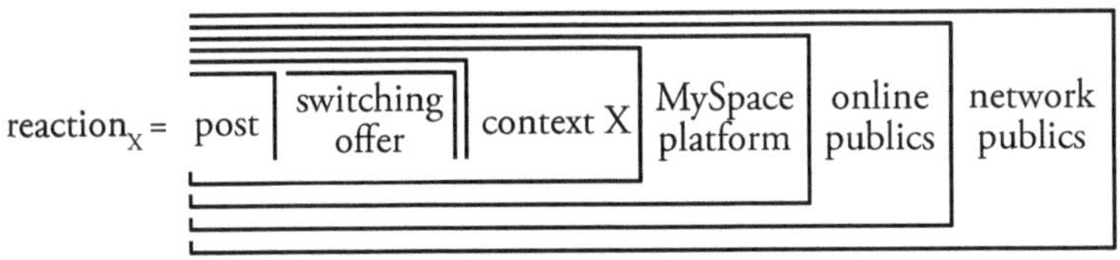

Form equation 3.1.3.e: The reaction by a member X as a post and a switching offer, in the context of the member X, following the rules set by the MySpace platform, in a situation of online public communication, which was embedded into the publics of the network structure of the field.

Using the same categories as in the analysis of comments on the artist O's MySpace profile page, we can see the same marketing focus in the comments on the label C's page. This is manifested in the relatively high ratio of comments including references leading away from the profile page at hand. There were no personal messages at all among the comments.

Notably, though, there was occasionally a high amount of references especially to external releases in the comments left on the page. This hints at a larger number of active musicians visiting this profile page. There were no comments in the two months prior to the last sampling date.

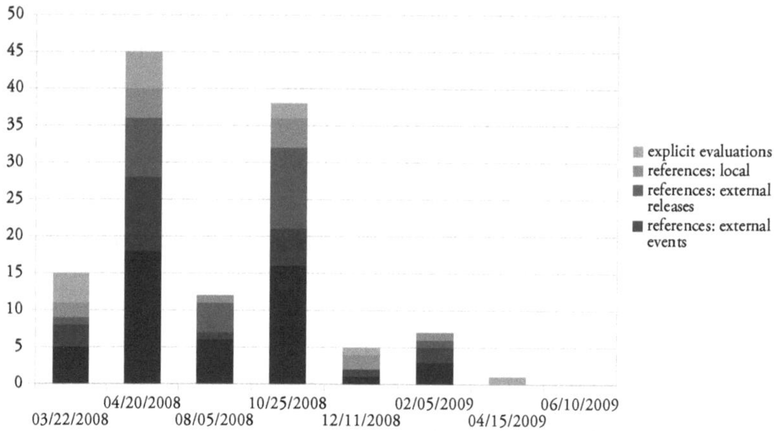

Types of comments on the label C's MySpace profile page over a period of two months prior to the sample date. Any one comment could fall into more than one category.

As on the artist O's MySpace profile page, explicit evaluations in the comments were sometimes scarce. The following table shows the number of comments per explicit evaluation:

Date	Comments per explicit evaluation
03/22/2008	3.25
04/20/2008	5.20
10/25/2008	10.00
12/11/2008	4.00
04/15/2009	1.00

The number of comments it took for one explicit evaluation to appear on the label C's MySpace profile page. The samples missing from the previous graphic mark periods without any explicit evaluations.

3.2 Facebook

During the research period, Facebook became the dominant so-called social network, not just in our field or the electronic music scene, but on the internet as a whole. This overarching change was reflected in our field, though: During the years 2008 and 2009, most of the participants in the field became active Facebook members. Usage of MySpace decreased during the same period. For the worldwide internet public, the quantitative break came around the end of the year 2008, when Facebook overtook MySpace in both cumulated recurring visits as well as the number of individual visitors (Quantcast 2011; Google 2011a; Google 2011b). Another interesting quantitative measure is the time visitors spent on their visits to each platform. The analysis of internet traffic data shows that, while MySpace and Facebook were in direct competition for users, visitors on average stayed roughly twice as long on Facebook than on MySpace (Alexa.com 2011).

A large proportion of the participants in the field was represented on Facebook during the research period. Many more members had representations there towards the end of the data collection, which coincided with Facebook's growth in both member count and inclusion of social metadata in general.

During the time of the data collection, membership on Facebook was tied to the notion of the individual person. In the process of signing up, new members had to declare themselves as natural persons (Facebook 2011g). So-called "pages" were the form of choice for representations of non-"natural" entities on Facebook, and "groups" were used as gathering places for members who shared certain interests (Facebook 2011a; Facebook 2012). A third format, that of the "event", was used to host metadata on a specific performance or party event, such as its date, time and duration, as well as information on the line-up and the venue. Only one date was accepted for a Facebook event (Facebook 2011f), so individual instances of an event series required separate Facebook events for each occurrence.

A Facebook event could be created by any member, who could then invite other members to this Facebook event. The invited members could state whether they would attend the Facebook event or not. In any case, the invited members were shown on the Facebook event's page, separated into groups indicated as "Going", "Maybe", and "Invited" (P3379). Members had to actively remove themselves from the Facebook event's page if they wanted to disappear after having been invited. The observation that the "Invited" group from which the Facebook event was awaiting reply was usually the largest suggests that members generally did not bother to remove themselves from the page for a Facebook event they had no interest in.

On the other hand, the statement of a member's attendance on a Facebook event's page did not mean that this person would actually show up at the venue. Attendance stated by members could therefore be seen as a sign of approval of and idealistic support for a Facebook event, but it did not justify the expectation that the members who stated their attendance at the representation of a performance or party event would also attend the actual occurrence itself.

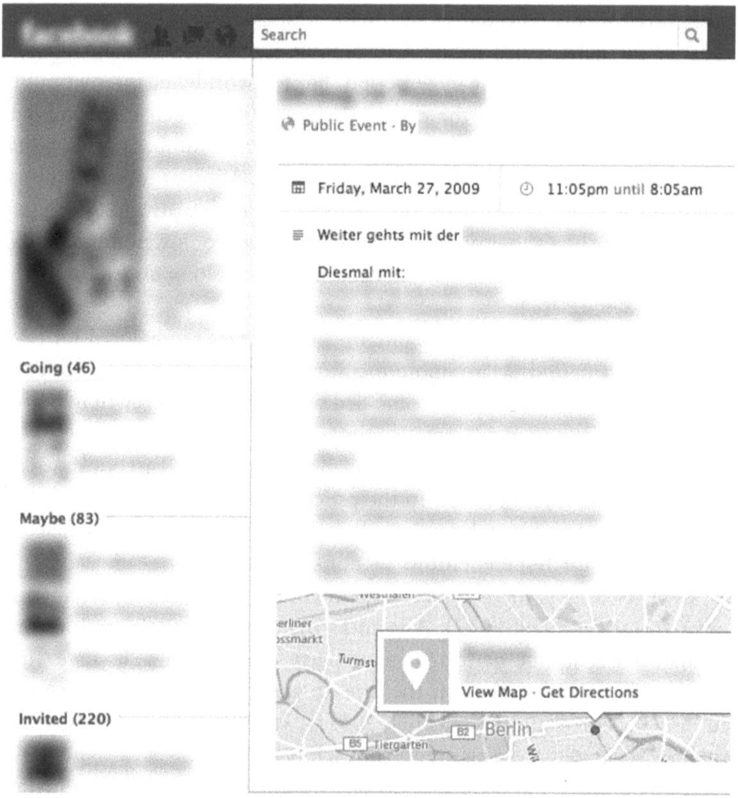

A Facebook event page by the magazine where the label owner H worked (P3379).

Facebook events were created as a subpage of either a member profile or a dedicated page representing a non-person entity, and this relation was visible prominently on the Facebook event's page as long as it existed. The Facebook pages themselves used a similar scheme of attribution. They had administrators, who had control over the official contents of the page. The creator of a Facebook page had to be a member of Facebook, and automatically became the page's administrator – a privilege he could give up later so long as there was at least one other member taking over. Such changeovers in a page's administration did for instance become necessary when the page was created by a member that did not have an organizational relation to the represented identity, and the page was then taken over by a member authorized – outside of Facebook – to administrate the representation. In the case of the label C, a Facebook page existed that looked completely official, with correct street address and contact email, but that was apparently not administrated by members of the label's organization team. Nevertheless, several artists from the label's roster had actively become "fans" of this page. The concept of "fans" was later abandoned by Facebook in favor of the universal application of "likes".

The Facebook group was a third means to represent non-member entities. It was intended to host joint interests by members, and could be closed off to outsiders (Facebook 2012). Members could join a group and thereby show their interest in its topic. I did not observe any groups started out of music-cultural practice, but artists did regularly join groups started by others outside of the scene, often out of protest movements. Facebook groups were similar to pages in that they had administrators who did not necessarily have to be the original creators of the group. The role of the administrators was similar to that of a moderator on a regular internet forum, as they usually showed continuous presence in the discussions among members.

The three different ways for non-members to have a representation on Facebook therefore established three different ways for members to communicate about the represented identities. I already mentioned that since a Facebook event was designed to be about a particular social occurrence at a certain date and with a certain duration, members were linked to this site through the notion of attendance at the represented cultural event. As mentioned also, the statement of attendance on a Facebook event's page was in some cases used actively for the creation of a link on Facebook only, with no intention of the members to actually show up at the occurrence.

On the other hand, members could not prevent being invited to a Facebook event and thereby automatically being visible in the "Invited" group of members shown on the site. The creator of a Facebook event could choose whether it was public or private. In the case of a public Facebook event, all Facebook members could post comments on a section of the page dedicated to this form of communication, called the "wall" (Facebook 2011d). All representations on Facebook – member profiles, Facebook events, pages, and groups – had a wall. On pages representing a non-member entity, a member visiting the page could choose whether to see all comments, only comments from the administrators, or only the comments made by other members who were already linked to the page through Facebook. If the administrators decided to make the page public, it was not only visible to Facebook members, but directly accessible on the internet, also showing up in search results of general search engines such as Google. Commenting and visibly linking was, however, restricted to Facebook members.

One of the core concepts of Facebook was the "like" button (Facebook 2011b; Gerlitz 2011). This button was available for every comment or activity item on Facebook, and clicking it allowed a member to make a generalized positive statement about the respective item. Thus, a member could "like" a comment by another member, or an activity item shown on another member's or page's wall, such as a new "friend" relation or attendance of a Facebook event. The "like" feature was used heavily in the field.

On Facebook pages, Facebook members had to actively become a "fan" (e.g. P2289) to create a link between themselves and the page. The notion of fanhood of an identity represented on a page was consistent with its most common use case as the representational home of organizations, products, or, dominating in our field, artist identities. Groups, on the other hand, had to be "joined" (e.g. P2724), again in line with the group's use case for discussions among members who shared a common interest. Becoming a "fan" of a page or joining a group was immediately reflected in an automatic statement on the member's own wall, while members had to actively confirm their participation on an event page for their relation to the event to show up on their wall. This was consistent with the fact that members could be invited to an event without their consent. Statements on walls therefore reflected active member behavior only. This activity was automatically displayed to each member in their news feed. This feed was composed on the basis of the relations between members, where seemingly important connections, e.g. with many mutual "friends", were prioritized higher and showed up more frequently in the feed (Hutter 2012).

A large proportion of the artists in our field used Facebook as a site for representation. Individual artists all used their own member profiles for this purpose, without creating a separate representation for their artist identity. Since most of them also used Facebook for communication unrelated to their artistic work, the comments on their walls usually mixed references to the artistic work and more personal themes. Bands mostly used pages instead of member profiles as representational sites. In the field, the proportion of individual artists using Facebook was much higher than that of bands or collaborative projects. Every member profile on Facebook displayed information on the pages the member was a "fan" of, and which groups they had joined. For the artists, this meant that if they had added such links to other artists on Facebook, this relation could spark a direct cultural comparison between themselves and the other artists. This did of course introduce a tendency of drawing attention towards the pages and groups, as a usual "friend" relation between individual members was not consistently featured on the member walls. It was, again, a means to enrich the current page which also drew attention away from it.

Facebook profiles or pages did not feature any sections customizable for use in specific cultural contexts, such as music. Unlike MySpace, Facebook did not offer a section predefined for the naming of influences and band members, for example.

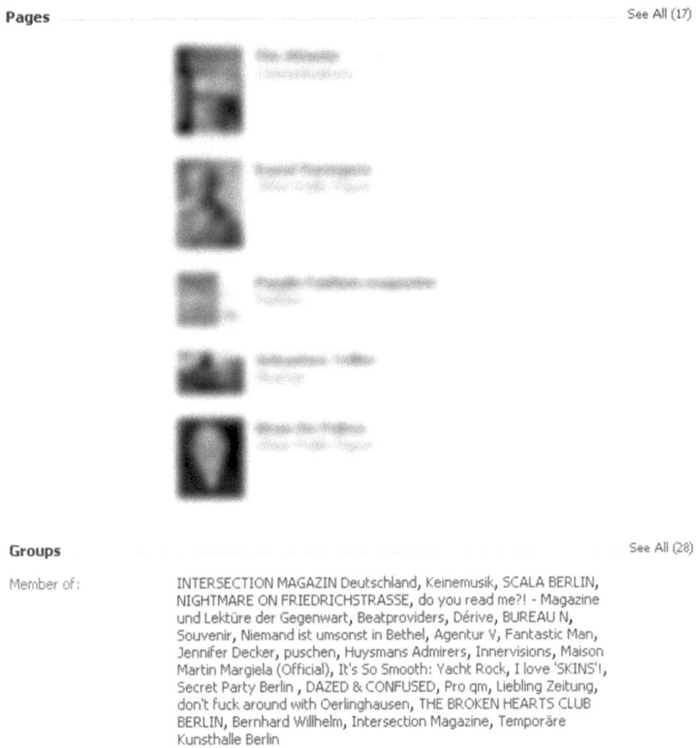

Listing of Facebook pages and groups the label assistant L was a "fan" of or had joined, shown in the info section of his profile page (P1416).

3.2.1 Facebook Case Study: Artist T

The artist T's Facebook profile, accessed in June 2009 (P1413), shows significant differences in comparison with O's MySpace profile (P445), accessed roughly a year earlier. First and foremost, the profile mixed artistic and personal information in the items provided by the artist himself (P1413). Overall, the amount of information that was static on the page was very small, especially compared to MySpace. There was a profile picture as well, in a position very similar to where it was placed on MySpace. The background was the standard white of Facebook, which could not be changed by the user. The top section also housed the platform's navigation elements, but the horizontal bar was relatively small compared to MySpace. Also, there was no external banner advertisement present there.

In accordance with Facebook's rules, the artist used his real name for his profile. In addition to the primary profile picture selected by the artist, there were two more pictures of him available on Facebook (P1422). The primary picture was stylized as a cartoon adaptation of the artist. Of the other pictures of him, one was a photo in his own album, while the other was uploaded by another Facebook member who had tagged the artist T in it.

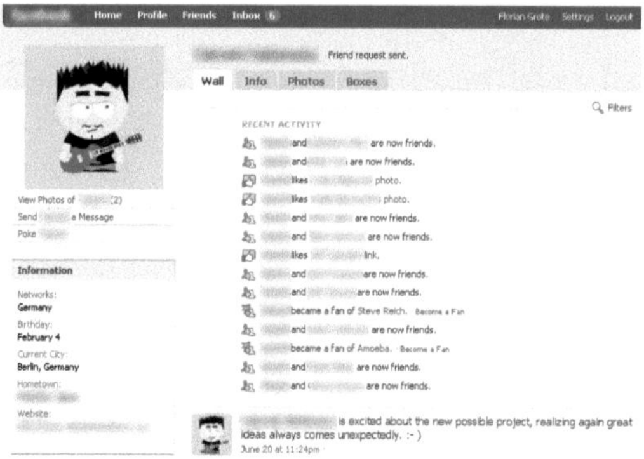

The Facebook wall of the artist T's profile page (P1413).

On the main profile page (P1413), the only additional information provided was in a dedicated box on the left side of the page, and included the artist's birthday date, as well as an entry called "Networks", which was a mandatory selection on Facebook. It was used here to communicate the artist's current country of residence. In addition, the basic information given here also made a distinction between the current city of residence, and the "hometown", i.e. the place where the Facebook member was from originally. The artist stated Berlin as his current city and a city in his home country of Japan as hometown. Below this, T provided a link to his external artist website.

By the time of access, T had 134 "friends", three of which he and I had in common. The mutual "friends" were shown directly on the profile page, as were six out of the 134 "friends" he had in total. These were not "top friends" like on MySpace, where they could be selected by the user, but they rather appeared randomly. Below the information on the artist's "friends" came a link to the photo album he had in his profile, and then another link he had shared in the past. Further information was available in the artist's profile via a dedicated "information" tab in the navigation section at the top of the page. Clicking on this link opened a new page (P1418) on the right side, while the basic profile information on the left remained static. The information page repeated the basic information on the artist's current residence and his origin, but added an email address for direct contacting outside of the Facebook framework. As additional personal information, the artist provided the college he had attended in the US, complete with a direct link to the school.

The "friends" section on the artist T's Facebook profile page, as seen logged into Facebook with my credentials (P1413).

Below this came a section with access to the pages the artist had become a "fan" of in the past, and groups he had joined. These included venues, artists or artist groups, as well as recurring cultural events like an annual design festival in Berlin. While all the groups were listed as text links directly on the information page, only a sample of five pages the artist was a "fan" of were shown, along with their profile pictures. For the rest, the visitor had to click a link, upon which a pop-up screen would open, showing a long list of the pages. This section concluded the information that was static on the profile page. While MySpace facilitated a separate blog on the profile page, which the artists usually used as a news outlet, Facebook was all about the posting of all information on a member's wall. Through this process of "sharing" (e.g. on P2273), every piece of information published here would automatically be pushed onto the walls of all of the artist's Facebook "friends". If any of them decided to share the information themselves, or if they commented on it or "liked" it, they pushed it to all of their "friends" as well, and so on. This way, a published piece of information could reach a public that was far greater than that of the publisher's own profile page. I will discuss the implications of such network effects in section 3.4.6.

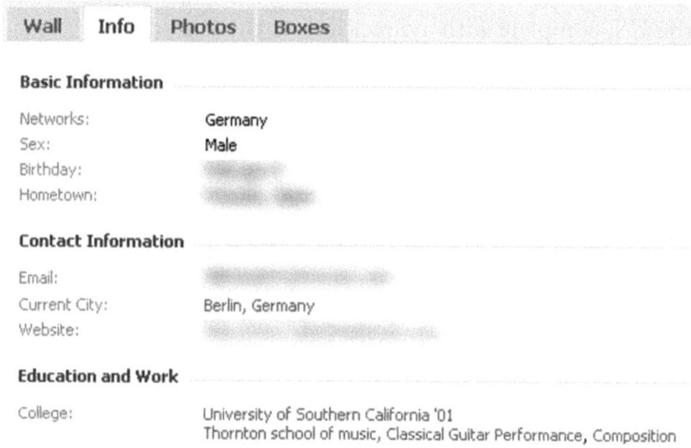

The "info" section on the artist T's Facebook profile page (P1418).

Post and subsequent discussion on the artist T's Facebook wall (P1413).

The information posted on the artist T's wall included reflections on his personal feelings and announcements of performances. Sometimes, it was a mixture of both, e.g. when he reflected upon his feelings towards writing music as a task at hand. Several of these communication offers received comments, some of them starting short discussions in which the artist answered a comment with another comment of his own. The principle of the sequence of offers and reactions in the discussion shown directly above can be expressed in the following equations:

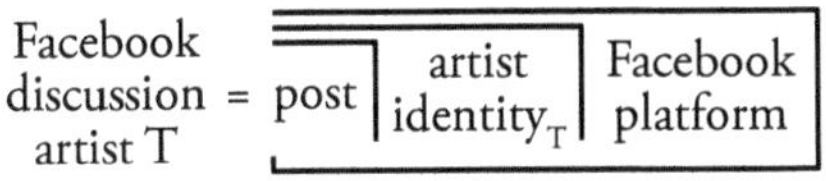

Form equation 3.2.1.a: The discussion started by artist T on his Facebook wall as a post observed in the context of the artist T's identity, following the rules set by the Facebook platform.

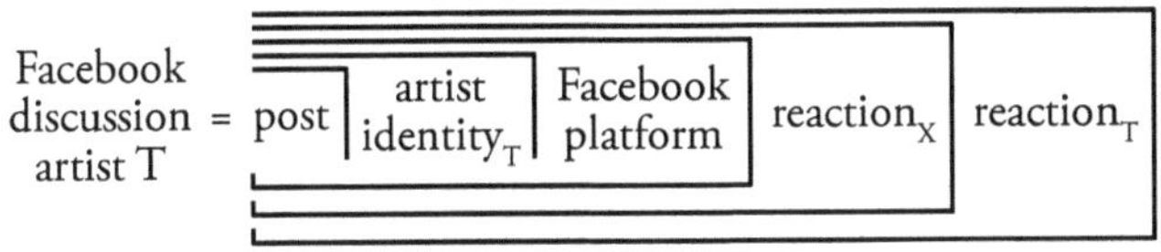

Form equation 3.2.1.b: The discussion started by artist T on his Facebook wall as a post observed in the context of the artist T's identity, following the rules set by the Facebook platform, observed in a reaction by member X, which in turn is observed in a reaction by the artist T.

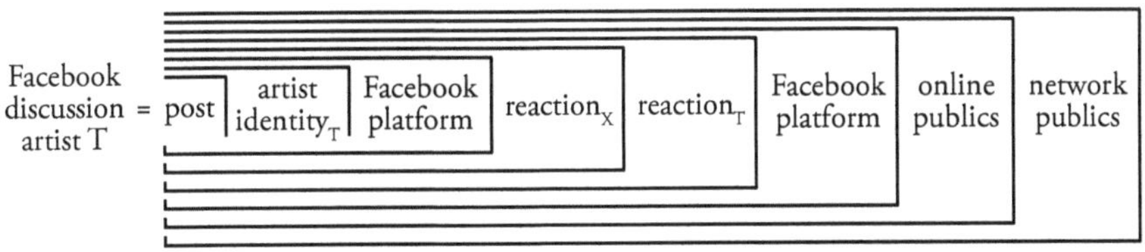

Form equation 3.2.1.c: The discussion started by artist T on his Facebook wall as a post observed in the context of the artist T's identity, following the rules set by the Facebook platform, observed in a reaction by member X, which in turn is observed in a reaction by the artist T, as a whole following the rules set by the Facebook platform in a situation of online public communication, embedded in the publics of the network structure of the field.

The artist T was relatively active on Facebook. I took an exemplary sample of his activity on June 26, 2009 (P1413), and in the two months prior to that date, he had accumulated a total of 107 activity items, including status messages and automatic notifications when he had confirmed his attendance at a Facebook event or had made a new Facebook "friend". I also counted explicit offers by T, such as links to music streams, cultural events, or other destinations, among the activity items. There were eight such offers. In a separate count, I looked at the reactions to these offers, of which there were 20. The distribution of these items is shown in the following chart:

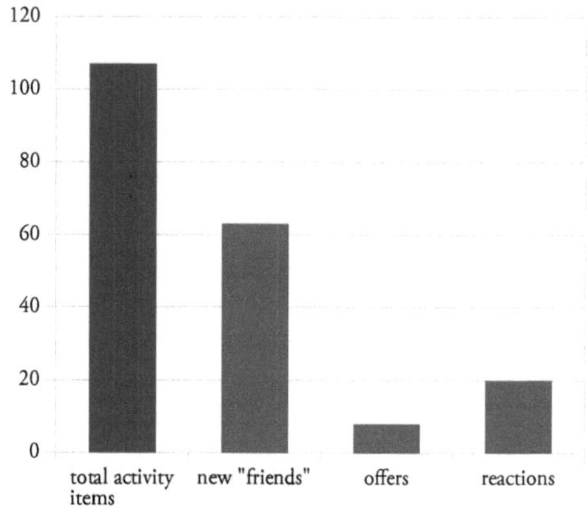

Types of activity on the artist T's Facebook wall over a period of two months prior to the sample date on June 26, 2009 (P1413).

The reactions to offers made on the artist T's Facebook profile page were distributed among "likes", references to external destinations, such as information on the posting member's own work, and personal messages.

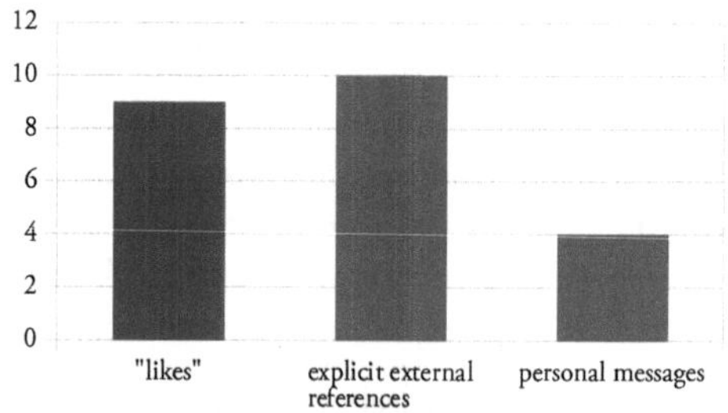

Types of reactions on the artist T's Facebook wall over a period of two months prior to the sample date in June 2009 (P1413).

As on the artist O's MySpace profile page, references to external destinations placed first among the reactions. However, "likes" came in as a close second, showing engagement with the offers. As on MySpace, personal messages played a secondary role in this situation of public online communication.

3.2.2 Facebook Case Study: Label C / Label Owner H

There were three different representations of the label C on Facebook during the time of research. In the beginning of the research period, there was a member profile by its name (P2723), but it appeared inactive. Some of the label artists were already "friends" with this member, but a "friend" request I sent was left unanswered. There was also a Facebook group using the name of the label C (P2724). It contained all official information (P2744), including the contact data and the artist roster, and several of the artists from the roster had joined it. Nevertheless, this group was also not maintained beyond a few news posts on the "info" page (Ibid.), and the group's administrator, who did not identify as a field participant, had posted to the group's wall only once (P2724).

This did, however, not mean that the label was not present on Facebook. Instead of maintaining a dedicated page or group, the label owner H took over the task of publishing information on label events via his own, personal member profile (P1415). As I have mentioned, the label owner was at the same time editor of a major German music and lifestyle magazine, and he used his personal Facebook profile to make announcements in this capacity as well.

The Facebook group with the name and logo of the label C (P2724).

The Facebook wall of the label owner H (P1415).

On his Facebook page, the label owner did not disclose detailed information on the different roles he fulfilled. As employers, he mentioned the music magazine and the radio station where he had his bi-weekly night show (P1419), but did not specify his roles inside of these organizations. The information he provided on events or new releases did not make these references, either. The different organizational contexts were not made explicit; instead, they had to be deduced by the visitors to the profile page. This was in line with the label owner's page not being visible to the general public, but only to his "friends". Nevertheless, in the posts on his wall, the different network domains in which he fulfilled functional roles were regularly present as topics. The differentiation structure of the communicational offers made by H on his Facebook wall is expressed in the following form equations:

$$\text{offers}_{\text{Facebook H}} = \overline{\text{posts}_{\text{H}} \;\Big|\; \overline{\text{radio host} \;\Big|\; \text{magazine editor} \;\Big|\; \text{label owner} \;\Big|\; \text{personal relations}}}$$

Form equation 3.2.2.a: Offers made on the label owner H's Facebook wall observed as posts by H in the context of his functional roles as radio host, magazine editor, label owner, and of his personal relations.

Form equation 3.2.2.b: The same differentiation structure as above, following the rules set by the Facebook platform.

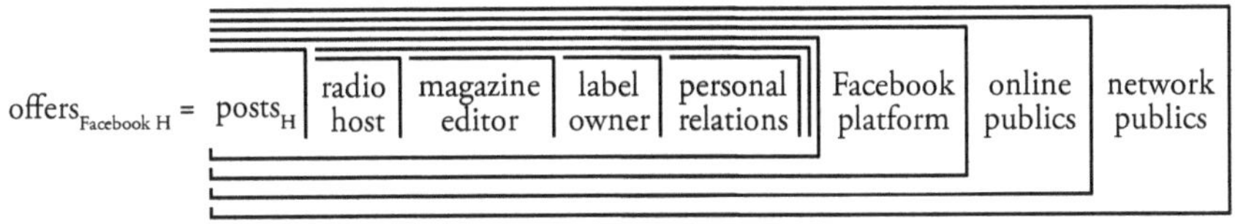

Form equation 3.2.2.c: Offers made on the label owner H's Facebook wall observed as posts by H in the context of his functional roles as radio host, magazine editor, label owner, and of his personal relations, following the rules set by the Facebook platform, in a situation of public online communication and embedded in the publics of the network structure of the field.

The context of the functional roles can be generalized:

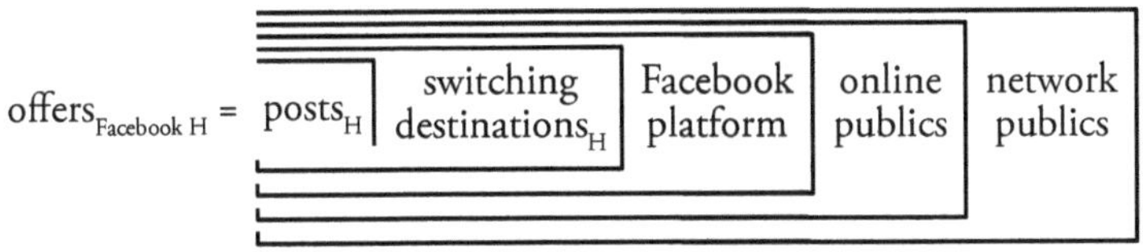

Form equation 3.2.2.d: Offers made on the label owner H's Facebook wall observed as posts by H in the context of switching destinations referencing H, following the rules set by the Facebook platform, in a situation of public online communication and embedded in the publics of the network structure of the field.

The only static pieces of information given on the label owner's main profile page (P1415) were his birthday, and "Germany" as his network. On the "information" subpage (P1419), he disclosed his sex as male, his hometown as "Berlin, Germany", and also provided a direct email address. The work information has already been mentioned, and below it, a random selection of five pages the label owner had become a "fan" of were shown, as were all six of the groups he had joined. All groups and most of the pages were music-related. Only one of the pages was related to a TV show, the other groups and pages were representations belonging to either musicians, music labels, or event organizers. There were three of the label's artists represented here, out of 11 groups and pages in total. Notably, H was not a member of the Facebook group with the name of the label C.

No clear functional distinction could be made between groups and pages represented on H's profile page; they were all used to publish information on the respective identities. The presentation form on the label owner's profile page was different, though: While pages were accompanied by an image, and thus took up more space, the groups only had text links with their names.

The label owner's Facebook wall (P1415) contained a mixture of posts by him and by his Facebook "friends". Directly after he had joined Facebook, several "friends" posted on his wall, welcoming him to the platform. He did not publicly reply to these posts, though. The first post he did stated that he was "picking records for his radioshow" (Ibid.), which was immediately "liked" by two "friends". The next post was about an interview with a very popular electronic music group, which he was about to conduct. This triggered one "like" and one reply. The third post was an announcement of an event organized by the magazine he worked for. This did not trigger immediate replies on the label owner's personal wall, but it was a Facebook event of its own, which he had shared to his Facebook "friends". Further comments were a mixture of references to TV shows he had watched, announcements of his bi-weekly radioshow, more events organized by the magazine he worked for, various personal statements, and information on new releases on his label.

In the first weeks of his membership on Facebook, the label owner mostly gathered "friends", while he did not start posting right away. After a while, he posted more and more, so that the posts by "friends" on his wall eventually became a minority, while most of the posts were by him. Also, while the first three statements he had published were dedicated announcements, he embraced a more personal style of writing after that. This was matched by comments from his "friends" that were mostly similarly personal, while touching subjects related to his work. In several cases, Facebook "friends" would both "like" a statement the label owner had published, and also comment on it. Essentially, the "like" feature here was used in a similar way as the generic comments that appeared regularly on the label C's and the artists' MySpace pages, where members simply stated "great music" (P1397), or something close to it. This sort of comment was made easier with the "like" feature on Facebook, and it also ensured that the commenter's identity was publicly linked to the origin of the statement the comment referred to. The generalization was already built into this feature, and did not have to be expressed by the users, while they could still achieve exposure for themselves. At the same time, the accessibility of the "like" feature facilitated network effects, where information spread via several participants in the network, potentially gaining as much or more attention as could have been achieved using traditional broadcasting media.

The expressive comments or statements on the label owner's wall were used by the "friends" to add statements of their own observations, publishing them to all the visitors to the label owner's Facebook profile. From a distinction-logic analytical view, they thereby added further distinctions to the arrangement already present on the profile page. This included adding their own distinction as observers to the arrangements perceivable by the public of the profile. The principle of the reaction's differentiation structure is modeled in the following equations:

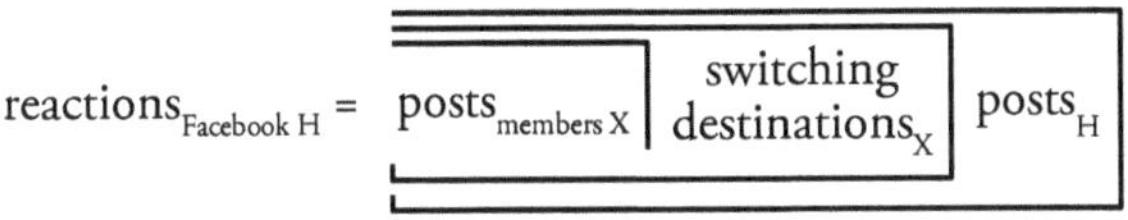

Form equation 3.2.2.e: Reactions on the label owner H's Facebook wall as posts by other Facebook members X in the context of switching destinations referencing these members X, in the further context of posts made by H.

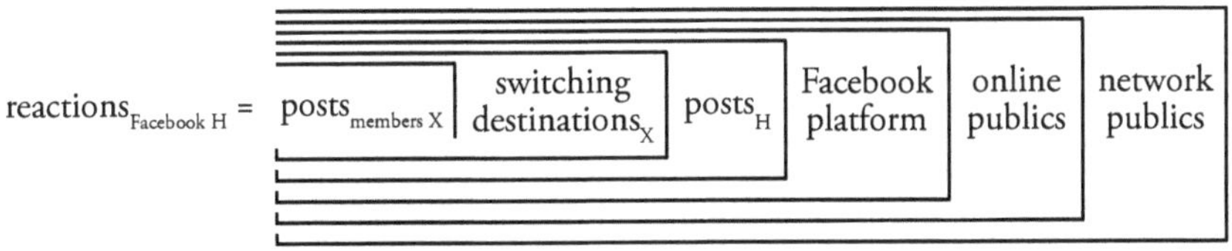

Form equation 3.2.2.f: Reactions on the label owner H's Facebook wall as posts by other Facebook members X in the context of switching destinations referencing these members X, in the further context of posts made by H, following the rules set by the Facebook platform, in a situation of online public communication and embedded in the publics of the network structure of the field.

In the following example, the label owner H posted a video containing music and visuals from an upcoming album by one of the bands that released on the label C (also in P1415). The video was hosted on Vimeo.com, and it showed up in an embedded view on H's Facebook page. Because the video could be included by merely giving the link to its position on Vimeo.com, the post had to contain more information than just the video itself. Originating in the notion of the status update, which had been the original idea behind the stream of information on a Facebook wall, the headline of any post had to be text. The announcement made here by H was rather neutral, as he did not give any explicit valuations with regard to the album. The metadata he provided included the name of the band and the album, the fact that it was a new release coming up on the label C, the release date, the formats in which it would be released, the fact that the material linked in the post was intended as a teaser for this release, and the name of the director of the visual material. There were no comparisons to other artists or albums by the same band, indeed no qualitative statement at all.

Post with embedded teaser video on the label owner H's Facebook wall (P1415).

In response to this post, four other Facebook members had "liked" it by the time of access in June 2009. The member names and their profile images were shown directly underneath the post. There was, however, no additional statement by the other members. They had simply clicked the "like" button underneath the post by the label owner H in the stream of posts by their "friends", or while visiting H's wall. This "like" function gave these other members the opportunity to show up alongside the post in the news stream of all of H's "friends". That way, they could integrate references to their own identity with the post made by H, getting their own names out to the public reached by him. At the same time, they also published the post they had "liked" together with the fact that they had "liked" it to their own "friends". This is expressed in the following equation:

Form equation 3.2.2.g: A reaction in the form of a "like" as the operational event of the "like" in the context of a reference to the "liking" member, following the rules set by the Facebook platform, in a situation of online public communication and embedded in the publics of the network structure of the field.

The next example contains an announcement of a performance event organized by the magazine where H worked as editor:

Announcement of a magazine-sponsored party and subsequent reactions on the label owner H's Facebook wall (P1415).

In this post (also in P1415), the label owner announced a party that was part of a series of events celebrating the publication of new monthly issues of the magazine he worked at. A separate Facebook event had been set up for the party, and the post on the label owner's wall consisted just of a link to this event. Internally on Facebook, items such as events, pages, etc. could be shared to all of a member's "friends", and the resulting post would then only contain the main information provided on the item's page as well as its main image. This was the case here, where the image essentially was a scaled-down version of the flyer for the event, including the line-up of performers written on it. Because the image had been scaled down to be used for the Facebook event, this information was not readable here. Three explicit reactions followed the offer, but they were off topic and did not appear to relate to the content of the offer. Nevertheless, this activity formed an offer and reaction structure that can be modeled as follows:

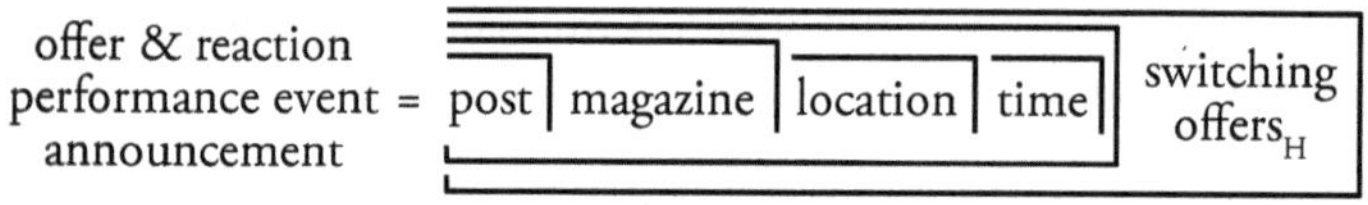

Form equation 3.2.2.h: The offer and reaction structure of the performance event announcement as the initial post in the context of the magazine's identity, and the further context of the specified location and time of the performance event, embedded in switching offers referencing H.

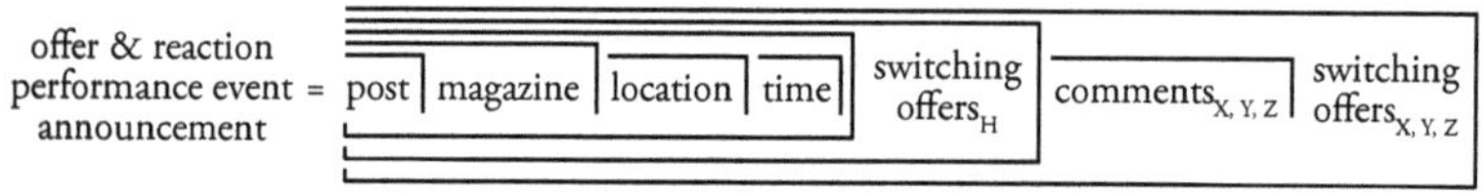

Form equation 3.2.2.i: The same differentiation structure as above, observed in comments by members X, Y, Z in the context of switching offers referencing X, Y, Z.

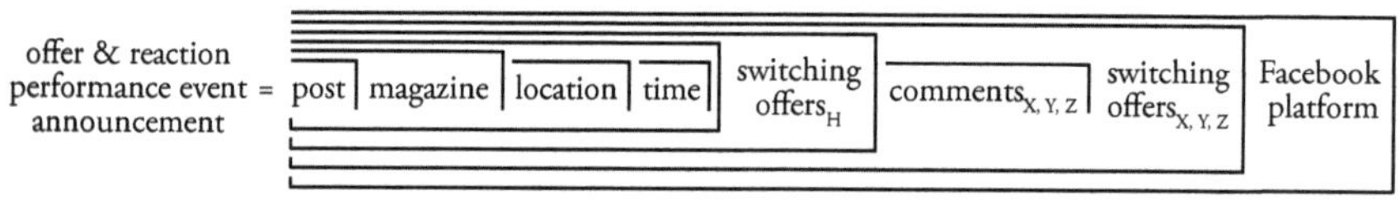

Form equation 3.2.2.j: The offer and reaction structure of the performance event announcement as the initial post in the context of the magazine's identity, and the further context of the specified location and time of the performance event, embedded in switching offers referencing H, observed in comments by members X, Y, Z in the context of switching offers referencing X, Y, Z and following the rules set by the Facebook platform.

As in the previous models, equation 3.2.2.j occurred in a situation of online public communication and was embedded in the publics of the network structure of the field. These differentiation steps are omitted here for reasons of readability.

To measure the label owner H's activity on Facebook, I took a sample on the same day as for the artist T, on June 26, 2009. In the two months prior to that date, H had accumulated 59 activity items in total (T: 107). He had made 43 explicit offers (T: 8), and received 77 reactions (T: 20). Thus, in direct comparison with T, H was overall less active on Facebook, but his activity was more focused on concrete offers, and he also received a higher number of reactions in total. On a relative basis, the artist T received 0.187 reactions per activity item, while H received 1.305. This activity / reaction ratio shows that H had a much more active and verbose community of "friends" on Facebook than did T.

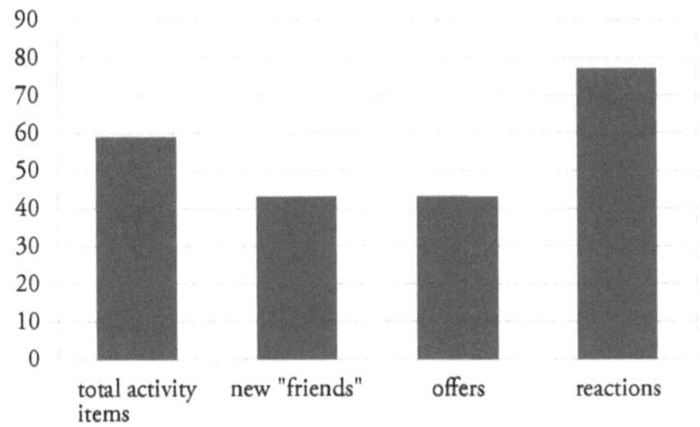

Types of activity on the label owner H's Facebook wall over a period of two months prior to the sample date in June 2009 (P1415).

The internal differentiation of the reactions on H's Facebook wall show a similar emphasis. Here, the "likes" took the lead as the reaction category with the most occurrences, but the references to external destinations were almost as important. Only a few personal messages showed up on the wall, and even fewer discussions occurred, where an explicit comment was followed by one or more other comments referencing the previous one. Other, almost negligible reactions were explicit negative statements about an offer made by H, and tags, where other members had stated on Facebook that H was in a photo they had posted.

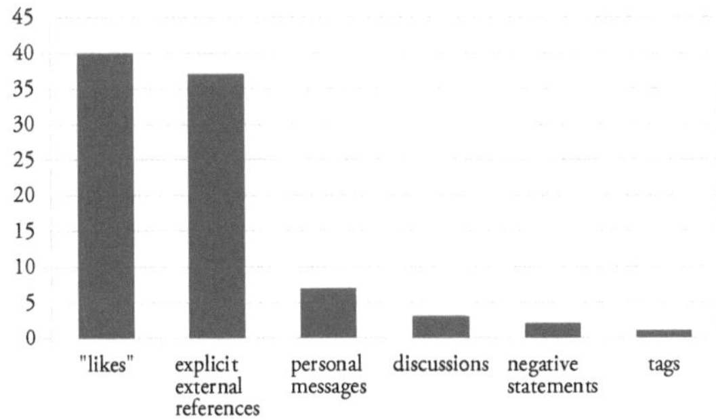

Types of reactions on the label owner H's Facebook wall over a period of two months prior to the sample date on June 26, 2009 (P1415).

Although the types of reactions show more diversity on the label owner H's Facebook wall, the emphasis on explicit external references and "likes" is almost identical to the situation on the artist T's wall. Both categories share the function of adding activity to the page where they appear, while at the same time also offering an opportunity to make a switch and divert the attention away from it. This dilemma was obviously shared among profile pages on MySpace and Facebook, even though the direct embedding of reactions underneath the posts resulted in a more associative flow of communication on Facebook.

3.3 Control Efforts

An analysis of the control structures involved in the creation and lifespan of profile pages on both MySpace and Facebook allows us to gain more insight into the possibilities for participants to switch between different contexts, add distinctions, and either indicate their perspective or remain unmarked on purpose.

The technological basis of all computer-based media, including mobile phone networks, was entirely in the hands of large-scale industrial corporations, layering a service industry of data transportation and hosting on top of the hardware of the global computer networks. In any case, these corporations had their own policies and were influenced by government policies, while in some cases, they were directly controlled by governments (Goldsmith / Wu 2006; Berners-Lee 2006). Platforms such as MySpace and Facebook made use of this layer structure and built their offerings on the foundations of a flexible and easily scalable technical infrastructure. Nonetheless, they were still embedded in the global infrastructure of the medium. They could only offer what their members' computers, their operating systems, and browsers could display, and they had to tailor their services to the bandwidth of the connections available to their members. Both platforms had millions of members from all around the world, with a broad variety of social backgrounds and differing access to the internet (Google 2011a; Google 2011b). Thus, any control efforts had to work with or around the technical preconditions of available internet technologies and their adoption among the platforms' target groups, as well as political influences. These preconditions were mostly controlled by multinational industrial corporations and governments. The next layer of control efforts was added by the design of the platforms' services themselves. Upon programming their offerings for their members to use, the owners of MySpace and Facebook implemented a set of social rules, some of which were implicit in the possibilities offered to the members, while others were stated explicitly (e.g. MySpace 2011c; MySpace 2011d; Facebook 2011a; Facebook 2011c). The rule that member accounts had to represent "natural persons" (Facebook 2011g), disallowing organizations to set up dedicated member profiles, is an example of such an explicit control effort on the part of Facebook.

A third layer of control efforts was handed to the members by MySpace and Facebook. They allowed their members to decide whether or not they wanted to allow any other member to post on their profile pages, or if they wanted to restrict posting to only their "friends". On Facebook, posting by someone else could be ruled out altogether, allowing only the owner of the wall to post on it (Facebook 2011d). On MySpace, an option could be activated requiring moderation of posts. This meant that any post on the page would not show up there automatically, but would have to first be approved by the page's administrator (MySpace 2011d).

By analyzing the pages, we can deduct some of the control settings used by the profiles' administrators. Notable in this regard is the abrupt absence of comments on the label C's MySpace page after February 2009 (P1085). This is a strong indication that the administrator had closed the commenting feature on the page, or enabled the mandatory moderation and then abstained from allowing any comments to be posted. The artists T and O both had comments on their MySpace pages well beyond that date, although their frequencies decreased notably.

On their Facebook profiles, all the members I observed allowed posts from their "friends". None of them restricted the access to allow only their own posts to appear on their wall. However, Facebook allowed for rather detailed privacy settings for each member's profile, and therefore, the exact composition of the control structure could not be deducted for all member profiles observed. The artist T and the label owner did, for example, allow for photos by other members in which they were "tagged", i.e. identified, to appear on their own walls. If a member did not allow for such posts to show up on its wall, I would likely not have been able to observe its existence. Comments on these images also appeared on the walls of those members "tagged" in the images, thus also adding their own observational perspectives and their distinction arrangements to these contexts (e.g. P1415), similar to the structures of "liking" described above. It has to be noted that on Facebook, posts, "likes", comments, and "tags" could also be removed by either those who published them, or, in the case of "tags", by those who were referenced by them. This was an important feature in general for images in which a member appeared in a way it did not want to be seen publicly (Facebook 2011d).

The technological control platforms such as MySpace and Facebook had over the social activity involving their offerings exceeded the definition of who was allowed to post on which wall. This control also included the selection of media formats which members could embed on their pages, as well as their file sizes, for individual assets and in total. This was important for the quality in which the members could embed original material on their profile pages, and the possible maximum length of audio or video streams, for example. First of all, it was important that the platforms allowed the label and the artists to embed audio material matching the length of the works they wanted to present. This was provided for on both MySpace and Facebook. Notably, though, neither the label owner H nor the artist T actually presented any original material as static information in their Facebook profiles. This could have been done on subpages, which were accessible via tabs at the top of the wall, using Facebook's own embeddable music player. This piece of software used a very simple user interface, and did not allow for comments on the material it held.

The second option was to post a link to a video hosted on the services YouTube or Vimeo. Similar to the MP3 link, Facebook would automatically create an embedded player for the video on the wall, with the same possibility for commenting. Technically, the material was played back from its original location, with Facebook simply acting as a proxy between the visitor and the hosting service (e.g. on P1415). As a third option, a link to audio material hosted on the platform Soundcloud could also be posted. Soundcloud offered online hosting and sharing of audio material in relatively good quality, with the special feature that comments could be posted directly onto the visual waveform of the material. This made it possible to comment not on the entire work, but on specific parts of its temporal structure. Soundcloud became a popular way to embed audio material towards the end of the research period.

The ability to render material from external sources directly accessible on the Facebook members' walls meant that the platform designers deliberately gave up control in favor of freedom for the users to embed their own material using a method of their choice. The form of the representation as well as its admittance on the walls was, however, determined by Facebook.

3.4 The Formation of Online Publics

The analysis of the cases of communication on MySpace and Facebook member profiles has shown how publics can work involving the networked computer as a primary medium. Information was offered in direct relation to its perceived origins, i.e. the artists and the label. Any member, in the case of MySpace or public Facebook profiles and pages even any internet user, could access this information without being hindered by significant transmission latencies or limited availability. Members could then react by publishing further information directly on the same pages (see section 3.1.2 and form equation 3.1.2.h). The reactions could include both semantic generalizations and additional structures. In any case, reactions on the pages analyzed here made the different observer perspectives explicit by including the names of the respective members who published the reactions, as well as direct links to their profiles.

The offerings on MySpace and Facebook, as I have described them here, were provided in public situations spanning across the entire accessible internet. The internet users had the choice among a multitude of websites, accessible either directly or via various search engines. The social complexity accessible to every internet user was, for all practical purposes, just as contingent as any meaning accessible through spoken language or writing. The structures of the online publics were different from publics utilizing other communication media. The internet protocols used to transmit messages, the computers, their operating systems, the actual code of the websites as well as the browsers displaying it, all had been conceived by programmers and engineers who never could have anticipated all communicative situations they would eventually be used in. Facebook as a platform for online communication has been described as attempting to take over more and more functions of the regular internet, such as searching, hosting photos etc. (see for example Siegler 2010).[15] In our field, such an attraction force towards Facebook was certainly observable. However, with the use of Facebook rising during the research period, social complexity on the platform also increased. For the social process, the technological foundation was unimportant, as long as it did not disturb. Of course, the chances for disturbances could increase if the technological basis for social processes was largely kept in the hands of just one company, as was the case with Facebook. In the end, to be part of the process the participants in the field almost had to become Facebook members. Since the platform was not walled-in – membership was kept free during the time of research and signing up was a relatively quick process –, Facebook was not separated from the wider internet, but remained a vital part of it.

The participants in the field used the internet for various purposes and different social undertakings in the respective network domains. For example, they were organizing artistic practice, discussing aesthetic considerations with the label owner H, or negotiating contract conditions. However, these uses remained invisible to others unless they were made explicit by their originators. The label owner H working directly with the record manufacturers and distributors was not a topic on Facebook, for example, until he made a comment about it on his wall (P1415). A large share of the communication using the internet in our field therefore happened in private or as direct communication among business partners, using email or chat services like Skype. In order to go public, communication had to enter a public situation explicitly, by creating artifacts for others to be found on websites or member profile pages. There, these artifacts could be noticed and discussed by other participants in this public situation, who might have had a similar background of functional network domains. The observation of how something was done in a specific network domain could then become a theme of public discussion, with the cultural dimension of comparing and weighing different approaches against each other.

3.4.1 Building Publics

Getting members of a public to take note and listen to one's music offerings, i.e. become part of the audience, was the primary function of the marketing efforts I

15 Siegler (2010) describes how Facebook started to make its "sharing" and "like" features available to other websites, in an attempt to have its users reflect on their activities outside of Facebook on their walls.

observed in the field. In order to listen to and subsequently evaluate a work of art on offer, it first of all had to be accessible. This was mainly achieved via online presentations, such as individual websites, and profiles on MySpace, Facebook, or Last.fm. With such online presentations, accessibility of original material, such as music or video, had reached a level far exceeding the possibilities available before the introduction of ubiquitous internet access.

Secondly, guidance to the accessible works had to be provided in an existing situation of a public. Only a small number of members of a public would access a work if they had to find it on their own. The chances of successfully building a larger audience increased with the guidance offered, so that works introduced by an artist could be found according to specific interests leading members of the public to the right places. On the online platforms mentioned above, guidance was primarily provided by peers, i.e. by other artists also striving to build potentials for their works by getting more members of the public interested. Sharing public interest in this way may seem counterproductive, yet it appeared to be one of the most sustainable ways to build substantial interest in one's offerings. The risk any participant in such a sharing game was taking lies in the very real possibility that the addition of another artist's identity as context could immediately drive away any interest in their own offerings and thus effectively prevent any building of an audience and, eventually, positive evaluations. Yet, it appears the potential and actual gains were well worth taking this risk, as online presentations took over as the dominant form of identity representations in the field. Indeed, observations sustain the impression of mutual transitivity of relations among peers: Exchanging public interest seemed to rely on a mechanism of give-and-take. On MySpace, the circle of peer artists on the label C's roster constantly kept each other in the selections of "top friends", which were featured prominently on the profile pages (e.g. P445; P447; P466). Some were more successful than others in this sharing game, as we have seen in the cases of the artist T and the label owner H and their differing activity / reaction ratios.

Other means by which members of the online publics could find presentations of artists and their works were explicit searches for artist, label, or track names, or indeed other keywords, as the search function on MySpace allowed for full text as well as direct name searches. Moreover, MySpace profile pages were entirely indexed by generic search engines, such as Google. A Google search for an artist, label, or track name would therefore return the MySpace profile page, among other results (e.g. P3103; P1008). The placement in the results was subject to the same ranking algorithms applied to regular websites, so the amount of traffic on the profile page as well as its connectivity to other relevant pages were important factors for its location in regular searches (Brin / Page 1998).

Without access to MySpace's server logs, it was not possible to discriminate the importance of individual technological means by which members of the public accessed artist and label profiles. Visitors were counted the same, whether they came directly from a MySpace-internal search or an external search engine, or were directed from another member's profile page.

3.4.2 Novelty and Selection

The music that was produced by the artists in our field was embedded into the temporality of cultural practice in its specific scene. Music releases were introduced at a certain publication date, and almost always kept at least the year of their publication as part of their metadata whenever they were referenced (see for example P445; P448). Via the explicit inclusion of time, a narrative of continuous cultural evolution unfolded, where works of art could be assessed retrospectively in the context of other releases published around the same time.

The inclusion of a date with reference to individual releases of recorded music is an indication of how these releases were perceived as adding something genuinely new to the cultural scenes in which they were embedded. Adding a concrete time reference was functionally equivalent to claiming that the work published was making a real difference to the state of the scene. Otherwise, there would have been no distinction possible between the time before and after the release had been published. By assigning this difference a temporal signature, the claim was made that the difference was, indeed, real. Thus, in the field we are analyzing, publications of works of art or the announcements of events were regarded as novelties.[16] They were placed as such in the context of online representations of artists and the label C (for example P428) as well as in relevant journalistic publications, both in print and online (e.g. P484).

Recall Niklas Luhmann's notion of communication referenced in section 1.4.3: The uttering of an information to be understood. In the operation of communication, these three aspects fall into one and cannot be discerned. After the fact, however, as we have proceeded through the act of communication, we can try to analytically separate the elements in another, separate act of communication. In the case of the introduction of works of art, we can attest that the message and the information can be attributed to the artists themselves or to actions on their behalf, while understanding remains opaque unless we find an explicit nexus, a further reference implicitly selecting a previous act of communication. This, as well, can only be done after the fact, encapsulated into an observation that is, again, uttered as information to be understood. This analytical view can be differentiated:

16 See section 2.4.2 for a discussion of how phenomena integrate novelty.

$$\text{temporal relation} = \overline{\overline{\text{communication}}\big|\;\overline{\text{origin of difference}}\big|\;\overline{\text{destination of difference}}\big|}\Big|$$

Form equation 3.4.2.a: Temporal relation as communication observed in the context of the origin of a difference and the destination of a difference.

This brings to light another aspect: By observing previous communication, the information marked in that operation is attributed to that which makes the difference and to that to which it makes a difference, as well as to the observer. Through observation, there is relation. Without observation, there would be no information and no relation. Offering information on the publication of a novel work of art was, therefore, a call to make observations of the novelty factor explicit. The original work of art that was published was of course not being observed for the first time. It was new in the context of public availability, but at least the artists who created it had observed it before, deeming it worth its publication and thereby already attributing a value to it. Any song that a musician released under his name could be assumed to have had at least one listener before it went public: the musician himself. By this expectation, the musician's identity was linked to the song; after all, he could be expected to withhold it from publication if he thought it was not good enough. The participants involved in the attribution of such values constantly run the risk of being held accountable for their public attributions.

Therefore, the musician's position in the network of cultural practice served to build expectations about the quality of music released: A bad song was not just a bad song in itself, rather, it was a separate disappointment that a musician who should have known better had released it. The same function could be used to create inverse effects as well: An artist with a very high standing in a network of cultural practice could hope to get a good reception for a music release that would not find similar public interest had it been released by an unknown newcomer.

If a label was involved in the publication of a music release, it took an even greater risk than the artist. While the artist was perceived as an originator, labels could be seen as curators (see section 4.2.1). This put them in a position where they could be expected to compare and assess thoroughly the material offered by the artists, and to only publish it if they saw it on par with the quality of other releases the label had published in the past. Therefore, they had to carefully select which releases they published.

For the reasons stated above, control over how an artist's identity was described in the network structure was highly important for the artists themselves and their agents. As long as the music was not entirely decontextualized, the producer's identity would inevitably be linked to any selection of artistic work in an observation. Moreover, the producer's identity influenced directly which selections could be made by introducing a frame for the information and the message, thereby ruling out some possibilities as to how communication could proceed in this context.

The risk I have mentioned manifested itself in the inability of artists, labels, and distributors to anticipate whether or not the claims they made about their music or about a release they published would find a following in the public discussion. Would others agree that their latest album or single was indeed a milestone in its own regard, or that it at least added something of relevance to the scene? Would listeners agree in their comments that an album did indeed fit in with the past releases of the label, and would they see it as a worthy addition to the label's portfolio? There was no way of anticipating the answers; they had to be derived from observations made of reactions in the public discussions after the release was out.

This brings into focus another aspect of how relations were built in the process of making selections: As we deal with stories or sets of stories, the observer making the selection of one among various alternatives in turn offered an evaluation of the selection, thereby adding information to it in a separate operational step. The most basic form of such an evaluation would be the affirmation or disaffirmation of the selection fitting to a value on which the evaluation was based. In the case of the evaluation of works of art, the observer could offer an evaluation on whether or not the selected work fit the expectations held towards a work from its particular background. Luhmann (2000, pp. 118) has described this as the basic code of communication in the art world. The instances of selections I could observe (for example described in section 3.1.2) were often clear in their positive evaluation, yet offered little in terms of differentiated reasonings for their judgment. This vagueness on the part of the commenters as to what exactly they liked about the music functioned as an all-inclusive affirmation of the presentations to which the comments were added. Therefore, the evolution of artistic styles did not usually produce changes via the selection of individual stylistic traits in pieces of recorded or performed music, or even of individual works. I did not observe cases were such detailed critiques of aesthetic aspects were given. Rather, the selections referenced the entire spectrum of work done by one artist, or even one label. Selections with positive evaluations did not provide consultation for the artists; they could only be observed as highly generalized symptoms of public affirmation. Also, they always included a reference to the contexts of the members making the evaluation, thus serving their interest in promoting their own activities as well.

On MySpace, positive evaluations could be observed in scarce verbose affirmations described above and, vaguely, in the number of visits to a page, as well as the number of times a piece of music had been played back on the page. As the latter two are numbers, no information was conveyed as to who made the selections, and whether the selections indeed resulted in a positive judgment. In fact, the generalized nature of these measures of success made them vulnerable to manipulation (Jag 2007).

The explicitly positive evaluations given on MySpace could be observed by all visitors to the respective MySpace page, whether they were members of the platform or not. On Facebook, the situation was different: Here, the commenters not only left an account of their judgment on the profile page where the artifact they commented upon was presented, but they also presented their selection as fresh information together with a link to the original material on their own profile page. Technically, there was no difference to providing original material of their own, and the selection was automatically visible in all of their "friends'" information feeds. Thereby, a selection made explicit on Facebook had a potential for a significantly greater proliferation than one made public on MySpace, even though it was possible on Facebook to restrict the reach of proliferation and the access to one's profile page. On Facebook, the information was pushed to the wider public consisting of an artist's network of "friends" and "friends of friends", whereas on MySpace the information had to be actively pulled by members of the public, requiring a preexisting level of interest.

Generalized positive evaluations could themselves be embedded into narratives. For example, the label or the artist could claim to have a great success at their hands, with a new release enjoying widespread public acclaim. A claim like that needed not refer to a quantifiable entity, but could be offered as a general qualitative observation.

3.4.3 Comparisons and Valuation Chains

I have described different cases of online presentations of artist's identities. In none of these cases do we find a self-sufficient description of the artist and his work that could make do without any further references. Instead, we find that in all observed cases, artists are presented and present themselves as embedded in a frame of references to other identities. This includes references to other artists as well as to labels, similar organizations, and distribution partners. The qualitative difference of such embeddings in the context of the networked computer as a medium of communication lies in the ability of any interested member of the public to check out all the other identities mentioned in the same context in full detail. The others' own presentations were only one or two clicks away. In many cases, presentations even included direct hyperlinks. In the modern society of mass media, before the mass-adoption of the internet, members of the publics had to accept the embeddings in a presentation as a given statement – for example, when comparisons among artists were made in printed articles –, and all they could do was engage in sometimes cumbersome research to verify or falsify for themselves the proclaimed statements of comparison. This does not exclude the case of the expert, e.g. a journalist or collector, who had already invested substantial efforts and resources to build up knowledge about a specific set of artists, and who could put this knowledge to use to immediately review the parts of the given frame of reference this knowledge covered. With the accessibility of the networked computer, building up expert knowledge had become much less cumbersome, with detailed information – including primary material – being readily available.

This resulted in a situation where the assessment of a given factual comparison – one artist's work being similar to another's – was no longer decoupled socially or in time. Print media featured experts, who, because of their positions, had access to exclusive primary material, such as pre-releases of upcoming albums, and therefore enjoyed a privilege to make assessments of qualitative similarities or differences in the artists' work. The format for such assessments was usually the album or concert review, which appeared in established print magazines. From the perspective of the public, assessments were therefore socially decoupled via the experts, while the print schedule of the magazines also accounted for the decoupling in time. The expert reviewer who received his commissions from print magazines was in the privileged position that he received CDs, vinyl records, and downloads of new material almost automatically. The labels, the distributors, and sometimes the artists would make sure that relevant reviewers within their musical genre would receive their upcoming releases, so that reviews already appeared in print magazines by the time the release could be bought. This mechanism was still in place in our field, but the social and temporal decoupling had already lost most of its functional ability together with the influence of the experts.[17] The original material was widely available in the public domain, and the technological basis of access rendered the social and temporal decoupling of the assessment of a factual comparison unnecessary.

Harrison C. White has described a type of social action that is based on comparisons as disciplines (White 2008: pp. 67). With White, there are three such disciplines as ways in which identities can be ordered: The first contains interfaces that structure processes of getting things done, the second arenas that structure orders of purity towards a certain value, and the third councils that act as mediators between different attempts at influencing overarching value orders. In the complexity of social situations, such disciplines never occur as singular, clear-cut structures. Instead, we observe multiple value orders in effect simultaneously, mutually and recursively influencing each other, and negotiating trade-offs between positions higher up or lower down the respective chains of order.

The function of these disciplines is to establish and maintain what White calls valuation chains, effective orderings of the elements observed by the disciplines. These

17 For a more general analysis of the changes the widespread adoption of the internet brought about for journalism, see for example Renner / Renner 2011: pp. 168. One of their main arguments is that traditional journalism had to cede its privilege of interpretation to the actual participants in cultural practice.

valuation chains serve to provide information as to whether one selection is preferred over another selection, with reference to the basis of the valuation. In order to make this possible, both selections have to be subjected to the mechanism of comparison. While I observed a multitude of comparisons in the field – a few of which are mentioned above –, entire valuation chains were not part of the operations, at least not explicitly. Instead, distinctions were referenced in which valuation chains could be expected to unfold. They would, however, not be observable at once, but rather event-based, like the rest of the network. Take for example the self-description given by the artist O on his MySpace profile (described in section 3.1.2). On the very top of the page, we have the claim that the work of this artist falls into the electronica genre. On the left side, we find the mention of influences on the artist's work, some of them from inside the genres referenced at the top, some of them from other genres. Via referencing these genres and other artists from within them, the artist O placed his work in a valuation chain with them and all other artists who could be observed as belonging to that genre. However, there was no observable entirety of all of these artists, nor was it possible to deliberately name them all, if an observer wished to do so. No one observer could ever claim to have exhaustive knowledge of all possible artists to be included in one genre, and another observer could always come up with a selection that differed significantly.

For any second-order observer, the entity in which an artist claimed inclusion via the self-descriptions mentioned above remained largely unspecified. If the claim was based on a comparison observable by the artists who made the claim, this was not conveyed in the message. As second-order observers, we can make out a rough set of artists and labels referenced in the self-description, which we can assume belong to a valuation chain as it was seen by the artist. To the observer, these points of reference formed a somewhat hazy value sphere, similar to what Michael Hutter has described in his paper on valuation systems (Hutter 2007).

If we take value spheres as areas of reference which we use to categorize artists, and which artists use to suggest categorizations for themselves, we inherently accept that explicit valuation chains played no direct part in these operations. Instead, it was enough to have a value sphere where one could find similar works to those of the artist one was observing, and that could be used as a category to place the artist in. Actual valuations of the form "work A is better than work B" were not necessary to achieve this. To the contrary: Any such explicit valuation could have backfired on the observer, whose judgment and, subsequently, whose entire standing could be questioned if his assessment was not affirmed among his peers. This risk could be avoided by accepting claims of belonging to a value sphere without further questioning, and especially without the need for an explicit placement in an observable valuation chain.

The comparisons I observed worked by claiming that one or more works of art could be included in a particular value sphere, such as a musical genre and its scene. Essentially, the claim was of the form "this work belongs into this category", and via the naming of influences, it could take on the more detailed form of "this work is similar to these other works". On the artist's profile page, visitors could leave comments, giving their judgment of either affirmation or negation. Individual comparisons, however, were usually not commented on; rather, comments usually expressed undifferentiated content with the entire presentation on the profile page or website, while negative statements were given only on very rare occasions.

If we as second-order observers look at a comparison in the field, we can attribute it to a specific identity. In the case mentioned above, or in the case described in section 3.1.2, this was the artist who suggested having his work compared with that of other, well-known artists in the field of electronica and more mainstream-oriented popular electronic music. The basic operational steps of such a comparison are identical to those described in section 1.5.1:

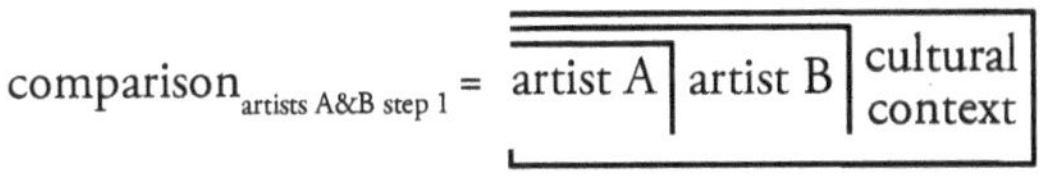

Form equation 1.5.1.a / 3.4.3.a: Step 1 of the comparison between artists A and B as artist A observed in the context of artist B and the wider context of the cultural scene.

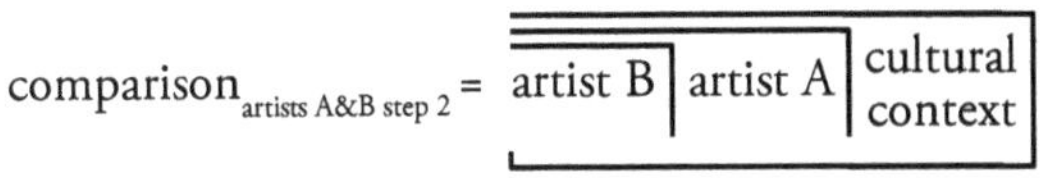

Form equation 1.5.1.b / 3.4.3.b: Step 2 of the comparison between artists A and B as artist B observed in the context of artist A and the wider context of the cultural scene.

However, instead of reaching a preference for one of the artists in the comparison, the social mechanism described here determines the suitability of the statements in their respective, or common, cultural contexts.

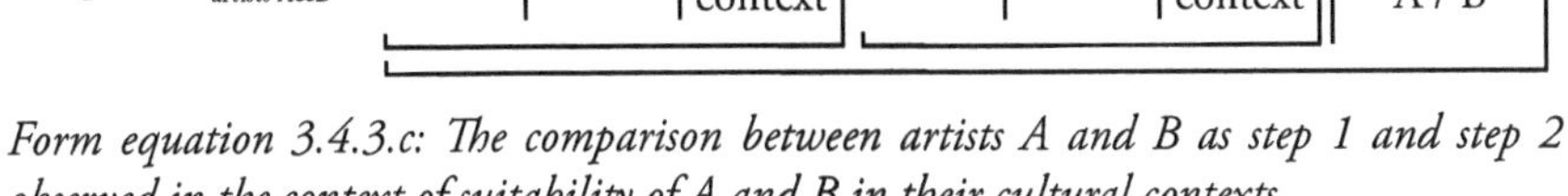

Form equation 3.4.3.c: The comparison between artists A and B as step 1 and step 2 observed in the context of suitability of A and B in their cultural contexts.

I have mentioned the specific situation of a public forming around the artists, labels, and their potential and actual audiences, as it has become possible with the use of platforms like MySpace and Facebook that allow for the presentation and accessibility of original material by the artists in the form of audio and video streams. Above, I have laid out the details of how I understand the workings of comparisons in the field, and why I think these operations were of great importance to the artists developing their identities. For the situations in which publics formed, it was crucial that both selections being compared could be judged independently. For this, visitors to a MySpace page, for example, had to be able to access the original material of both the artist making the comparison – which was provided directly on the page – and material by other artists suggested as comparison. In the case of MySpace, such material was usually easily accessible either directly on the same platform, if the other artists had MySpace pages themselves, or via other sources, such as their websites or videos with their music on YouTube. If searches on these sources did not bring the desired results, there was still the option to prelisten music releases commercially available in iTunes or other online music stores.

The direct accessibility of source material is paramount to this new type of public situation. The key to achieving this accessibility was the inclusion of the relevant source material on the websites and profile pages, so that a situation of full connectivity (White 1995) could emerge, where all participants had full access to all information relevant to the public in question at any time. With the material available online, interested members of the public could access it from their desktop and laptop computers, but also from their internet-connected mobile phones. In addition, using the same technological means, the participants could also communicate with the providers of the material and with each other without further hindrance. Thus, full connectivity was established.

3.4.4 Different Potentials

One method of gaining public interest was to be referenced from places where it already existed. In the field of music, this meant being mentioned in information on other artists that had already drawn interest. This could involve being mentioned in comparisons, i.e. on the other artist's list of "top friends" on MySpace, or being mentioned as a collaboration partner in music production or performance. Examples of such mentions include co-productions as well as remixes of works by another artist, or being featured in a production as a vocalist or instrumentalist.

Comparisons, therefore, served two functions for the identities in the network: Firstly, they suggested a valuation for the material associated with the identities if the subjects of the comparison were known to the public and had a standing there. Secondly, they directed interest towards the included references, whether the artists referenced there were already known or not. Being included in a comparison by another identity in any case served to build a potential for an identity. Releasing music on different labels had a very similar function for most of the artists in the field. Even though labels usually did not have a strong following any more (P47: 59), interest for one artist also drew interest to the label and from there to other artists releasing on that label.

When observing the building of potentials, it has to be kept in mind that the underlying network processes are ephemeral, event-based social constructs (White 2008). They are nothing that any identity could rely on, and thus, the same holds true for the potentials we try to analyze. The decline of MySpace over the course of the research period shows just how fragile potentials were. Although MySpace was still around by the end of the research period, social activity on the artists' profile pages had decreased significantly. When analyzing potentials, therefore, one has to take into account their relative instability, and avoid making the mistake of taking aggregated numbers, as they are readily available online, as measures of the size of potentials. Huge public interest in the past may have left its imprint in the numbers of visits displayed on a website or profile page, but it may have long since moved on, leaving the actual potential at the time of the observation much smaller. A better way to measure the potential gained by a certain offering is to look for the velocity of relative changes, for example in the numbers of comments or plays of songs over a certain time period (with caution, keeping the possible fraud mentioned in section 3.1.1 in mind).

So far, we have only looked at potentials built through online presentations. The more traditional offline media built potentials as well, of course, and they continued to fulfill this role for the artists during the time of research. However, the relative size of the potentials the artists in the field could get through print magazines as well as radio and TV appearances could not easily be measured in detail in the absence of traceable audience counts.

At performance or concert events, the potential was equal to the number of visitors. As I will lay out further in Chapter 4, the number of visitors did not necessarily equal the audience at an event, as in several cases I observed, a large part of the visitors did not engage in listening or watching the performance at all. On the other hand, to become a member of the audience, one had to already be a visitor at the event. The potential at hand in these cases was the actual public interest in a concrete offering.

The topics of public interest determined how the artists could build potentials for their audiences. Had there not been public interest in the electronica music genre, comparisons within this genre would not have helped the musicians to acquire audiences. In this regard, the rise of the production-oriented publics I have described in section 1.2.3 was of great interest to the musicians. It gave them another opportunity to be featured in different contexts, and thereby gain interest for their own work.

3.4.5 Music Releases

I have described how artists made use of online platforms to publish material they produced. These platforms offered an easy method by which the artists themselves or their labels could publish any material they wanted to. This possibility was used by all the artists and the labels in the field. Notably, though, the format in which the material was published on these platforms was that of individual pieces, most of which had no direct inherent relation with each other. Music was, for example, not published in the traditional album format. The material was provided as an audio stream and could, for the most part, not be downloaded. The embedded players for the audio streams provided a name for the individual stream and its length as additional information.

The publication of new material on an online profile page or on an artist's website was, however, not regarded as a release in the sense that a label published releases. MySpace, Facebook, and the artists' own websites were places for the publication of information regarding the artists' work, but not a primary channel for the public release of their works. Releases still made use of traditional album formats and were organized differently. Also, only four to eight pieces could usually be accessed on an artist's or a label's profile page at any given time, while a regular album release usually held upwards of eight pieces (e.g. P648). While a regular album usually summarized a selection of new material which one or more artists had worked on over a defined period of time, the pieces presented on a profile page often deliberately brought together pieces from different periods in the artist's working biography (as on P445).

In the field, publications of works were usually summarized into releases. The forms of these releases were influenced by technical requirements of their physical incarnations, i.e. the maximum length of the material they could hold. In the cases I observed, the forms of the releases often followed the restrictions of the vinyl record: An album had to fit on a 12" record with a playback speed of 33 rpm, while singles had to be compatible with either 7" or 12" records playing back at 45 rpm (Millard 1995). A third format in between the single and the album was the "extended play", or EP release, which also utilized the 12" physical format, but fit more pieces onto it than a single would, with pieces that were usually considerably longer (e.g. P649).

The categorization of the formats album, single, and sometimes EP was usually followed in the release policy of the label and its artists. This meant that the formats implied by the physical releases were inscribed into the digital incarnations of the releases as well. On iTunes, Boomkat, and other online music stores, these formats formed the most prominent product categories, with relatively stable price points (e.g. P599; P613).

In the field, material was therefore often released in forms that were based on the technical restrictions of physical media. These physical media had of course been conceived and implemented in social action, and therefore the objectifications of releases as I observed them have to be categorized as conservative, in the way they were preserving the system in which recorded music was published in the era before music became accessible as pure information.

3.4.6 Switchings

Artists and other participants in the field offered numerous hints and links that invited visitors who came across their online representations to engage in the perception of works of art. Music was provided directly on websites and online platform profile pages, next to photos and videos that dealt with the work of the artists. The material was mostly available in streaming formats, not allowing for the original files to be downloaded. This meant that the material had to be played back directly from the websites and profile pages, and therefore the players were embedded directly into the code of the pages and appeared in prominent spots. The players thereby served as indications outlining original material, i.e. works of art, in the context of the vast assortment of metadata supplied with most online representations.

The metadata provided with these online representations were invaluable as indications guiding expectations towards works of art. However, at the same time, they were also invitations to switch away again. The destinations of such switchings were usually similar social entities, i.e. other artists and organizations. The visitors could evaluate such hints and links for useful information both on the artist or organization whose profile they had originally visited, as well as follow the links and do the same at the destination of the switching. The catch with this was that these other artists' and organizations' profiles had to be similar enough, so that they were directly comparable from the visitors' point of view and the visitors did not feel misled. At the same time, these profiles had to be significantly different in some relevant way, so that a potential comparison between the source and the destination profile of the switching did not risk coming across as a mere copy.

Online representations were not provided for individual visitors, of course. They were designed and published to appeal to many visitors with a similar set of interests, as anticipated by the creators. As mentioned above, Harrison C. White (1995) has described this notion of multiple switchings among sets of densely connected offerings as the activity of publics. And Dirk Baecker (2010) has warned against the notion of stability in the publics addressed by an artist's offerings, pointing out their restlessness in the continuous search for interesting places to switch to.

The set of interests in a public that a designed representation could try to appeal to was usually not specific enough to be served by only this one representation. Instead, it was served by a larger number of representations and identities. Publics were usually not just interested in one artist, but in a loose set of artists that could be seen to fall into some identical category. Such a value sphere can guide members of publics switching back and forth among the various representational offerings, keeping the entire variety of what was on offer in terms of original artistic work as their horizon of possible selections. Such publics are rather specialized, offering similar switching destinations. Although it would appear counterproductive for artists or organizations to send visitors to competitors that appealed to the same set of interests while also trying to establish and maintain an audience, the answers given in the survey among MySpace "friends" of the label C show that one of the main interests of visitors was the discovery of new music. Hence, being included in a group of artists who all linked to each other could be beneficial for every one of them.

The links offered on the label C's website and MySpace page mostly stayed within the realm of its own neighborhood in the cultural network, directed towards the artists and the distribution and sales chain. The artists, on the other hand, offered mostly links to other artists, while also sometimes including links to different labels (e.g. P443; P445; P447; P466).

The cases of member profile pages we have analyzed have shown various differences between MySpace and Facebook as the most commonly used platforms for online communication. MySpace was mainly designed for publication of information that was more or less static, or at least only slowly changing information. This information was arranged on the top of the page, very similar to a traditional website. Having the comments at the bottom of the page made them comments on the entire page. Indeed, I did not observe a single case where a MySpace comment discussed a specific item on the page. Rather, if they referenced the work of the member at all, they expressed very generalized opinions and evaluations. Altogether, though, only 15.4% of comments on MySpace I observed in the analysis referenced the work of the member on whose profile page they were posted. They were grossly outnumbered by comments that referenced the commenter's work, mostly either music releases, or concert events where they either participated or which they organized. 56.5% of all comments in the analysis were such marketing comments. They were potentially destructive for the communicative efforts of the owner of the profile page, as they were attempts to divert away attention from the page they were entered on. They were blunt offers to the visitors of the page to immediately switch away again. About 8.2% of the comments on the MySpace pages in our analysis contained personal messages, i.e. messages that addressed the owner of the profile page directly, not just referencing the work. The rest of the comments were short notes of the "thanks for the add" (e.g. on P1400) type.

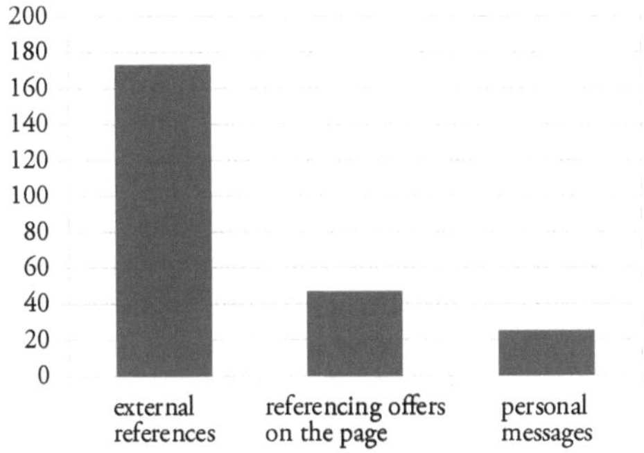

Overall distribution of comment types on MySpace profile pages in the analysis.

The situation with comments was rather different on Facebook. Here, the comments were added to individual items on the page by design. The entire structure of the pages was different, as there was very little possibility to enter static information on the main page of a member profile, or an artist or organization page. The front pages of any such representations were dominated by their wall, with the latest entries at the top, and therefore primarily contained information with some sort of news value. The information given on the main pages on Facebook was much less descriptive than on MySpace, and was rather mostly tied to actual topics. Descriptions of an artist's or an organization's work were provided on Facebook as well, but only on subpages of the main page. Therefore, most social activity took place on the main page and its wall.

In the field, it was usually indicated on Facebook walls that they were in sync with cultural practice. References to current or upcoming social events were the means to communicate this. Differing from MySpace, these references did not have to be cultural events in which the owner of the page participated in some way. However, in order to add a certain news value, references to the page owner's own cultural production were regularly woven in. The cases we analyzed showed relatively regular updates, with relatively small announcements or statements made in each update. Especially on the member profiles, many of these updates referenced lifestyle aspects rather than aspects of cultural production, but this has to be seen in context: The member profiles on Facebook were based on the notion of personhood, and therefore the wall updates usually reflected multiple facets of an artist's identity. A clear distinction between private and public aspects does not seem appropriate in many of the observed cases. Some published items would have to be attributed to the member's private lifestyle, while others could have been published as a news item in a music magazine. At the same time, the term "publication" here usually meant making information accessible to a more or less select group of Facebook "friends". Even though these relations were not all close friendships, the member at least had points of reference for what to expect as reaction to any item he or she published. After all, each "friend" request had been accepted manually, so the member would have a general overview of who might be reached directly by a publication. Therefore, the situation in which an item was made accessible was not necessarily the same as that in which a magazine article, a blog entry, or even an item on a MySpace profile page was published. Still, the potential network effects – a published item being "shared" by many other members – made it likely that an item would spread further, to members not directly connected with the artist. A "like" or a comment on the artist's wall were traces of such spreading. Items published on a Facebook wall were therefore not published to an anonymous, broad public, but, at least initially, rather to a relatively limited public of which the publisher had at least a vague notion.

The topics of communication on Facebook mixed elements which the modern society would have considered private with others that would have been considered destined for public accessibility. The situation in which they were made accessible certainly fits the definition of a public by Harrison C. White (1995), as I have been using it throughout this study. All participants were fully connected in the situation, and they were engaged in switchings between different network domains. However, this public situation was not necessarily distinguished from the realm of the private any more. The entire dichotomy did not seem relevant in these cases. Rather, topics that would have been considered as private before, such as what an artist felt after waking up (P1413), were now published as information on that artist's lifestyle. The information made accessible in this public situation did not usually reference its greater social contexts. For example, the label owner H posted information on upcoming label releases as well as on events organized by the magazine he worked for, without including further references to the roles he enacted in each context. The same was the case for the posts that would have been considered private before: There, too, the publishers did not mention where and with whom they had been waking up. Also, I did not observe a single case where a commenter would have asked about such things. In the cases analyzed above in section 3.2, the external switching offers brought about by the member owning a page therefore remained largely unmarked and unused.

3.4.7 Generalizations and Casual Intimacy

In the cases observed, semantic generalizations occurred in several different ways. The most obvious mechanism facilitating generalizations was that of the "like" feature on the Facebook platform. Other incarnations required explicit statements in the form of comments, but they worked in a similar way. They all collated rich semantic structures into easily understandable generalizations, and often coupled them with an explicit evaluation. This form of evaluating phenomena required generalization. Only by means of omitting a large part of the specifics of an observed phenomenon could it be made comparable with other phenomena, thus actualizing a category. The judgment whether such a generalized phenomenon was suitable for its cultural context could then serve as a mechanism to reinforce and perpetuate the generalizations.

The public online communication as analyzed in the case studies above exhibited a mixture of intimacy and distance, both focusing on a specific topic while remaining entirely general. This generalization cumulated in the function of the "like" on Facebook, where a positive statement was entirely generalized, yet focused on something very specific. Nevertheless, even the most generalized statement was a trace of visitors on a page, showing that they had taken note of the content on offer there. I will call this mode of communication "casual intimacy", where a large number of more or less generalized statements keep a community of participants in similar or the same cultural and artistic practices informed about the very details of each other's activities, without employing the dichotomy between public and private. The term casual intimacy highlights both the intimate, seemingly private nature of the information and its casual presentation, in which other topics can and will become more relevant at any time. Naming the entries on Facebook walls "status updates" (Facebook 2011e) was therefore very fitting, as they and their counterparts on other platforms ensured that participants were always up to date about the current activity status of other participants they were interested in. This mode defined the online public communication in the field, which is expressed in the following equation:

public online communication = communication | casual intimacy | online publics

Form equation 3.4.7.a: Public online communication as communication in the mode of casual intimacy, embedded in situations of online publics.

Online publics can be defined as public situations using online communication media. One property of this was that communication occurred asynchronously, i.e. offers and reactions were decoupled from each other. This was due to their technical implementation, where users could access the offers at any time and leave their reactions behind. When a field participant published a post on his MySpace or Facebook profile page, he could never be sure if and when a reaction would occur, and what a potential reaction might entail. This uncertainty had to be taken into account when making statements, and it was an important element of what I am describing as casual intimacy, as it prevented participants from getting too involved and too specific. Since they could not foresee how their statements would be recontextualized by subsequent reactions, they kept them casual so they could always draw on their ambiguity.[18] Nevertheless, the sheer amount and frequency of statements in the form of switching offers meant that they could still be close to the actual activity, and therefore, intimate. This principle of casual intimacy is expressed in the following equation:

Form equation 3.4.7.b: Casual intimacy as switching offers in the context of asynchronous accessibility.

Substituting the term of casual intimacy in form equation 3.4.7.a with 3.4.7.b, we obtain the following equation:

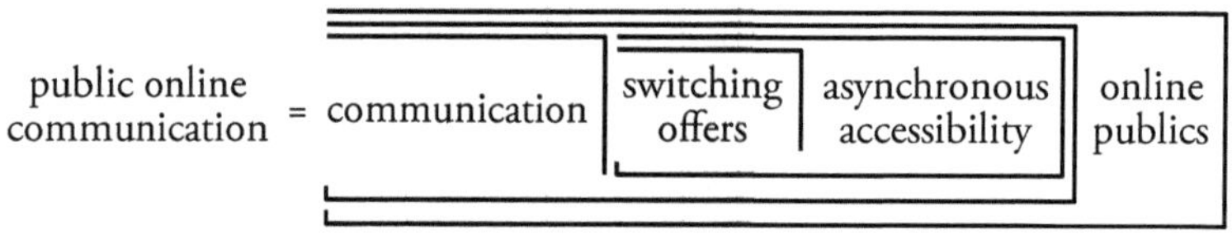

Form equation 3.4.7.c: Public online communication as communication in the mode of asynchronously accessible switching offers, embedded in situations of online publics.

Thus, public online communication in the field can be described as centered on switching offers that were accessible asynchronously, which had the quality of a situation of casual intimacy in our field. This highlights a constant situation of restlessness, where users are confronted with offers to direct their attention away from what they are currently concerning themselves with. The primary message of observable activity in one area is often a hint at other areas. Especially MySpace, but later also Facebook, excelled at embedding multimedia material directly on users' profile pages. Thus, switching away from one page to check out a new track or video on another page, inevitably became an attractive choice. This may sound problematic for the owner of the original page, but there is a different side of the story: Even posts that were primarily intended to draw attention away from where they were placed were indeed observable as social activity at that very place. Thereby, they increased the attractiveness of the offer from where they were intended to draw away the attention. This mode of reception, where artifacts are presented in the context of narrative

18 See Baecker 2011 for a discussion of ambiguity on Facebook.

embedding and in a situation of restlessness in the light of attempts at luring away attention, has been described by Walter Benjamin as "Zerstreuung" (Benjamin 1963: pp. 40). Similar to his examples, which include cinemas and architecture, the offers in the analyzed public online communication were aimed at casual reception. The publics, on the other hand, were often more interested in the information surrounding the offers than in the offers themselves. This mode, combined with seemingly private information, is what I refer to as casual intimacy.

Chapter 4:
Performance Events: Cultural and Artistic Practice in Social Space

While the artists in our field provided their material online, both on commercial download platforms and in excerpts for free on their own websites and profile pages, all of them also played live in front of audiences. The two realms of online information processing and interaction at live events were closely linked, as we will examine in the following sections. Both realms profited from each other, potentially building audiences in the respective other realm. However, while audiences could not be observed directly in online contexts, the interaction situations at live events allowed for the direct observation of those engaging in listening and watching the performance. The attention that was paid to providing detailed information about the events online hints at the perceived importance of the publics that could be reached there, and at the possibility of harnessing the online potential for the live events. One of the differences between the two realms adds a context in this situation: While there were no immediate economic gains to be had for the label and the artists on the online pages where they offered information to the public, the live events clearly had an economic background. At the same time, the websites and MySpace pages were often referenced in printed material accompanying the live events.

4.1 Format I: Label Event with Live Performance

The first event format we look at integrated a live performance with dedicated DJ sets into a longer evening. It was hosted not by the artists themselves or the venue owners, but rather by the label C as an external organization. During the research period, I attended six performance events of this format. Before getting into the detailed analysis of the case study, I will discuss the basic configuration of performance events and their underlying interaction systems.

4.1.1 Interaction Systems and Performances

The following is an account of an observation I made at one of the performance events of format I (P1192).

The door opened to a large room, the chatter of voices layered on top of loud synthesizer pop music. The music had been audible walking up the staircase, and it was the only indication that we actually had found the right entrance. Outside, on the street leading up to Berlin's Kottbusser Tor, we had not seen a single sign hinting at either the performance event or the venue itself. With me was a technology journalist from New York, who had visited me during the day and wanted to experience the Berlin electronic music scene first hand. Armed just with the description of the venue's location in relation to a nearby grocery store, we had finally found the correct staircase, after two previous attempts at other staircases in the immediate vicinity had failed. Now, with the warmth of the heated inside embracing us, I spotted a few familiar faces at the bar and the windows. Still, there was no sign at the door naming the venue or the performance event, and the entrance was not guarded or controlled at all. There were about 100 people inside, most of them flocking around the bar or sitting in the somewhat separated, almost triangular area in front of the small stage, furnished with lounge sofas and barstools. The room was cut in half by the bar, blocking our sight towards the stage as we entered. The entrance area was almost empty, just a few people sat around two tables in corner booths. These booths were made of wood and designed in a traditionalist bar fashion. The area behind the bar, seen from the entrance, was almost full with people standing or sitting in groups, engaged in conversation. The interior design was entirely different in this area, with art photographs on the walls and modernistic lounge furniture. Only the lamps were the same all over; they fit the traditionalist style of the entrance area and seemed a bit out of place in the crowded, second area. There was a DJ booth by the window close to the bar, where the label assistant L, the local event manager for the label C, was spinning vinyl records of synthpop music. I waved hello to him, then turned towards the bar to greet other visitors I knew, some of them label artists. I bought beers for my guest and myself, paying the required extra Euro on the first drink as a fee for the artist. The artist T was sitting at the bar, engaged in conversation. With our beers in hand, we greeted T and joined the conversation (P1192).

Direct interaction played a significant role in the cultural processes in our field. Various systems of interaction could be observed at all performance events mentioned in this study. Such systems rely on the co-presence of all participants, and have the advantage that all themes relevant to the participants can be negotiated immediately (see section 1.1.2 and Luhmann 1984: pp. 551; Luhmann 1995a: pp. 405; Luhmann 1997b: pp. 816; Goffman 1959; Goffman 1963). Co-presence here means that all observers have to assume that they are observed by all other observers they can observe. This synchronized recursivity coupled with full inclusion – every communicative offer can potentially be observed by all observers – creates a situation rich with multiple semantic contexts that cannot easily be controlled by any one participant

(Luhmann 1984, pp. 561). The unavoidable co-presence in an interaction system also means that the background contexts of all participants can potentially be addressed in the interaction, as long as they are known. The potential gains for the artists are high, as references to their work can spread out away from any one performance event, far across the different network domains of the participants, possibly growing the attention focused on the artist and thereby building the potential for audiences. In the absence of mass media coverage for the artists in the field, the spreading of references to their identity triggered by a live performance event was one of the ways they could grow their fan base. We have seen similar efforts in the analysis of artist representations on MySpace and Facebook in Chapter 3.

If we take interaction as communication on the condition of mutual presence, then the public interaction at the performance events we are analyzing here added the context of a located public situation to the equation. This can be modeled as follows:

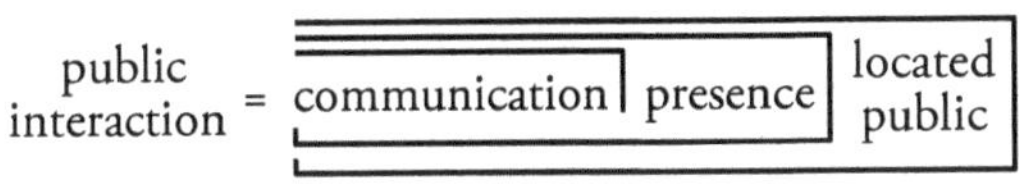

Form equation 4.1.1.a: Public interaction as communication on the condition of presence, embedded in a situation of a located public.

At the same time, interaction also brought together participants from different functional network domains, as defined in section 2.3.1. In the interaction itself, the association with certain network domains was suppressed in the way Harrison C. White (1995) has described, i.e. they were not relevant for the interaction to function, yet they could be a topic of communication. Presence in this context enabled participants to observe each other as they were switching between different topics, and follow the change of topics in realtime. Thus, this specific situation can be characterized by allowing for synchronized access to switching offers.

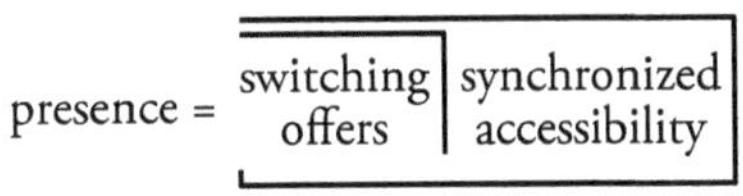

Form equation 4.1.1.b: Presence as switching offers observable in a context of synchronized accessibility.

If we substitute the term "presence" in form equation 4.1.1.a with its definition in form equation 4.1.1.b, we obtain the following equation:

$$\text{public interaction} = \overline{\text{communication} \,\big|\, \overline{\text{switching offers} \,\big|\, \text{synchronized accessibility}} \,\big|\, \text{located public}}$$

Form equation 4.1.1.c: Public interaction as communication on the condition of switching offers observable in a context of synchronized accessibility, embedded in a situation of a located public.

Direct interaction remained a vital form of communication in the field. Interaction and performance did not simply facilitate and support each other, though. From the audience's perspective, the live performances could either be seen as an experience of the reception of art, or as a distraction from communication with other visitors. Both views could be observed, and they expressed partly contradictory expectations for such performance events, leading to different evaluations.

4.1.2 Case Study: The Label C's "Allnighter" Event

The first type of arrangement we look at was entirely self-organized by the label C. Between 2007 and 2009, this performance event was held regularly – save a few exceptions – on the fourth Wednesday of the month. Called the label's "Allnighter", the label C was the most prominent reference in the name as well as on the artwork on the printed flyer. The term "Allnighter" was used mostly by labels in the electronic music scene for club events that were designed and organized entirely by one label. As in our case, this could include a live performance by a single artist or a group, but it also referenced an opportunity to engage in interaction that went beyond the framing of a concert. Naming a performance event a label's "Allnighter" therefore hints at a club situation with DJ sets in a certain realm of musical style related to the label's artist roster. In this context, a live performance could be expected as one highlight during an event that lasted over a longer timespan, enabling interaction systems to be sustained over the course of several hours.

According to the label owner H, the idea for the monthly performance event formed because of pressure from the artists releasing on the label to have a regular basis for their performances and for promoting their releases. In an interview (P47), he explained how the situation for live performers with this style of music had worsened over the years. He attributed the largest negative effect to the closing of the secondary floors in some of the bigger clubs of the city. During the 1990s and early 2000s, these floors housed the more experimental performances, music that was not strictly functional as music for the dancefloor – as it was still played on the primary floors of the clubs by the time of research – but that could be listened to in a concert-like situation. The club that was explicitly mentioned was the WMF, and the label owner pointed out that on a regular weekend, there would have been a dedicated crowd that visited the club only because of the secondary floor. In his assessment, an entire form of "underground" (P47: 71) culture has disappeared together with these floors.

Since then, he pointed out, the club landscape in Berlin had changed dramatically, and he expressed special disappointment about the development of the club NBI, a club that he had followed from location to location for over a decade, but that had changed so much he would not want to organize a regular label evening there:

> "Well, in the 90s you had clubs like the WMF, they opened their second floor on every weekend, where everything was possible and there was an audience only for the second floor, because they were just looking for experiments and things beyond the dancefloor, but this whole culture is completely gone, that doesn't exist anymore. And at the same time, this, this underground culture, or, let's say, this somewhat dingy culture is totally changed as well, you know, who wants to still do something at NBI, who wants to still be there, that's not a place where you'd want to organize something on a regular basis, you know." (P47: 71, transl. FG)

The artists, on the other hand, had high requirements in the view of the label owner, especially towards his role as event sponsor. He stated: "They want a cozy atmosphere, good sound, low prices, but of course they also want a high fee [for themselves, FG]." (P47: 71, transl. FG) This combination of requirements, he continued, was impossible to meet, especially in a city like Berlin "where the bass drum rules" (P47: 71; transl. FG), and the clubs were only booking big-name live-acts for performance events. As a result, he decided to turn away from clubs altogether, and instead opted for a small bar as venue for the monthly label event. In our interview, the reason he gave for this decision had to do with managing expectations on part of the artists: "Either the people [artists, FG] are up for it and have fun there, or they can say upfront that they don't want to play there." (P47: 71; transl. FG) The latter was the case with a planned performance event celebrating the album release of one of the label's artist groups: According to the label owner, the artists told him they would be happy to DJ at the performance event, but that they did not feel that a performance by them as a band belonged in this type of venue (P47: 71).

Regarding the expected audience, the label owner saw the regular label events as a chance for the artists to introduce their music to new people. He did get confirmation from the venue's owners after the first two label events held there that the audience was indeed different from the crowd they had on a regular bar night (P47: 75). He expressed hope that some of the regular visitors to the bar would also show up for the label event, though, and discover an interest for the music. At the same time, he expected people who already knew the artists would drag friends along, who then in turn would also get interested and start to research the musical style and eventually buy records.

So far, we have analyzed the perspective of the label owner H, who received the requirements directly from the artists and then had to consider them. His views on the development of the club scene in Berlin and the venues for live performances reflected this considerate process, which was carried out in dialogue with the artists. It is important to note that the label owner considered such performance events only for Berlin. He made it clear that Berlin was his home ground where he was in charge of such performance events for the label, but that he did not get involved with any performances that might get organized outside of the city. Such concerts received support from the label, for example in the form of promotional material for local media, but otherwise the entire organization was left to the respective local booking agency (P47: 65). The label owner assumed a responsibility to facilitate artists releasing on his label with the means to grow their fan base. He saw the benefits for the artists or artist groups, but he did not believe that labels had fans and followers any more like he observed it up until the 1990s (P47: 59). Despite this fragmentation of the label's identity into a back-end for individual releases, naming the regular monthly performance event the label's "Allnighter" was in keeping with a more corporate way of identity building and maintenance, creating a frame for the performances by very different artists from the label's roster.

The notion of the label's "Allnighter" event as a situation for interaction systems to form and be sustained was explicitly expressed by the label assistant L. The label owner H had commissioned him with organizing the performance events on the detailed level of coordinating and supporting the technical setup for the artists as well as entering the metadata of the performance events on the label's MySpace page. In an interview (P1160), this label assistant shared his observation that the typical performance events in the electronica scene were too focused on live performances relying entirely on music playing back from computers, thus being indistinguishable from DJ sets or even CD playback at home (P1160: 16). This meant that, for him, the live performances and, indeed, the music itself did not serve as attractors any more, and as a result, he lost interest in such performance events. His motivation for his role as organizer of the label's "Allnighter" was, in his own observation, the possibility to interact with other members of his wider network at the performance events (P1160: 21). Consistent with this function, the label assistant L rationalized the selection of a very small bar as the original venue for the performance events with the intention of increasing the potential for "intensity" (P1160: 16; transl. FG). In addition to this, the venue was located in a particular area of the city, at the Kottbusser Tor in Kreuzberg. This part of the city was described by the label assistant as a less cleaned-up area, distinct from the established venues in the Mitte and Prenzlauer Berg districts. Cultural events in these areas were characterized as "harmless" (Ibid.; transl. FG), while attending an event at Kottbusser Tor was considered more exciting and brought with it a higher level of alertness. This environment, the assistant stated, should serve expectations towards the scene's "subcultural" (Ibid.; transl. FG) heritage, thus helping the scene and the musicians to get back to a "basis" (Ibid.; transl. FG) from which, in his historical assessment, the entire scene had departed around the end of the 1990s or the early 2000s.

The original venue for the "Allnighter" events could only be reached via a platform hidden away from the street. This platform was also used by the local drug scene as a place to gather and consume drugs. After some close encounters and a spectacular police raid directly in front of the venue's entrance, it was decided to move the performance events to a somewhat larger bar next door, which could be reached via an enclosed staircase that directly connected the street and the venue's entrance.

The entrance to the original venue (P1290).

Both venues had a bar as the central element of their functional layout. The layout of the original venue was almost triangular (P1223: p. 4). The longest side of the triangle consisted of windows with a bench running along its full length. This bench was the most popular place during the "Allnighter" events, with all seats being taken almost immediately after the first visitors arrived (P1362). The bar occupied a prominent part of one of the other sides. With barstools in front of it, the place around the bar was highly popular as well, and mostly crowded during the label events (P1365).

The remaining side of the layout featured the DJ booth in a central location, while the stage for the performances was tucked away in the corner between the bench at the windows and the DJ booth, on the far side across from the bar (P1354). The speakers of the sound system were flown (P1349), i.e. they were hanging from the ceiling, in the two corners on the side of the layout with the bar. I observed the room as being very small, and it felt crowded with around 40 people inside. The large windows helped mediate that impression, looking out at the overground subway station directly across the street from the building and on the same level as the venue on the first floor (P1346).

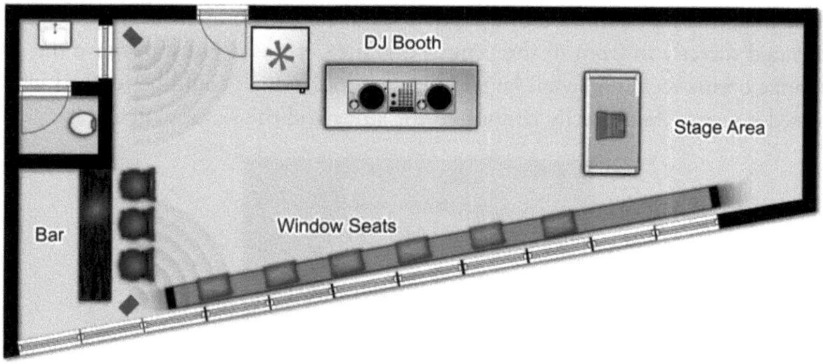

Reconstructed floor plan of the first venue.

The second venue for the label event, where it moved after interaction with the local drug scene seemed inevitable at the original venue, was located in the same building complex as the original venue, also on the first floor, but it was accessible differently. It shared a similar window front as the original venue, but was considerably larger (P1466). It essentially consisted of two parts, with a rectangular bar in between them (P1447; P1450). The sound system only catered to the part of the venue where the stage was located, while audience members in the other part could only perceive the music from a distance.

Although the venue could hold more people, the stage area was actually smaller at the second venue. It was, however, elevated by one step (P1461). It was almost impossible for more than one person to be performing on the stage, especially if a table for the music technology was necessary. The part of the layout that included the stage was almost triangular in shape, with the stage area occupying the shortest side that almost closed to a tip of a triangle. Again, one of the longer sides consisted of windows looking out onto the street and at the overground subway station (Ibid.), while one side of the bar marked the far side of this part of the venue's layout. There were barstools in front of the bar and, grouped with tables, along the other side of this part of the venue, at the wall opposite from the windows. Small cubes where placed as seats, also in groups, in front of the windows (P1450). The DJ booth was placed on the side with the windows, close to the bar (P1471). The DJs could face the audience either towards the bar, or towards the stage. At one of the "Allnighter" events I observed (P1192), celebrating the record release of the artist M, two visual artists were placed beside the DJ booth, facing the stage and performing to the music (P1460). Their visuals were projected onto the wall behind the stage (P1447).

The artist M playing live at the second venue (infrared photo, P1466).

The other part of the venue's layout span between the other side of the bar, facing away from the stage, and towards the entrance. The window front continued through this part, and there were chairs and tables arranged in groups along the windows and the wall on the opposite side (P1450).

The layout of this part was similar to the other part, only mirrored roughly at the bar. At the longer side of the layout was the entrance to the venue. It had a metal door, connecting the inside of the venue with the enclosed staircase leading down to the street. The door was not marked on the outside, and there was another door on the same level, also not marked. This door was always closed when I passed it. Inside the venue, next to the entrance and the windows, a pinball machine was placed close to a group of chairs. This machine was active, but did not get much use during the performance events.

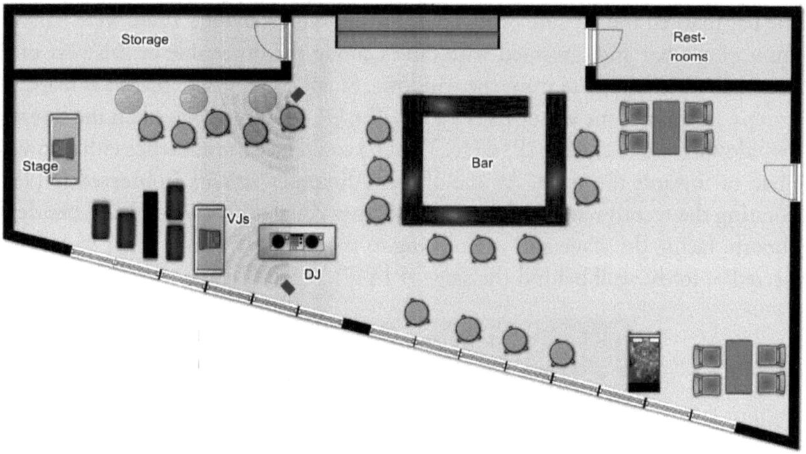

Reconstructed floor plan of the second venue.

There was another area, in between the two parts of the venue's layout, located between the bar and the wall opposite of the window front (P1449). It was receded from the rest of the layout by a protrusion in the wall, and so neither the stage nor the entrance could be seen from this area. Nevertheless, it was a popular place during the performance events I observed. Along the back wall, three rows of stairs were usually used as benches or as a place to deposit coats and bags, as there was no cloakroom inside the venue. The restrooms were also accessible exclusively through this area.

The bar area inside the second venue (infrared photo, P1450).

4.1.3 *The Social Form of the Performance Event*

From the previous descriptions out of interviews and observations, we can already deduce that there were different areas of action at work in each of the cases. Dirk Baecker (2010c), with reference to the situation in theaters, has suggested to analyze the inner workings of this institution and their relation to society as a coherent social form that arranges, in the case of the theater, the three distinct areas of the stage, the organization, and the audience. In our cases of musical events, we can observe a very similar structure, albeit with a special focus on the individual, event-specific performance.

The first of the distinct areas observed in our cases was the realm of the artists who induced the idea for these performance events by pushing the label into providing a structure in which they could perform in front of an audience. Such performances required a cultural event as a semantic framework for further social action. The notion of the cultural event was in turn required for the artist's own planning and rehearsing of their performance, and it was referenced in communication in different network domains (see section 2.3.1), such as friends, fellow musicians, technicians, business networks, etc. At the cultural event, the area of social action associated with the performance had a special standing, supporting the auratic character of the artistic part itself. While the live act was playing, the musicians became performers, decoupled from the surrounding social action, and available for social embedding only in the mode of listening. The distance of this decoupling (White 2008, pp. 36) manifested the aura of the performance. During the performance, the performers were entirely on their own, as any reconnection with non-artistic social action would have required a break in the performance. It was therefore crucial for any social action connected to the performance – before, after, or during the performance – to ensure that the performance itself was not disturbed. The performances can be described as the offers made at these cultural events, as they were the defining element for the locating of the public situation at the venues, and for references to the cultural events in online public communication. The performing artists placed their own identities and their contexts as possible themes in the interaction at the venues. This is modeled as follows:

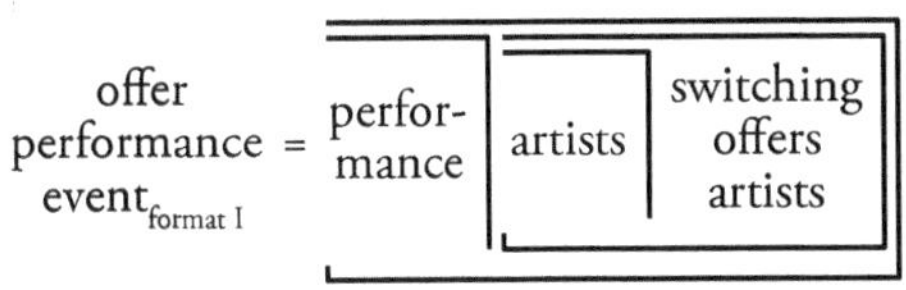

Form equation 4.1.3.a: The offer at a performance event of format I as the unity of the difference between a performance and artists observed in the context of switching offers referencing them.

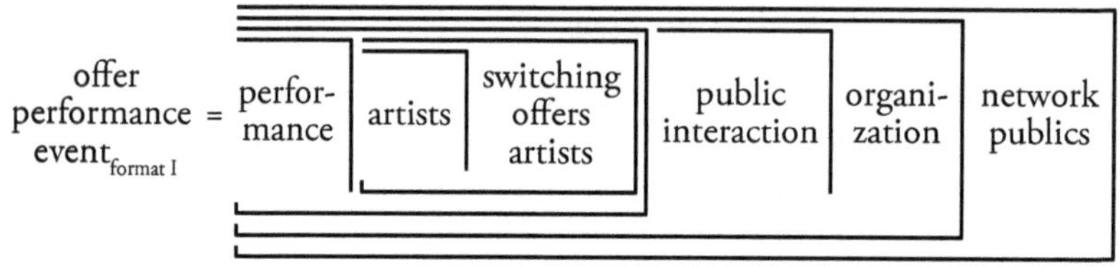

Form equation 4.1.3.b: The offer at a performance event of format I as the unity of the difference between a performance and artists observed in the context of switching offers referencing them, in a situation of public interaction conceived by an organization, embedded in the publics of the network structure of the field.

As a reaction to these offers, audiences formed at the performance events. Artists planned their performances with the audience as external reference, and they counted on the event making the forming of a specific audience appreciative of the performance likely. The performance event had a footing in social meaning, and this footing allowed the audience to form. Whether or not the audience then fulfilled the role expected by the performing artists is another question.

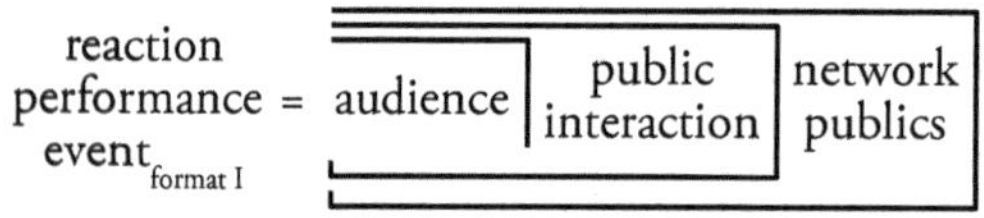

Form equation 4.1.3.c: The reaction at a performance event of format I as the forming of an audience in a situation of public interaction, embedded in the publics of the network structure of the field.

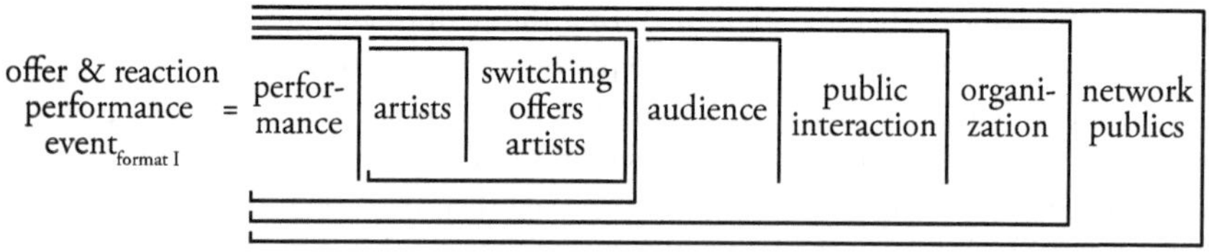

Form equation 4.1.3.d: The offer and reaction at a performance event of format I as the unity of the difference between a performance and artists observed in the context of switching offers referencing them, in the context of an audience as reaction in a situation of public interaction, influenced by an organization, embedded in the publics of the network structure of the field.

The organization of the performance events had to facilitate both offers and reactions, similar to the function of the online platforms MySpace and Facebook. As we observed in the interview with the label owner (P47), inquiries from the artists to facilitate their performances were given as reason to instigate the organization of a framework to hold both the performances and an audience. The organization developed and maintained the footing of the performance event, as I mentioned above, and offered information on this footing in communication. To be able to sustain this footing for the performance event, the organization had to include the venue staff, provide the technical setup for the performance, and enforce the time schedule for the event. Additionally, the organization framed the formation of the audience by providing a context for interaction.

Social action concerned with offers and reactions was not confined to the processes at the performance event itself or its organization before and after. Rather, the semantic association with the performance event was also utilized to develop and maintain identities outside of the immediate realm of the event, and outside of the reach of direct interaction at the event. All social action occurring at the performance event was tied to identities in network domains that extended beyond the semantic realms of individual events. Examples of such identities in our research field included the identity of the label C itself, the identity of the artists, the qualitative assessment of performances in relation to similar performances, and the personal identities of visitors. All of these identities in play were constantly actualized and maintained, and any situation of mutual observation – such as at a performance event – inevitably produced self-descriptions expanding on the participant's own identities. It also triggered descriptions by others on how social action by participants and performers fell in line with what had been known about their identity, and how it deviated from it. In our analysis, we will keep an eye on this orientation towards the wider network of identities participating in the cases by taking the publics of the network structure of the cultural context into account.

For the organization, one important consideration in the social domain was which participants it wanted at the performance event and who it rather would have excluded. At club events, doorkeepers regularly fulfilled the function of executing the organizer's inclusion/exclusion regime. The role of the doorkeeper was usually combined with a staffed entrance counter, where the entrance fee was collected and the guest list was kept and maintained. At the performance events I attended, there was usually no doorkeeper on duty, while an entrance counter was put into place in a number of cases. At the label's "Allnighter" events, however, I did not observe either a doorkeeper or an entrance counter. There was no obvious inclusion/exclusion mechanism in place directly at the venue; essentially, everyone could just walk in. At one of the first "Allnighter" events I attended, I observed several groups inside the venue who explained that they mistook the venue for another club in the area, and walked out after a short while (P1474). At the same time, both of the venues used for the label's "Allnighter" were essentially hidden from the rest of the social activity in the area.

There were no signs announcing the performance events, nor any hints at the venue's location at all. Both venues were located on the first floor above shops on street level. To get to them, one needed to use an open staircase in the case of the original venue, and a closed, in-house staircase for the second venue. The open staircase leading up to the original venue was completely unlabeled, while the one for the second venue carried the name of a Turkish culture club that could be reached from there as well. The respective doors to the venues were not labeled, either. At my first visits to these two venues, I had trouble finding them in both cases (P1192).

The omission of any indicators, such as signs giving directions or even just the names of the venues at their entrances, guiding potential visitors from the transit ways – the street or the nearby subway station – to the venues effectively served as the execution of an inclusion/exclusion mechanism for the label's "Allnighter" events. Guidance in the form of directions was only provided in the invitation emails and on the flyers that had been distributed in a few select record stores and cafés (e.g. P1159). These directions included the official street address as well as information above which grocery store the venue was located. With these directions, it was possible to spot the venue's windows by looking up from the street, but there were still several staircases and entrances to choose from (P1192). Digital versions of the flyers were sent out prior to the label events with the invitation emails, and were also available on the label's MySpace page (e.g. P443). On the label's own website, only the name of the venue was given, without any concrete directions. The email invitations were sent out as a mass email to all subscribers of the label's newsletter. The subscription to this newsletter could be completed for free via the label's website. Therefore, inclusion and exclusion were not based on personal preferences by the event organizers; instead, inclusion could be achieved easily by action on behalf of interested members of the publics. Nevertheless, this mechanism effectively served as exclusion of most people present in the immediate vicinity of the venue on or around Kottbusser Tor. Indeed, the visitors inside the venue during the label's "Allnighter" events had a social background that differed considerably from the social context I observed in the immediate vicinity. As mentioned above, several visitors were imported into this area from their own neighborhoods in Prenzlauer Berg, Schöneberg, Friedrichshain, or other parts of Kreuzberg.

Officially opening at 9.30 p.m., the venue filled up between 10 p.m. and 11 p.m. at the label events I observed, and concerts typically started between 11 p.m. and 11.30 p.m. With around 60 people present around 11 p.m., the original venue was filled entirely, while the second venue was only loosely filled with the same amount of people present. Interaction systems formed with between two and five participants. Generally, the size of interaction systems in a club context is influenced by the volume of the music played back in the venue. In the cases I observed, the volume level during the DJ sets before and after the concerts was low enough to accommodate conversations among a maximum of four to five participants, whereas larger groups would split up into different interaction systems. At the same time, the volume level of the music was also high enough to fill pauses in conversations.

An open platform outside of the original venue also accommodated social interaction during the label events. Here, no music was played back, and disturbance of interaction by the exchange of participants could be suppressed through decoupling by distance. Inside the venue, the fact that it was filled up directly before the start of the performances also meant that participants in interaction could decouple easily by casually turning around and joining another conversation. This was usually not possible on the outside platform, where a more directed movement towards the participants would have been required. All introductions to people I had not known before happened inside the venue, while more intimate conversations on personal views and business matters took place on the outside platform. I was engaged in longer discussions on topics including the music industry, music technology, and journalism in both areas, while standing outside on the platform. Also, I observed similar, more dedicated conversations, among other visitors at this location. The inside of the venue was usually too crowded for such interactions. There, I mostly overheard more casual conversations, covering more personal topics.

As already mentioned, the fact that this outside platform was freely accessible, yet hidden away from the street below it, attracted the local drug scene as a place to hang out and consume and deal drugs directly in front of the venue, while visitors were walking around outside, smoking, chatting, or making phone calls. Drug scene members were also sitting on the stairs leading to the venue a number of times, including when I got there early one time, accompanying two artists and helping them carry in their instruments and equipment for the concert. The owner of the venue tried to clean the staircase and the corners of the outside platform with buckets full of chlorinated water, but stains and a subtle smell of urine usually remained (P1477). I did not observe a single incident of visitors and the members of the drug scene engaging in verbal communication, but a situation of tentative mutual presence certainly emerged. The presence of the drug scene members was actualized as a communicational theme among visitors. I observed the situation as requiring caution, but not as dangerous, and I did not observe any expressions of fear or worry among the visitors. However, the situation did eventually turn more spectacular with a particular incident during one of the "Allnighter" events (P1477): Several members of the drug scene came running onto the platform, one of them with his pants down, being chased by one person who screamed and tried to beat the other persons. They were immediately followed by several police officers, who managed to tame the attacker and secure the situation (P1336). Several visitors had been on the platform when the situation emerged, and rushed back inside the venue immediately. Nobody walked outside while the police was busy keeping the situation under control and arresting some of the drug scene members.

In an interview (P1160: 69), the label assistant L mentioned this incident as one of the reasons why they decided to move the label's "Allnighter" events to another venue. He stated that after this incident, the owner of the first venue did not want to open with only one employee any more, and that two employees would make sense economically on weekends, but not on weeknights. As I mentioned, the second venue could only be accessed via an enclosed staircase with a door on street level. Although this door was not locked during the label events, I never observed any members of the drug scene inside the staircase, or even around the door leading to the street. In a newspaper interview (P3380), the owner of the original venue stated that he had tried to reach out to local social organizations and the city administration as the owner of the building complex to discuss possible solutions for the problems caused by the presence of the drug scene in the neighborhood, but that the only outcome was that the city administration decided to install metal gates at street level in front of the open staircases leading up to the venue's platform and neighboring platforms. The venue owner criticized this effort as a selective solution that would not lead to an overall improvement of the situation in the entire building complex.

An extensive set of communicational themes present at the label's "Allnighter" events was concerned with the technological setup used by the artists for their performances. I was able to observe the setup process in detail on one occasion (P1224), when the artist O came to Berlin to play live at the label C's "Allnighter" event. His performance was not related to an actual release, but he had released an album with the label in the previous year. O brought along a guitarist, also from Hamburg, for the performance, and they stayed overnight at my apartment before returning to their home city by car on the next day. We met early on the evening of the performance, and I had to give them directions to the venue. I was present for the entire process of setting up the music gear and testing it prior to the opening of the venue.

In our email conversation leading up to the label event, O had told me he had been in contact with the label owner H about the organization of the event, who then referred him to the label assistant L as the coordinator for the local organization at the venue. Email was the only medium used in this process. The venue was locked during the technical setup, with the venue owner and the label assistant L present in addition to the artists and myself. The label assistant assumed responsibility for acting as an interface communicating the artists' wishes and requirements to the venue owner, who operated the installed sound system and provided the label assistant with a key to a storage room outside of the venue, where the artists left their luggage and retrieved a table and chairs for the stage setup. An elevated stage was asked for by the artists, but the venue owner replied that, despite promising such a stage to the label assistant beforehand, he now could not find the stands for the stage elements. The artist O had brought along his own mid-sized sound system, but decided it was not needed as the installed system was adequate for the room. After the stage layout was complete and the technical setup was under way, the barkeeper for the evening showed up and, after having briefed him, the venue owner left. The label assistant L kept the key to the storage room and coordinated the removal of unneeded cases and equipment parts after the sound check was complete.

In addition to the live performance, which was communicated as the main act at the label's "Allnighter" events, each of the events also hosted one or more DJ sets. These sets were usually played either by other artists releasing on the label, or by DJs associated with the artist performing at the event. The DJs were also mentioned on the flyer for the event (e.g. P1159). The DJs for this particular performance event, (P1224) where I observed the technical setup, showed up shortly after the announced opening time of the event, and they started to play music from vinyl records right away after being given a brief introduction to the technical setup by the label assistant L. One of the two DJs had released an album and individual songs on the artist O's own label before, so they already knew each other well. At other "Allnighter" events, other artists from the label's roster played DJ sets in support of fellow label artists who performed at the events. Also, the label assistant L himself played DJ sets at several occasions after the label event had moved to the second venue (e.g. P1208). I could not observe a direct musical relation between the DJ sets and the performances, and in the case of the performance by the artist O and his support DJs as well as in another case of both a local artist and a local DJ, the artists told me in conversations that they had no knowledge of what exactly the other performers would play prior to the event (P1208).

In the process of preparation which I observed directly before the start of the label event (P1224), the social roles of all participants were functionally determined, with the relation between the artist O preparing the performance and the label assistant L as the local organizer having been established via email conversations beforehand. Additional relations developed from there on out, with the label assistant introducing the venue owner to us and the artist introducing the guitarist and myself to both the label assistant and the venue owner. While the guitarist was introduced in his function as performer, the artist introduced me as a friend. The barkeeper was introduced in his functional role as well, while one of the DJs, as already mentioned, filled his functional role but also had a stronger link to the artist through his involvement with the artist's own label.

Just as with the artists and the performance, the notion of a directedness is inherent in the definition of an audience as well – an audience has to be the audience of something. Hence, an audience needed, for its self- as well as external descriptions, the distinction from an area of artistic activity. The understanding of audience is therefore a reduction to a function in a social context: Being the addressee in a public situation with an artistic performance present. However, at any given time during a performance, this was only true for a part of the total number of visitors at an event. While some visitors listened and watched, thus having made the switch to becoming part of the audience, many others remained engaged in interaction, without actually following the performance. The situation of the public was thus sustained while an audience formed, and the visitors could observe each other either switching into the audience or not. The notion of an audience therefore implies another distinction: The public situation in which the audience formed, and into which the audience could dissolve again.

The beginning of a live performance by artists inside the venue usually meant a disturbance for the ongoing public interaction among the visitors, but it did not necessarily end it. Rather, an audience would form in front of the stage, where visitors listened to the music and watched the artists performing, while interaction within small groups continued in the back of the room, at the bar, and on the outside platform in the case of the first venue. The beginning of the concert therefore provided a means to decouple from interaction and switch over to being part of the audience. On the other hand, this means had the potential to remain unused, with the public interaction maintaining relative stability under the influence of being disturbed by the performance. Nevertheless, a stable subset of visitors did engage in listening during all of the performances I observed at the label's "Allnighter" events. The visitors at the "Allnighter" events also observed the organization through the context of the framework it had designed for the event. The visitors reacted on certain choices made by the organization, for example by deciding whether and what to consume from the bar and where within or around the venue to place the interaction.

4.1.4 Artistic Practice and Technology

Various different forms of technology were used in connection with the label C's "Allnighter" events, some more, some less apparent to the observer. Among the more apparent forms were the technologies the artists integrated into their performance. In the case of the performance by the artist O (P1224), the sound of the music was essentially generated on a standard laptop computer brought to the stage by O (e.g. P1461; P1230). On this machine, O could produce sounds and arrangements with the help of dedicated software programs (see section 1.2). The result was generated first as a digital code, which then was translated into variations of an electric current at the output stage of the computer's audio converter. This modulated electric current was still not observable directly by the members of the audience; instead, it needed to be translated into changes in air pressure by means of the venue's sound system. I already mentioned the lengthy and detailed process of the sound check before the performance of the artist O started (P1224; P1225), as well as the observation that within this event format, the performing artists brought along their own set of speakers to use in case the venue's installed sound system would not have been adequate in their own evaluation.

With reference to a different concert at the second venue of the label's "Allnighter" event, the label owner H expressed (in an interview, P1165: 43) his dissatisfaction with the setup of the sound system at the venue, adding that he could not have been there for the sound check at this particular label event, but would need to go there for future performances. He criticized the label assistant L for not ensuring the proper setup of the system at the venue. In particular, the label owner's critique was aimed at the volume of the music being too low. In my own observation (P1192) of the event he referred to, I noticed the low volume level in the entrance and bar areas, while the music did seem louder directly in front of the stage. This was in contrast to the performances at the first venue, where, at least while the artists were playing, the music had been considerably louder. These different volume levels had direct social implications: The low music volume level allowed for verbal communication within interaction systems, while a volume level far above the loudness of the human voice prevented it. The different perspectives and evaluations in the statements by the label owner H and the label assistant L are contradictory: The label owner mentioned the forming of an audience as a goal, while the label assistant was interested in the communicative process in interaction systems. The latter is, however, likely prevented if the former was to be carried out to the label owner's satisfaction. During the concert by the artist O at the first venue, the volume had been high enough to successfully disrupt most of the interaction among visitors, whereas at performances inside the second venue, a comparable volume level was only reached in the direct vicinity of the stage.

The performance by the artist O and his guitarist at the label C's "Allnighter" event (P1224) brought together very different sounds, mixing acoustic instruments with electronics and computers. The set was based primarily on pre-produced loops of different lengths, which the artist O played back in the sequencing and performance software Ableton Live. Most of the loops combined rhythmic and melodic elements. They served as playback for the two artists performing with their acoustic and electro-acoustic instruments on stage. Some of the drum-based rhythms in this performance were clearly influenced by the tradition of hip hop music. The inner structure of the musical bar exhibited a clear focus on the 1st beat, with a bass drum that was very present, and a snare acting as rhythmical counterpart on the 2nd and 4th beat. The 3rd beat usually brought in another, merely supportive bass drum. The sounds used for these functions were also selected in accordance with the hip hop tradition: They were based on what had once been recorded acoustic drums, perhaps sampled from a funk or jazz recording, but had been processed extensively, thereby attaining a distinctively electronic character. The micro structure of the bars was usually repeated more or less unchanged. In hip hop, the vocals would have added musical variety; in the performance of the artist O and the guitarist, it was their playing of various instruments. While the drum-based rhythmic structures had their origins in hip hop culture, which also influenced the choice of sounds being used, the live playing of instruments referenced classical instrument training. The artist O played his cello during many, mostly relatively short passages of the performance. It was placed on the floor by his side, where he carefully picked it up for playing and placed it back afterwards. The sounds used for the rhythmic patterns became more and more electronic during the set. In one piece, the rhythm was generated by a sampled part of clicking noises, which was looped in a fixed temporal distance, thus creating a macro pattern out of elements which already formed their own micro pattern. This strategy, and the sounds used here as well, could be seen as a reference to the aesthetical principles of the clicks & cuts genre, where artists used found or deliberately produced errors of digital signal storage and processing technology as musical elements in their works. The elements used here by the artist O were clearly discernible as clicks, i.e. as elements that did not originate from acoustic instruments or tried to mimic them. However, the rhythm created using them again resembled a hip hop beat.

The rhythmic structures through the entire set originated from hip hop culture, yet the sounds used to create them were rooted in the aesthetic world of electronica or experimental electronic music. This was the sound world native to the audience at the performance event, while the hip hop element in the beats was an import for the setting in which it was presented. Although the visitors at the performance event were certainly not unfamiliar with the aesthetics of hip hop, it was not their primary, defining culture. The same was true for the label C, which had released music with similar elements from hip hop culture before, while staying within the realm of its native electronica style. Hip hop beats were aesthetically out of the frame of expectation for the label C's "Allnighter" events, while the sounds used for the beats were clearly part of the aesthetic realm in which the music at all of these events positioned itself.

Similarly, the artist O and the guitarist he performed with imported the canonic cultural disposition of their respective acoustic and electro-acoustic instruments into the setting of their performance. The generation of sound in a musical instrument typically consists of two parts: the exciter and the resonator (Roads 1996[19]: pp. 268).

19 In his excellent Computer Music Tutorial, Curtis Roads (1996) explains the basics of sound generation against the background of their synthesis. Nevertheless, the book serves as a standard source of information on the inner structures of sound from all origins.

The exciter generates the original impulses for the sound, such as the stick on a drum (single impulse) or the bow on a string (multiple impulses). The resonator carries these impulses further, amplifying them and thereby adding its own spectral characteristics. An acoustic instrument is formed as a combination of exciter and resonator where all components work by physical vibration only, i.e. without translating vibrations into electric current, or vice versa, at any point. If such a translation occurs at any point in the system, we could speak of an electric instrument. However, in all cases relevant to the scene in our field, the translation of vibrations to electric current was only the first stage of a signal processing chain using various instances of electronic logic and amplification circuits. Instruments using such processing circuitry as the dominant element of sound generation, such as synthesizers, where all elements of the sound are generated and shaped electronically, are therefore referred to as electronic instruments. Finally, electro-acoustic instruments combine physical vibration with electronic signal processing. In such a system, any stage may be either acoustic or electronic, although the combination of acoustic exciter and electronic resonator is more common in music practice, for example in the electric guitar, which should be called electronic guitar since it is typically used in combination with an amplifier.

Digital systems typically work with numeric models of electronic circuits and their signal processing capabilities. Over time, processing techniques have taken hold in music practice that were hard to achieve with analog electronic devices, but were relatively easy to implement on digital systems. In order to hear any sound that was electronically generated or shaped, the sound signal has to be translated into vibrations of air pressure, which can be picked up by the human ear. Loudspeakers as the devices usually used for this translation therefore can be seen as a part of the system comprising an electronic instrument.

The artist O used a cello and a glockenspiel during the performance, while the guitarist played an electric guitar and a chapman stick, a form of guitar that is reduced to only the neck and a pickup, but with ten instead of the regular six strings (see www.stick.com). For both artists, their instruments were at the center of their performance. They used them with their traditional playing techniques, e.g. sitting down and playing the cello with a bow. The guitarist also played sitting down, thus adhering to a classical or jazz disposition rather than to that of rock music. In his playing technique, he combined playing with his fingers, a guitar pick, and an e-bow, a battery-powered device that induced vibrations of individual guitar strings, allowing for notes with infinite sustain (see www.ebow.com). The artist O played mostly recurring patterns of relatively short duration, typically between four and eight bars. Each piece they performed contained several such patterns, and O switched between them according to the overarching structure of the piece. The pieces were mostly arranged in a traditional ABAB format. O played patterns of similar length on either the cello or the glockenspiel, sometimes switching between them. The guitarist played mostly patterns that supported whatever O played, but he also had parts where he improvised freely. On both cello and guitar, the patterns changed between long notes and either arpeggios on the guitar or pizzicato riffs on the cello. On the chapman stick, the guitarist mainly played arpeggios of short notes.

In addition, O also used a game pad and the hand-held synthesizer I mentioned in section 3.1.2 during the performance. The game pad was a regular input device for computer games, coupled with the computer running Ableton Live via the bluetooth wireless protocol. The movement of the two small joysticks on the gamepads and the triggering of its buttons was routed to various musical parameters. O used it mostly on drum and percussion sounds, as a means to add effects on top of the loops that were playing in the background throughout the performance. The performance started out with a solo loop of percussion sounds onto which O added a stuttering effect via the game pad. He controlled the depth of the effect and its internal temporal structure – i.e. the length of the stutters – by moving the joysticks back and forth. Later on in the set, this effect was repeated a number of times. During one part of the set, O also controlled a filter on a synthesizer sound via the game pad. The way the game pad was used in the performance was atypical for the established use cases of the device. As a controller for computer games, it was commonly used in front of a screen, with the user controlling actions in the game world. As a wireless device, it could be used at a greater distance from the screen than the typical wired devices, while also allowing for greater flexibility of movements. In the performance, O did not look at the screen of the computer on which he was controlling musical parameters with the game pad. He took advantage of the wireless flexibility, moving his body with the music and also visualizing the parameter changes with gestures. For example, he bent down sideways a number of times, exaggerating the movement of the joysticks on the game pad. That way, he connected the visual presence of the performance with the sonic result. Since the game pad was a small device to be held in both hands, body gestures incorporating the device looked like dance moves rather than like the gestures involved in playing a more traditional instrument.

The hand-held synthesizer was an instrument that looked similar to the game pad when played on stage. It was also held in both hands, and its sound was controlled by finger movements. However, unlike the game pad, it was a self-contained instrument: Effectively a one-oscillator synthesizer, it operated on a battery and had its own loudspeaker. That way, it was independent from an audio mixer and did not need a cable. The oscillator could be controlled via metal contacts on the top of its case, which had to be touched in order to close the circuit and connect the oscillator with the loudspeaker. The pitch of the oscillator was determined by the skin resistance of the player. The instrument was designed and built by the art institute in Amsterdam where O and I had worked together during a research residency. O played the instrument similar to the game pad, exaggerating his body movements to visualize the movements of his fingers on the surface of the instrument, yet he was restricted in his movements by the need to stay close to the microphone he used to amplify its sound.

With the different instruments they played, the artist O and the guitarist accompanying him offered significant visual variety on stage during the performance. O used two computers for sound generating purposes: One to play back loops and apply realtime effects to them, the other to process the sound coming from the microphone he used on the cello and for announcements. They were placed on the side of the stage and the display lid of at least one of them was half closed. O scarcely diverted attention to the computers, effectively only turning towards the computer used for playback to start a new piece. The guitarist did not operate the computers at all. However, despite this freedom, O and the guitarist did not engage in much visible interaction with the audience. O often turned towards the guitarist, observing his playing and conducting the start of new parts. The guitarist was mostly watching O, following his musical movements in his accompanying improvisations. O did make announcements towards the audience, but they were sometimes hard to understand as the effects processing was still on the microphone. Also, they were restricted to the breaks in between pieces. During the pieces themselves, O and the guitarist seemed to perform without paying much attention to the audience.

The audience, on the other hand, was mostly listening to the music and closely watching the performers. During the performance, the visitors in the back of the room started to talk more and more, so it became harder for the audience members to listen to the music. At the same time, the room was entirely filled with about 30 to 40 people. The audience members did not make any attempts at dancing, despite the relatively clear rhythmical structures in the music. This somewhat countered the cultural import of the hip hop beats in the performance, as these beats clearly referenced the body-conscious, dance-centered performances of hip hop culture. However, I did not observe dancing at any of the events I visited in the "Allnighter" series. The music and the movement on the stage certainly provided a significant amount of variety for the audience to perceive and to remain entertained. At the same time, the artist O did not make loud and commanding announcements in order to draw more visitors into the audience. The music itself did not feature vocals, so the conversations in the back of the venue were not obstructed, and the rhythmic and melodic structures of the pieces were repetitive enough to serve as background music for the visitors who did not listen to the intricacies of the composition and performance.

4.1.5 Control Efforts

We have seen so far how the case of the label-organized event with music performance consisted of several distinct areas of social action. Actions in any of these areas usually did not reference only a single event, but rather operated with further distinctions within their respective network structure inside the wider cultural scene. Network domains and their roles, attributed to identities such as artists, the label owner H, or the label assistant L, bridged different performance events and instances of interaction. Therefore, efforts at controlling specific aspects of the performance events can be observed as work on identities in a broader context.

The enactment of control efforts was most visible in the realm of the organization. Here, the performance event was conceived of as an idea, then conceptualized and, eventually, operationalized. Such operationalization was only possible if the organization could assume enough freedom in its actions to independently take the necessary steps on the way to make the performance event happen, and also to observe their outcomes at the event, with potential readjustments at hand. The label owner H, his assistant L, and the venue owners with their staff acted together as organizers for an event, and their areas of control mostly complemented each other. In planning for a performance event and taking steps to implement them, the organization had to account for contingencies owed to the inability to anticipate actions by the other parties involved in the event, i.e. the artists in charge of the performance, and the visitors. In addition, any of its own efforts at taking the audience's or the artists' actions into account would have inevitably led to different actions by these parties than what the organization had accounted for. This recursivity added contingency to any anticipation in planning.

The organization's most prominent control effort in the temporal domain was the setting of the opening and closing time of the venue for the performance event. In doing so, the organization decided to place the performance event on a weeknight, and to set the opening time to 9.30 p.m. With this opening time, the performance event started early compared to other, similar events in Berlin, for example the "Killekill" event series which also took place on Wednesday nights, but started at 11 p.m., with the main performances typically beginning around midnight (P1503).

As I mentioned above, the first venue for the "Allnighter" was closed when I arrived there early with the artist O and his guitar player on the evening of their performance, and the key to the door was kept by the venue's owner. The venue was scheduled to open for the label event at 9.30 p.m., and this time was mentioned in the electronic communication as well (P1494). However, the DJs for the evening only showed up just in time for the opening, starting their set immediately without further preparation or consultation with the label assistant (P1224). Also, the sound check for the performance had been completed only about 20 minutes before the official opening time, with the label assistant pushing to move unnecessary items such as instrument cases out of the audience area before 9.30 p.m. Although some audience members arrived early at this and other "Allnighter" events, the venues did not fill up before 11 p.m. The largest number of audience members was present between 10.45 p.m. and 11.30 p.m. In the case of the performance by the artist O, the label assistant L asked O to wait with the performance when he wanted to start shortly after 10.30 p.m. O told me that this was the time the label assistant had asked him to start at in an email discussing arrangements for the event. The performance eventually got under way around 11.15 p.m. (Ibid.).

At one of the label nights (P1477), I also observed the label assistant L discussing starting times for performances with the artists, although in those cases, it was about getting the artists to start no later than 11.30 p.m., when they were still talking to visitors shortly before that time. Similarly, the changeover between the support DJs, if there was more than one DJ for the evening, in some cases had to be moderated by the label assistant (e.g. P1208). These control efforts had the effect that the venue was open with the sound check completed at the announced time in all cases I observed, and the starting time of most performances roughly coincided with the peak time of visitor presence. Nevertheless, some visitors expressed their dissatisfaction with the running time of the performances if they went on until after midnight (P1477). At one of the label events (Ibid.), the venue owner asked the label assistant L to get the artists to start the performance in time so that visitors could observe the performance and still get the last subway train home. As the label event was scheduled on a weeknight, the last trains departed around 1.00 a.m. from the station directly in front of both venues.

The organization also selected which factual elements were present at the performance events, taking into account the anticipated reactions on these decisions by the artists and the visitors. The frame for what was generally possible was set by the owners of the two venues, as they could ultimately be held accountable for any illegal activity inside their venues. The artists in charge of the performance and the label owner and assistant had the freedom to add elements to the venue, but the organizers mostly made do with the elements that were already available. As mentioned above, both venues for the label C's "Allnighter" events had predefined, fixed stage areas, which were relatively small compared to other stages used by artists from the label's roster. Both venues also had a sound system installed that was aligned with the placement of the stage. This general setup was not changed in any of the performances I observed, so any further decisions involving the artists were taken in acceptance of the factual arrangements made by the organization concerning the placement of the stage and the sound system. Further elements of the factual arrangement included the bar, the audience area, seats, and the light system. Because there were no changes to any of these elements, the label owner H implicitly decided on their presence at the label events by selecting the venue. The label assistant L pointed out (P1160: 16) the importance of the venue accommodating social interaction, while he did not mention the importance of the venue allowing for great music performances. This prioritization implied some other factual choices: The bar had to operate during performances, for example, and the visitors had to be able to – at their will – decouple listening from interaction among themselves, i.e. both modes had to be possible in parallel during performances. The latter requirement in turn had implications for the sound system: Had it been too loud, it would have prevented interaction in the medium of speech. At the same time, it had to be loud enough so that audience members who were listening to the performance, as well as the artists themselves, were not distracted by the ongoing interaction among other visitors. In addition, the stage had to be set up so that the entrance/exit was not blocked by the performance itself or the members of the audience.

The organization tried to select the visitors for a performance event by targeting the information it offered beforehand. As I have mentioned, the inclusion/exclusion mechanism for these events worked not on the basis of on-site, ad hoc selection, as was the case in many club contexts where the role of the gatekeeper was crucial, but rather via restricting the availability of information about the performance events to channels where only members of the public who already had an interest in the label C or the performing artists could be reached. This outsourcing of the crucial inclusion/exclusion mechanism to network processes had the effect that a large number of visitors to the events had ties to a similar cultural background, and it effectively prevented any integration of local audiences native to the social context of the building in which the venue was located.

While the artists' performance as a separate entity at the event was embedded into the schedule of performances and DJ sets during the event, its internal structure was decoupled from control over the event. The performers could claim the freedom of artistic activity to pursue their own control efforts. This special standing of the artistic practice could even, in some limited instances, enable the artists to claim priority for their control efforts over those by the organization and the visitors. The internal temporal structure of the performance was largely controlled by the artists.[20] Although the organizers and the artists usually agreed roughly on the length of a performance, it was up to the artists to decide how long to play exactly. Only an extreme overtaxing of the appointed length would have provoked an intervention on behalf of the organization – or even less likely, the audience. I have not observed such occurrences in any of the

20 Silke Seemann (2010: p. 229) has described a similar decoupling for feature presentations at movie theaters.

cases mentioned here, as all performances stayed within a timeframe of roughly one hour. Controlling the temporal structure of the performance was considered a core artistic capacity. This included the decision which pieces to play when and for how long – decisions that were not negotiable as the performances were mostly planned in advance with the artist steering the technological setup and adding elements live. The end of the performance was again solely determined by the artists – the organizers and audience members could disturb the performance, but they could not terminate it without the risk of conflict.

The soundcheck before the opening of the venue for the performance event can be seen as a negotiation between the organization and the artists in charge of the performance, finding the final form of the factual arrangement of the performance. This factual arrangement included the placement of elements such as instruments and the performers themselves on the stage, the placement of any visuals if they were present, the fine-tuning of the sound system, and, importantly, its overall level. Decisions on these elements were constrained by other decisions made by the organization, including the venue owner. As already mentioned, the space allocated for the stage area and its placement were not left up to the artists. The artists could only place their elements on the stage they were provided with, but within this frame, they were free to decide which elements to have on the stage at all and where to put them. As the stage areas in both venues were relatively small, there was only a limited degree of freedom to place a table carrying the computer and other devices while at the same time allowing the artists to face the audience. The case of the artist O was an exception insofar as he placed both computers off to the side, having them run in the background and requiring only rare user interaction (P1276). With two performers, four acoustic/electro-acoustic instruments plus the technology used for sound synthesis and processing of the live sound, the stage area was entirely crowded in this case.

The artists had the expectation that social interaction among visitors would seize during their performance. The artists' control efforts at getting the visitors engaged in listening differed widely. In the case of the artist O and his guitar player (P1224), O made an explicit, although not very loud, announcement before starting the performance. In an interview (P1165: 64), the label owner H referenced this announcement, stating that he liked it for its effect on getting the audience's attention, while also hinting at criticism that some visitors disliked the announcement because they understood it as the artists taking themselves too serious. In any case, the announcement made by the artist from Hamburg was the only one of its kind I observed at any of the label's "Allnighter" events. The label owner, in the same interview (Ibid.: 58), criticized other artists who played at the events for not announcing the start of their performances, and then being upset about a lack of attention from the audience.

The notion of the visitors as potential audience was present in most, if not all decisions made in relation to the event by the organization and the artists in charge of the performance. Prominently, the organization had to plan the timing of the performance event, the size of the venue, and the availability of drinks at the bar accounting for the anticipated needs of the visitors. The artists, on the other hand, had to anticipate the attention span of potential audience members listening to their performance, and also take a possible encore, depending on the audience reaction, into consideration.

I already mentioned that the peak time of visitor presence at the label's "Allnighter" events was between 10.30 p.m. and 11.30 p.m., on a Wednesday night. There was no official starting time for the performances, and visitors took the liberty of coming and leaving at their will. As a result, the ad hoc majority of the visitors was in a position of control over both the organization and the artists, as both chose to wait with the performance until the venue was full enough and the public situation had settled into a state of interaction that could be disturbed again by the start of the performance. The decision to leave the performance event at a certain time was a matter of discussion among visitors. In my observation, visitors almost never simply left. Rather, the decision to leave was prepared and rationalized beforehand. Reasons given included having to get the last subway train leaving at Kottbusser Tor station around 1.00 a.m. Indeed, I observed in all cases of the label's "Allnighter" events that by 12.30 a.m., audience attendance had dropped to approximately half the number it was at peak time about one to 1.5 hours earlier. The label owner told me about another observation he made of a difference in visitor attendance between the two venues for the "Allnighter" event: At the original venue, he noted the presence of a hard-core group of visitors who stayed at the bar until very late (P1165: 67). This he did not observe at the second venue; rather, he observed the venue emptying relatively quickly after the performances were over.

As mentioned above, several of the factual decisions made by the organization already included the notion of the visitors as potential audience members. These factual decisions included the setup of the sound system and the stage area, as well as the bar and its offerings. Observing this configuration and placement of elements, the primary choice made by the visitors was to either accept or boycott it. This means they could either observe the performance on the stage, thus being part of the audience, or stay engaged in interaction outside or in the back of the room. However, they could not negate the existence of the stage at all, or declare their own stage and start their own performance. Doing so would have drastically changed the meaning of the entire performance event. Also, they had the choice to either drink from the bar or not at all, but could not consume any drinks they might have brought with them. I did not even observe this on the outside platform at the original venue. As visitors of the performance event, they accepted the selection, configuration, and placement of elements at the event, as it was made by the organization including the venue owner and the artists in charge of the performance.

4.2 Format II: Concert Events

While cultural events such as the label C's "Allnighter" offered a means for both the label and the artists to position themselves, not least by associating their respective identities with each other, they also forced both sides to make compromises in terms of the aesthetic composition of the performance event, as well as its temporal, factual, and social elements. Some of the artists who performed at the "Allnighter" events also played at different other events during the research period, and in some cases, they were much more involved in the event's organization. The second format of live events we analyze is such an event format, where the artist or the artist group was directly involved in the organization, sometimes taking it over entirely.

This format of concert events differed from that of the label evening with added live performance (format I), the "Allnighter" events, in that the performance was the core element of the event, playing a central role in the alignment of its operational structure as well as its semantic framework in the temporal, factual, and social dimensions. One of the most obvious effects of this dominance of the performance was that these events were much shorter than the "Allnighter" events, usually ending almost directly after the performance. Their positioning in the context of the Berlin nightlife was different as well, as their short duration allowed visitors to move on to other cultural events afterwards.

Even with this focus on the performance, interaction among the visitors remained prevalent, but was confined temporally to the duration of the event before and after the performance. Notably, interaction including the artists was much more visible than at the format I type of events. During the research period, I attended 19 performance events of this format.

4.2.1 Case Study: The Duo Concert

The concert event I want to analyze as prototypical of the second format took place on March 27, 2009 (P1219). The duo that was to perform that evening consisted of the artist T and another artist well established in Berlin's live electronic music scene, who had also appeared on releases of the label C (P1504). This particular concert event took place at a venue that, in it's owners self description on its MySpace page, "is not a concert venue or a club!" (P926), thereby separating itself from multi-purpose venues and their typical social functions. Instead, the owners described the venue as "a private little studio where good friends meet[, ...] a quiet place for contemplation and listening [...]." (Ibid.; insertions FG). The artist T had sent out an invitation email three days before the concert, and in it he had asked the invitees to "Please remember that the [venue name] is a private place for music – only friends are invited!" (P1502; insertions FG). In the same email, the artist stated that the concert event was part of a concert series which was "curated" by the "music curator" (Ibid.) of a local artist network that supported concert events by Japanese artists.

Being officially announced as part of a concert series organized by an ethnic-cultural network, I expected a large part of the visitors to share the same ethnic background as well. However, this was not the case at this concert event. At other events (e.g. P1441), which were organized by another organization with a similar focus on Japanese artists, a large number of the visitors had shared this background. In this case, however, the ethnic organization was not visible at the venue at all. In addition to this ethnical connection, the artist also mentioned the label C in his invitation email (P1502). He stated that both he and his duo partner had released music on this label individually and as parts of other music projects. All of these projects were named in the email, and internet addresses were included in the form of links as well.

This concert was my first visit to the venue (P1219), and from the prominent indication of privacy, I had assumed there would be a restrictive entrance policy in effect. However, this was not the case. As with the venues of the label C's "Allnighter" events, the exclusion mechanism was only implemented as a network function. There was no sign indicating either the name of the venue or hinting at the concert. I found the venue by its street address, and chose the correct door simply because it was the only one that was half-open to the street. The building itself was a run-down apartment building on the border to one of Berlin's better residential areas. It was located on one of the major streets in the northern part of the city, and on ground level, most neighboring buildings housed small businesses and stores. This might have been the case once for the building in which the venue was located, but now all of the windows on the ground floor were secured with wood panels covered with posters. The half-open door led directly from the street to a relatively small front room that was completely empty. The walls were white, and there was no furniture. After crossing this room, I entered another room, also on ground level, which was not much bigger than the first one, but completely full with people. There was a bar on one side of the room, opposite from the entrance to the concert room, which was closed off with a curtain (P1510). The concert was scheduled to start at 9 p.m., and there were about 15 people inside the venue when I got there shortly before the official starting time. There was no control at the entrance, nor did anyone collect an entrance fee.

The artist T was present in the bar room, standing in a crowd of people next to the concert room entrance. Having greeted him, he introduced me to some of the members of the group standing around him, all of them colleagues of his at the music software company. I had talked about this concert to my colleagues at work, and some of them were present in the bar room as well. Both companies were direct competitors in the field of music technology, especially software. The situation felt a bit awkward to me, and I did observe that the artist T was not too comfortable with it, either. Throughout the evening, it turned out that most of the visitors were office colleagues of his. My direct supervisor was there, as well as the artist T's team coordinator. Although the situation at this particular concert was peculiar because there were so many employees of the competitor to my own employer present there, I had experienced this same subcontext of the duality of roles in interactions many times before at events in the realm of this scene (e.g. P1192). My supervisor had touched the topic a number of times at similar occasions, stating that he saw no problem with the people working in the other organization, only with the behavior of the company as a whole. Before the concert started, I remained mostly engaged in interaction with my colleagues, and we discussed work matters as well as several other, more personal topics. Also, my supervisor and I had planned to attend another cultural event that evening, and we discussed this event as well.

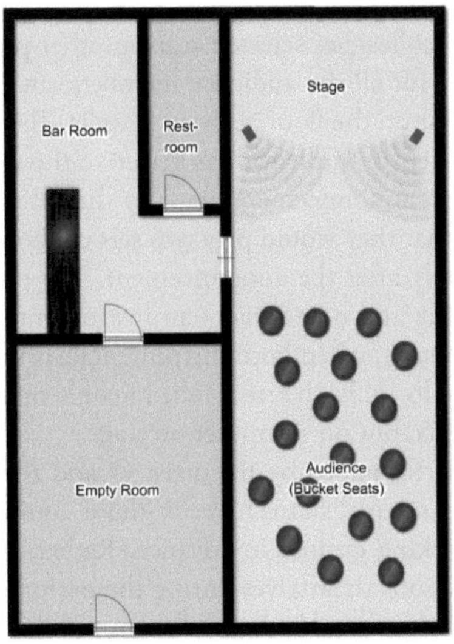

Reconstructed floor plan of the venue.

The artist explicitly postponed the start of the concert twice, without giving a direct reason. Leading up to the concert, I mostly remained engaged in interaction with my supervisor, another colleague of ours, and his girlfriend. The artist decoupled from his engagement in interaction only sporadically, for example at the two occasions when he announced the postponing of the concert start. My colleagues and I did not talk to him much before he and his fellow performer started playing. In the meantime, more visitors arrived. When the concert eventually was about to start, there were around 45 people inside the venue.

Directly before the start of the performance, the visitors moved from the bar room to the concert room. Although this was likely initialized by a signal from one of the artists, I did not observe this directly. My colleagues and I entered the concert room with the rest of the visitors. The concert room was distinctively different from the bar room or the front room through which I had entered the venue. While the other two rooms had shabby walls with worn out paint that had stains all over it, the all-white walls of the concert room were meticulous (P1505). Also, the lighting in the concert room was directed at the stage, which took up the area along the short side of the room left of the entrance to the room. To the right of the entrance, buckets were placed upside down on the floor. Audience members immediately accepted these buckets as seats, and I took one for myself in the central back of the room, as seen from the stage. There were two gas heaters inside the room, and I felt almost uncomfortably warm there. My colleagues selected seats in other places of the room. There were not enough buckets for all the audience members, and several people stood in the back of the room or sat on the floor at the side walls. The two performers entered the room shortly after the entire audience was placed to the right of the entrance, and the concert started with an announcement made by the fellow performer of the artist T. He told the audience that they would play two sets of about twenty minutes. They started to play immediately after the announcement. The music was very quiet and ambient, with subtle shifts and occasionally an instrumental solo. This changed in the second part of the concert, when both instrumentalists assumed more solo parts, mostly in improvisational form. Both artists relied mainly on their instruments, using additional electronic effects, but no computer on stage.

Unlike in the duo performance by the artist O and the accompanying guitarist, both performers had an equal status here. Without computers or other playback devices, there was no backing created in advance. Rather, the two performers had to create all musical functions themselves during the performance. One of the most important pieces of technology used by both of them was the looper effect. Both used this effect in the incarnation of a pedal board they kept on the floor, where they could operate it while playing their primary instruments. The looper effects essentially sampled a part of the audio captured either from the microphone in front of the clarinet or the pickup of the electric guitar and then continuously repeated – looped – this part. The looped audio could then be merged with further audio recordings, allowing the loop to become more and more complex as additional layers of audio were added in. With the push of a button, the loop could be stopped and restarted, and the audio memory could also be cleared to allow the performer to start building an entirely new loop. The looper pedals allowed for relatively complex musical performances created from just one or two instruments, and thus they were widely popular among solo players, especially guitarists. The artist T used his looper pedal in many of the solo performances I observed.

The concert room (infrared photo, P1506).

Using looper effects promoted the creation of multi-layered, slowly changing musical arrangements. Quick breaks and changes between different parts could not, or at least not easily, be achieved with this technology. Also, it could be hard to create straight beats, because there would likely always be a slight difference between the beat in the playing of the instrument and the recorded sample that was played back by the looper effect. Although such a difference may have gone unnoticed once, the looper effect would repeat it with every restart of the sample, pointing out the error with its machine precision. Looping arpeggiated notes of guitar or clarinet playing, and then layering more arpeggiated notes of the same instrument on top of that, helped mask the effect and create a consistent and organic, yet clearly rhythmic musical structure. However, changes were subtle, and the two performers mostly improvised on top of the layered sounds they had created. During the first half of the performance, solo parts were scarce, with the artists mainly adding and shifting layers of arpeggiated notes in pieces that were slowly evolving. The second half of the performance brought more soli, played alternatively by the two artists.

The two performers played their instruments facing the audience, rarely looking at each other to synchronize the beginning of a new part or piece. Nevertheless, they were very concentrated on playing, and did not engage in any further interaction with the audience. The only announcement was made at the very beginning, stating that the performance would be split in two parts. There was no further announcement at the beginning of the second part. At the end of each part, the performers thanked for the applause, but did not say anything else. The audience, on the other hand, was entirely focused on the two artists during the performance. The situation was as frontal as it could possibly be, with the entire audience facing the artists, and the artists directly facing the audience most of the time. The music they played did not include any functional elements in the direction of dancing, and indeed, the two artists almost did not move. This becomes especially apparent in contrast to the performance by the artist O and the guitarist, where O moved around on the stage a lot, sometimes even starting to get into faint resemblances of dancing moves.

During both parts of the concert, the audience was entirely quiet. All interaction among audience members had seized directly after the announcement, and the audience members maintained their engagement with the music performance until the end of the respective set. During the sets, there were no breaks in between pieces. Both parts of the concert were performed as coherent sets. The applause after both sets seemed long, definitively longer than after individual songs at comparable concerts. Between the sets, the artist T stood next to the open door connecting the concert room and the bar area. He was engaged in interaction with about five people, and I joined in as well. T introduced me to several of his colleagues, and they asked me about my role with my employer. The topics mostly covered technological developments and rumors about new products in the music technology market. Meanwhile, other visitors were engaged in interaction in small groups of two to five participants in both the concert and the bar rooms. After about twenty minutes, the artist went to the backstage area in the concert room and soon after, the visitors were asked to take their seats again.

The second part of the concert lasted another twenty minutes, as announced before the first part. Afterwards, interaction formed again immediately in both rooms, but I also observed several visitors leaving the venue right away. My group of colleagues had planned to go to another music event directly after the concert. This one was sponsored by the magazine where the label owner H worked (P1217), and my supervisor pressed us to leave soon after the performance had ended. I agreed to come along with them, and so we walked up to the artists while they were breaking down their stage setup and told them we were leaving. T seemed surprised and asked us if we didn't have time for a beer after he was finished with his stage work, but my supervisor told him that we had to go to the other venue straight away. T uttered understanding and so we said goodbye and walked out.

The core distinctions comprising the performance event were identical to those of the event format I, the label C's "Allnighter" event series. However, the arrangement of distinctions I could observe differed in the role fulfilled by the artists, as they were directly involved in the organization of the performance event. This is expressed in the following equations:

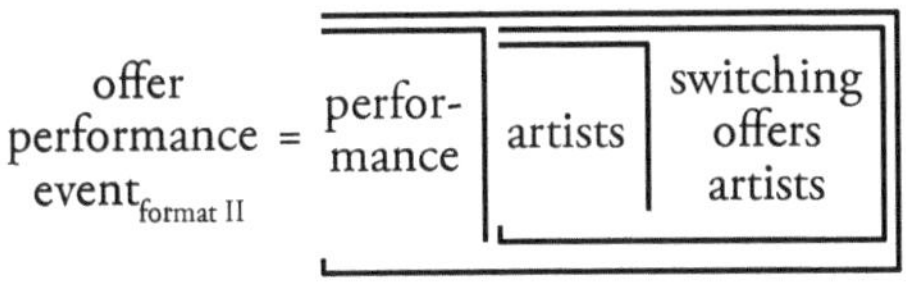

Form equation 4.2.1.a: The offer at a performance event of format II as the unity of the difference between a performance and artists observed in the context of switching offers referencing them.

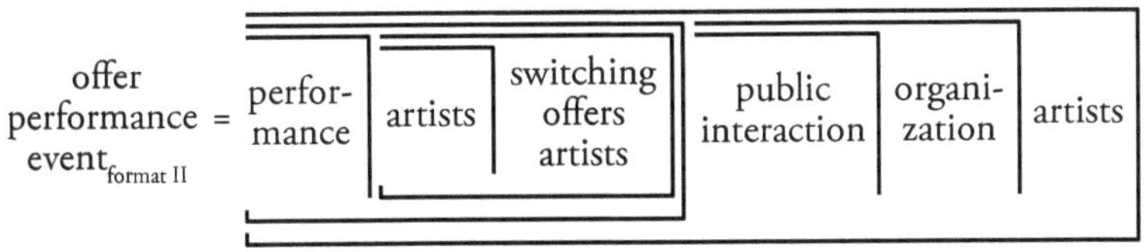

Form equation 4.2.1.b: The offer at a performance event of format II as the unity of the difference between a performance and artists observed in the context of switching offers referencing them, in a situation of public interaction conceived by an organization in the context of the involvement of the artists.

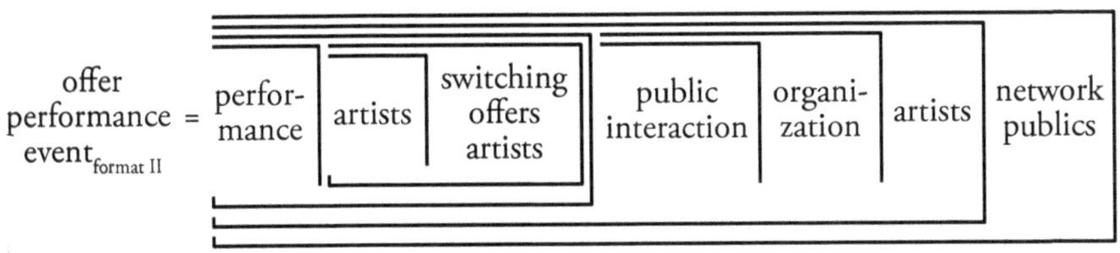

Form equation 4.2.1.c: The offer at a performance event of format II as the unity of the difference between a performance and artists observed in the context of switching offers referencing them, in a situation of public interaction conceived by an organization in the context of the involvement of the artists, embedded in the publics of the network structure of the field.

The reaction at the performance event of format II was similar to format I in that it also included an audience and a situation of public interaction. However, both realms of social action occurred with equal weight, decoupled in time.

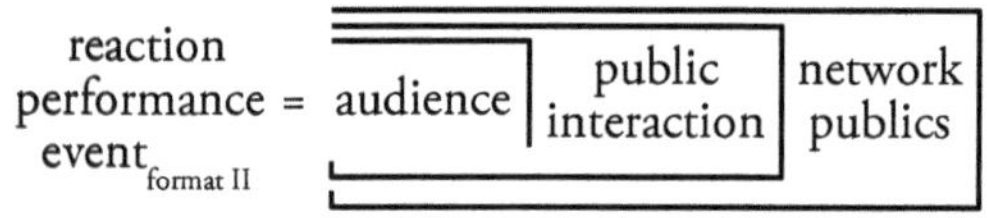

Form equation 4.2.1.d: The reaction at a performance event of format II as the audience and the situation of public interaction in the context of the publics of the network structure of the field.

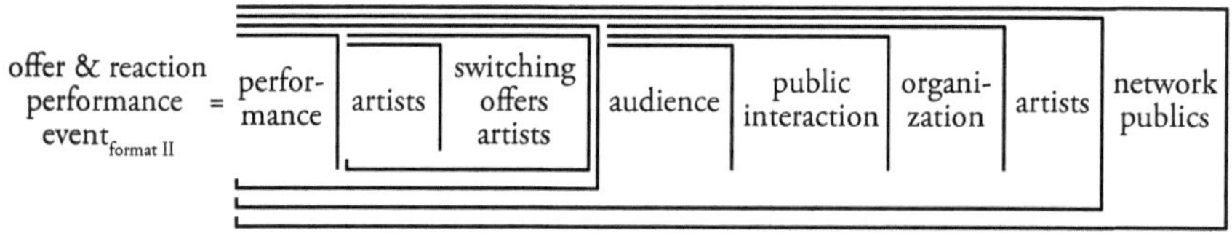

Form equation 4.2.1.e: The offer and reaction at a performance event of format II as the unity of the difference between a performance and artists observed in the context of switching offers referencing them, in the context of an audience as reaction in a situation of public interaction, influenced by an organization in the context of the involvement of the artists, embedded in the publics of the network structure of the field.

The organization of this concert event (P1219) was dominated by the artists. I have mentioned that in the announcement (P1502), the event was placed in the semantic realm of an organization which featured local Berlin artists with Japanese roots, and that this ethnic background was shared by the artist T, but not by his fellow performer. The word that was used to tie the concert event to this organization was "curated". Using this word as description for the tie between event and organization provided an allusion to the realm of fine arts, where curating means selecting the content for an exhibition and identifying with it (see Greenberg / Ferguson / Nairne 1996). I encountered the same notion in a conversation (documented in P1441) with the manager of the similar organization I mentioned above, which shared the focus on the same Japanese ethnic background and also was involved in cultural events featuring, among others, the artist T. This manager told me that he was thinking about new ways to distribute music. In an effort to go beyond offering CDs and downloads through the established channels, he had started to talk to art galleries in Berlin. His idea was to try to establish a new notion of originality for a recorded piece of music, negating the fact that it could be copied digitally without any loss of information, and instead exhibiting and offering it as a one-off piece of recorded music, with one original and no copies. In line with this idea, which he himself described as rather utopian, he told me he had also started to broaden the scope of his label work to include video and photo works of his artists, and that he saw himself more in the role of a curator than as a label owner who commissions releases of recorded music.

As I mentioned, the organization "curating" the event analyzed here did not show any presence at the venue itself (P1219). The starting time of the concert as well as the duration of the break were announced by the artists, and I did not observe any negotiation between the artists and the bartender, the only other person obviously occupied with the organizational side of this event. Nevertheless, the artists had to follow some conventions set by the venue owners and the embedding of the concert event into the general scheme of the Berlin nightlife. On the venue's MySpace page (P1392), the sole source of information directly published by the venue owners, 9 p.m. was given as the regular start time for all concert events. As stated above, the event was not communicated as a party or club event, but, rather to the contrary, as a private listening session (Ibid.). It was held on a Friday, and all of the colleagues I met at the concert event had plans to visit other venues that evening. Also, during the break, several visitors asked the artist T, who was engaged in conversations, to continue with the concert.

The notion of an organized concert event was mostly carried through the announcement of the event that was sent out via email (P1502). There, the association between the artists, the organizations, and the concert event was established as metadata for the event. The external organizations were not needed for any actions at the event itself. Their function was solely in the building of an identity for the event decoupled from its actual operative structure. Since the artists also fulfilled operational roles, their freedom between artistic activity and operational functions was limited. Fulfilling their roles as artists, they enjoyed freedom in their musical activity on stage. The exact musical style of the performance had not been communicated prior to the concert event. Hints at the musical style could only be derived from the meta data in the invitation e-mail. As I have mentioned, the two parts of the performance differed significantly in style, but this was not explicitly announced before the concert.

The inclusion/exclusion mechanism at the concert event of format II was similar to the mechanism I observed at the label C's "Allnighter" events, and so a great number of the visitors already had established ties to the artists and/or the cultural organization focusing on the ethnic background of the artist T. Several visitors were work colleagues of T, and therefore represented a densely connected network domain of its own. In the public situation at the performance event, this network domain was not hermetic, but rather offered potential for the establishing of new ties to other visitors through the utilization of different social contexts of individual members. My colleagues and I represented another densely connected network domain, and some of the visitors had ties linking both domains through personal connections – as did I with my connection to the artist T. In the public situation, T had to switch between his roles as work colleague, as artist, and as organizer, for example. Similarly, my colleagues and I engaged in interaction with work colleagues of the artist T, and discussed, among other things, our roles at the two companies.

The setup at the venue was aimed at consumption by the visitors, and the bar was frequented before and after the concert as well as during the break. As at other venues, visitors did not bring their own drinks. During the concert, all visitors were inside the concert room and seemed engaged in perception of the performance. There was no separate area in the back of the room or outside of the venue, as I observed it at the venues where the label C's "Allnighter" events were held. The bar area at this venue was directly connected to the concert room, and the music was rather quiet, so that any talking would have conflicted with the engaged listening of the audience. The audience was facing the stage, so any recursive mutual observation among the audience members was severely restricted. Any deviation from this dominant behavior would have had an outstanding impact, as it would have been observable immediately by the entire audience as well as the artists. At a similar concert event (P1478), where this artist played a solo concert in a similarly quiet musical style, I observed how some visitors attempted to maintain their interaction during the concert, but were quickly corrected by members of the audience, asking them to be quiet and join in listening.

4.3 On Formats

At the performance events, an area of communication becomes observable that can only be made out by its traces in public online communication: The actual audience of the artists, i.e. the field participants who engage in the reception of the music. At the performance events, the audience communicated its reception via embodiment of attention directed at the performance. However, as I have described, the situation at least in format I was again filled with offers to switch away and concern oneself with topics discussed in various interaction systems present at the same time. Again, this could be described using Walter Benjamin's term "Zerstreuung" (Benjamin 1963: pp. 40).

Cultural events such as the cases we analyzed were constructed out of contributions by different parties with distinct interests. In our cases, these parties were the artists, the organization, and the visitors. The primary operative interest of the artists was to bring visitors to engage in listening and observing their performance, thus forming an audience. These three parties and their possible subdivisions, such as venue owners, bartenders, instrumentalists, visual artists, etc., could not exist if there were no such cultural events at all. The three parties implied each other. Whenever the identity of an artist was distinguished from everything else in society, the outside of this distinction implicitly carried further distinctions from itself and from everything else in society. Observing the identity of an artist meant to also observe an audience that referenced this identity, and in addition to observe the organization embedding this identity of an artist into other processes of society, such as the economy – e.g. establishing an entrance fee for a performance – or the judicial system, e.g. choosing a professionally run venue where all eventualities are insured. Observing the identity of an organization meant to also observe the artists this organization worked with, and the publics it catered to. Such observations typically included asking whether the artists the organization worked with all fell into the same category, and where a hierarchy of values – some artists getting more acclaim from critics or drawing larger audiences – might be detected. Finally, observing an audience meant to also observe the artists it referenced, as otherwise it could not be called an audience. The organization came into play as well, acting as the coupling device between the audience and the artists.

On the grounds of these intertwined observations from different perspectives, we can therefore assume that the three parties observed were indeed parts of one and the same social form integrating artistic and cultural practice. We have seen that each realm could observe its own dependency on being observed by the other realms, which is why we have to understand our overarching form as being constructed from recursions. The logic of the analytical deconstruction of the performance and concert events is purely technical unless the variables used to name the insides of the distinctions are filled. In the field, this happened in a recursive process for all the communicative realms involved. Each realm was observed and evaluated by the other realms, including their compliance with control efforts by the observer's own and the other realms. As a result, each realm was constantly referencing the other realms it had to deal with, as well as itself as a reflection in the actions of the other realms.

Although it may seem as if all realms were concerned with the performance event itself, another variable decoupled from the inner workings of the performance event proved to be highly important for all realms concerned with the event. This was the reference to the publics of the wider network of cultural and artistic practice, which connected the actions focused on the event with processes outside of the realm of any particular event-instance. This ability to semantically connect with processes outside of the situation at hand itself was vital for all realms involved with it, because it enabled them to utilize observations referencing the performance event for the development and maintenance of their identity in their relevant network domains. Each realm's efforts at exerting at least some control over the actions of the other realms, the recursive mutual observation of compliance, and each realm's efforts at assuming a certain degree of freedom from being controlled by the other realms led to a precariously balanced construct of social control, including the exploitation of limited areas of freedom. All cultural events featuring an artistic performance would include the artists, the organization, and visitors as realms, but the specific nature of the volatile balance between exploitation and control, or between blocking action and getting action (White 2008, pp. 279), allows for the definitions of different formats of instances of cultural and artistic practice.

The analysis of the two event formats has shown several important differences. However, they were also very similar in that they were deeply embedded into the online communication of their relevant publics. Without the metadata that had been available almost exclusively online, the visitors would not have known about the performance events, nor would they have found them. Of course, some visitors were also brought along by others and did not look up or receive this information themselves, but these network effects were already factored into the setup of the events. The inclusion/exclusion mechanism for both event formats worked via the implicit restriction of access to the relevant – and necessary – metadata. The restriction was implicit because there were no technical limitations in the accessibility of the information: Even though some of the more detailed information on the event of the format II (P1219) was only distributed via email, there was still enough information publicly available on the venue's MySpace page, for example, to find out who was playing where and when. However, access to this information was implicitly restricted because no further pointers to it – such as mentions on larger event schedule websites for Berlin, or magazine advertisements – were released to the general public. Another similarity can be found in the fact that all performance events of the two formats were held at venues that already had a stage setup and a sound system in place, and these factual elements were utilized for the performances without any major changes.

The most important difference between the two formats was openly observable: At the label C's "Allnighter" events, the audience was never all-inclusive, i.e. there were always visitors who did not listen and watch during the performance, but who remained engaged in the situation of public interaction. At the concert event described as format II (P1219) and at similar events (e.g. P490; P1201; P1206; P1517), public interaction seized almost entirely during the performance. Still, the notion of co-presence among the audience members was upheld during the performance, which also meant that as the applause faded, the visitors could return to public interaction in a self-organized process of simultaneous switching. Despite the focus on interaction, visitors at performance events at some times did observe the need for an audience to be present while artists were performing. In one case, the applause in between songs faded, this fading was observed and additional applause was explicitly given, which then faded again. Although ultimately unsuccessful, this case was an effort to deliberately balance the control structure between artists, audience, and visitors engaged in interaction at the public situation of the performance event. The performing artists certainly had to put more effort into events of the format II, yet the effort paid off for them in the form of an audience that was fully concentrated on their performance. The artist O had expressed his dissatisfaction with performance events where audiences were unstable and visitors kept switching back and forth between listening and interaction (P1175: 92-95). For him, a situation where visitors kept talking inside the venue during his own performance was very discouraging.

Leaving aside the artists' sentiments, the network function of a performance event where the situation of public interaction remained steady during the performance was not necessarily different from a situation where it paused. Even though the second case study shows that different formats of performance events could successfully suppress interaction during a performance, it was still present as a frame before and after the performance, and during intermission. It can be stated for all performance events I observed that interaction was indeed one of the most important factors for the situations in which performances were embedded. Why this relevance of interaction? Looking closer at the communicational process, it became clear that in interaction, many different topics were brought up in the discussions, topics were changed, and risky topics were brought up regularly. Risky topics included discussions about participants' memberships in organizations and their competitive environment, but also differentiated critique of music releases or other performance events. It became apparent that the field participants treaded carefully in these cases, moving slowly towards statements, while keeping the possibility of recontextualization within reach. All of this was only possible because interaction operates as synchronized communication, so that any reactions to offers made could be observed and reacted on directly. For the network of cultural practice, the communicational switchings between the different network domains represented by the visitors of a performance event were of much greater importance than the question whether or not a significant part of the visitors had actually listened to the music performed there, at least as long as visitor behavior was not widely seen as problematic. The most obvious topics that were regularly called upon in the interaction were those of the roles the participants fulfilled in organizations. These could be music technology manufacturers, as was the case for the artists T and M as well as myself, or music and lifestyle magazines in the case of the label owner H and his assistant L. These and similar contexts became prevalent topics of communication at all of the performance events I observed, yet they were rarely mentioned in the communication based on online media.

The social spaces of the performance events we have analyzed here fulfilled a communicational role within the field. Their construction was guided by the expectations among those who could exert control over the layout as to how interaction and performances with audiences should be facilitated. In the case of the label C's "Allnighter" events, the interaction and the performances with the audiences were not separated, and visitors could switch back and forth easily. This resulted in loud conversations being continued during the performances, a situation the artists and the label owner did not approve of. This was solved by the different, more traditional approach of the performance event format II. There, the artists could exert enough control to ensure that the performance and the opportunity for interaction were decoupled, both in time as well as in social space. They moved the visitors from one room to another, thereby indicating the change in the social situation from interaction to audience and back. This approach was successful in that the audience was all-inclusive for the visitors, while there was also opportunity to engage in interaction before and after the performances. The locations also differed significantly between the two event formats. The label C's "Allnighter" event was deliberately located away from the expected area for such cultural events, in an area where few, if any, of the visitors actually lived. It was also not an area frequented by tourists, but rather a center of the still more foreign culture of Berlin's Turkish community. In addition, especially the building in which the "Allnighter" events took place was a hotspot of the local drug scene. These two factors together contributed to the insular character of the venue during these evenings. As a result, visitors usually stayed close to or inside the venue, increasing the social density, and without a spatial decoupling of interaction and performance, the interaction carried on. In contrast, the analyzed performance event of format II and similar events were located in areas where the visitors likely spent their evenings anyways. They were much more embedded in the calendar of events of the interested publics, and so it was easier for visitors to leave and come in again. This was countered with a strict inclusion of the visitors into the audience, i.e. those who were present at the beginning of the performance were all included, and those few who were late had to wait in the hallway until the performance was over.

The goals of artists and members of the publics appear contradictory. While the offers made by the artists were betting on the continuous presence of an audience, any reactions in publics mostly came with the interest of being able to switch away from the offer at any time. This contradiction was resolved into an operative paradox, consisting of an oscillation between granted attention of an audience and a potential switch to other topics. Either part of the oscillation was possible only in the context of the other part. Attention was only granted in the context of a possible switch, but the switch itself also depended on a situation in which a cultural event such as a performance had attracted enough attention in the publics to make switching worthwhile.

The main social function of the performance events we have analyzed therefore was the facilitation of interaction systems. The actual situations I observed and took as the basis for analysis all helped to establish interaction among field participants. Similar observations could presumably be made about intermissions during opera or symphonic performances. However, unlike these cultural events, the performance events in our field attracted groups of visitors who were regularly in touch about the very same cultural and artistic practices they encountered at these events. Therefore, they did not have to spend much time and effort in interaction at the events to update each other on the status of their activities, but could rather venture into the exploration of other social contexts the participants held stakes in, e.g. issues of technology or organizations. This they did at all instances of performance events I observed, while actual listening and watching of the performances were optional choices, at least at the label C's "Allnighter" events.

In any case, the performance and the artists were set as a theme that would come up in the public interaction happening before, during, and after the event. This is especially interesting since different network domains were represented in those interactions. As mentioned, several participants worked for larger manufacturing organizations, others were journalists. When I attended one of the "Allnighter" events together with a journalist (P1192), the topics of communication with the artists at the venue were dominated by the technology market and the developments inside the manufacturing organizations where the individual participants worked. The situation was awkward, as none of the participants – including myself – knew exactly how to handle the fact that they were theoretically not allowed to discuss topics regarding these organizations with the same level of detail as the processes of cultural practice. The situation settled on a discussion on a more general level, referencing not only the manufacturers where some of the participants were employed, and which the journalist had been visiting, but also other aspects of the technology market.

Within the interaction systems, accessibility of very different social contexts served discussions of organizational processes involving technology manufacturers and journalistic organizations, and thereby grounded the cultural practice of the scene in the vicinity of these organizations. This added a sense of scope to the performance events, adding outside references that were important to most visitors. Making such references as well as the number of visitors directly observable turned the performance events into a means of self-reassurance for the scene. Participants – visitors, organizers, and artists – could get a sense of whether or not their offers were relevant in the other contexts they could expect to be represented at the events. This was the case especially as all performance events I observed also had to establish themselves in the context of the busy schedule of cultural activities on offer in Berlin during the research period.

The "Allnighter" performance event of format I was discontinued during the research period. The label owner H expressed his discontent with the event series in an interview (P1216), rationalizing his decision to discontinue it with the money he lost with each individual performance event. The discontinuation of the label C's "Allnighter" series of performance events shows that a structure of control efforts as described in 4.1.5 can work on an operational level per individual performance event, but not in the greater picture of identities and control efforts in the field. I have described how the performance event series was viewed from two fundamentally different perspectives, one focusing on the artistic performance, the other on the public interaction during the evening. At the "Allnighter" performance events, the dominance of the public interaction was apparent, and its efforts at negotiating a coexistence with the artistic performances were largely unsuccessful. The artists and organizers concerned with the performances were therefore unsatisfied with the event, and the label owner H as the field participant in charge of initiating each individual performance event in the series decided to discontinue it. This shows how a structure of control efforts such as this series of performance events can be observed as off balance, and therefore as unattractive, even though the individual parts of the series were successful on an operational level.

In the field, the perspective that viewed a performance event primarily as a structure facilitating an artistic performance which had an audience prevailed. Of the two competing perspectives, the field settled on the one associated with format II, at least temporarily towards the end of the research period covered in this study. The artists and the organizers directly involved with the performances enforced their position of control over those visitors who primarily wanted to engage in public interaction during performance events. Their interests could not be disregarded altogether, though, as they were needed as visitors who could potentially be recruited for an audience. This was solved in performance events of format II by the temporal decoupling I have described: Periods of artistic performance were framed by periods of public interaction. This decoupling was enforced via clear announcements, which were echoed in social pressure, should individual visitors try to exclude themselves from the audience and reestablish interaction during the performance.

Chapter 5: Integrating Online Publics and Performance Events

The field we have analyzed in this study can be described as a mesh of artistic creativity, social interaction across very different media, technological advancements and versatility, and general innovation in lifestyle concepts outside of any usual career planning. The musicians in the field were experts in many areas, and they had to be. Producing works of art was the basic prerequisite for their existence, but most of them could not rely on the help of experienced studio owners and sound engineers, as the generations of professional musicians in the 20th century had done. And the activities required for getting themselves and their works known among the publics they targeted were fulfilled only in part by mass media organizations struggling for their own survival. Most of the publicity-gaining work was left to the musicians themselves. The ability to sell large numbers of physical representations of music releases with an equally large margin to support huge production, distribution, promotion, and, indirectly via marketing budgets, journalistic organizations, was gone entirely for this scene. At the same time, the means to pursue their careers on their own had more or less all become available to the artists in our field. The means to both produce and promote, and even to sell music had all been made available as information in the form of software running on networked computers that had become ubiquitous. While reflecting on these phenomena, it should not be forgotten that while the social processes utilizing computers, networks, and software may well lead to a post-industrial cultural economy, the electronic substrate providing the technological layer on which this process was built was manufactured under highly industrial conditions (for an example, see Dean 2007).

The wide availability of computer-based music production technology had enabled large parts of the music-interested publics to gain their own experiences in using these means. The potential to produce material of a technical quality on par with the semi-professionals or professionals in our field was available to their publics and audiences. And indeed, as the comments and statistics especially on MySpace show, reactions in the publics in many cases involved the promotion of musical activities by other members of the platform. These publics can therefore be called producer publics. Nevertheless, creating and promoting art in a certain socio-cultural context involved more personal effort than most amateur producers were able to invest. For this, it was still required to publicly define oneself as an artist. Building an identity to support this claim was sometimes cumbersome, as the examples in this study show.

5.1 Experienced Potential-Builders

The targeting of production-oriented, technology interested publics by the musicians in our field made them interesting collaborators or even employees for the companies manufacturing this technology. In many cases, the musicians and their audiences used the same software and hardware, and the recording or performing musicians could be expected to have in-depth knowledge of the programs and devices produced by these manufacturers. This combination of them being part of the manufacturers' target groups themselves, while also having built experience on how to reach further parts of these groups, constituted their value for the manufacturers, aside from any individual skills and knowledge they might have brought to the table in addition.

As I have mentioned in section 2.2.2, two of the artists I observed closer worked for a music software company, one of them in customer support, the other as a freelancer in the website content team. Several other artists in the vicinity of the label I observed also had jobs at this company or similar companies. During the research period, I worked for a different music technology manufacturer myself. The situation was specific to the cultural setting in Berlin, at least for Germany, because Berlin was home to a cluster of music technology companies, providing more job opportunities in this sector than would have been available in other cities.

The areas in which the artists worked did not involve traditional public relations (e.g. P1439). The companies had public relations positions – I held one myself during the time of research – but they primarily dealt with the mass media outlets, such as magazines, newspapers, and occasionally radio or TV stations. Many of them also had official Facebook and sometimes MySpace presences (e.g. P2221), but this was also not the area in which they utilized the artists they worked with. The artists were most important as multipliers of the social operation of publishing information online, carrying selected bits further into the target groups, and thus creating the positive network effects I have described in section 3.4.6. From the perspectives of the publics interested in the artists' musical work, their professional relationship with the music technology manufacturers had a potential of drawing more interest and attention towards their offerings. However, the artists' positions in between the companies' interests and their own credibility were risky as well. I have mentioned the importance of being perceived as "independent", in the sense that the activities of the artists were not determined by any outside influences other than those they chose to allow. They had to maintain this position of idealistic independence, otherwise they would have risked losing their credibility, and thereby the public interest in their work.

The building up of potentials for audiences was an important activity for artists both in the cases of online publics and at performance events. However, also in all of those cases, it became clear in the analysis that this importance existed mainly for the artists themselves and for the label owner H. Other participants involved in the public situations surrounding these cases did not share the same interest in building up an audience for the artists. Rather, their focus was on building and maintaining interaction systems in which they could participate.

5.2 A Casual Intimacy

The public situations we have analyzed differed considerably between online publics and publics built on direct interaction, as was the case at the event formats laid out in Chapter 4. Although all of the public situations described in this study usually shared a portion of their members, they were still operationally, and thus, socially, decoupled from each other. If we follow Harrison C. White (1995) and take the switching among network domains as the primary function of publics, the notable difference is that social action leading up to this switching itself was only observable in publics when interaction was involved, but not in online publics. These online publics can therefore be seen in line with other media based on writing, which moved the social action embedding the switchings out of the publics and into the private realm. Reading printed material in private and then discussing it publicly is a similar process. At first sight, the public situations based on print and online media might seem quite similar: In both cases, participants read privately, then carry their opinions out into the public where they are discussed. The discussions again require writing and reading to continue, and so the mix between public statements and their private preparation ensues. However, print media were broadcasting media, requiring a large production apparatus that could only be financed if the words written by very few authors and compiled by even fewer editors were paid for by a large number of readers. This had changed dramatically with the widespread adoption of online media. In our field, public discussions took place not in the one-to-many configurations of broadcasting media, but in the peer-to-peer configurations typical of online platforms.

This had several implications: First of all, the number of members of the public who followed a discussion on Facebook was much smaller than it would have been if the medium was a print magazine, for example. Then, participation in discussions was almost instant, without the production latency of print media. New posts in a discussion could be published in a matter of minutes or even seconds, yet they were decoupled from each other in that the participants could not observe each other's presence. The most important difference, however, was perhaps in the perceived intimacy between the participants in communication on the online platforms versus the situation with print media. The publication frequency of the online platforms resulted in a qualitative decrease of importance accredited to any single published item. The novelty value that had been established with the printed news media still mattered in the online publics – all postings had some sort of news value –, but any single item on MySpace or Facebook was, on average, less significant in the process of cultural practice than an editorial item in a print magazine. Yet, they appeared more often, and were usually very close to the activities of the participants involved. This sharing of smaller, less significant, but up-to-date bits of information established a sort of casual intimacy among the participants in communication on the online platforms and, potentially, among many members of the online publics following these postings. This allowed the scene to operate as a loosely coupled network of part-time participants, who regularly re-actualized and enriched their connectivity in the interaction-based publics of cultural events.

Another aspect that separated performance events from online representations was that online, the audience became invisible. At the performance events, the audience engaged in the perception of the performance could be observed, either by members of the audience themselves, or, more general, in public interaction among visitors present during the performance. This was not the same when online media were involved. In Chapter 3, I have described in detail the representations of both the artists and the label C on MySpace and Facebook. The availability of original material had a stronger focus on MySpace than on Facebook, where hints at actual releases to be listened to and bought elsewhere, as well as performances, were more prominent. But even in the case of MySpace, the actual audience that listened to the material so readily available remained invisible. The audience left traces, like the number of times a song or track in the player embedded on the MySpace page had been played back, but the disposition in which this material had been listened to, if at all, remained opaque. Instead of the audience, the publics were very visible in the context of these online representations. From the members of the publics came the comments, offering, among other things, opinions on the available material, and thereby hinting at the existence of an actual audience for the online material. The number of page views and "friends" on MySpace as well as Facebook, and the number of comments they left behind, could give an estimate as to how large the public was a given artist could reach with his profile.

We have explored the different formats of performance events in the field. The differences that set these formats apart were for the most part found in the control structures allowing certain groups participating in these performance events – namely the artists, the organization, the visitors, and the audience – to influence the actions of the other groups. The performance event was described as a prototypical public situation in section 4.1.1, so the different control structures made out in sections 4.1.5 and 4.2.1 amount to an inward differentiation of public situations.

We have analyzed online publics as well, and found them to be variations of a specific situation allowing for the immediate and direct comparison of primary material, with a focus on its suitability for a value sphere rather than explicit preferences. While the public situations at performance events were based on interaction, the connectivity achieved online utilized technological media in the form of software and computer hardware. With this dependency, these new formats of publics stand in the tradition of non-interactional technological media like print, photography, and phonography, which highlighted the reproducibility of material. Having taken the step into reproduction that seemed to work, for all practical purposes, independent of its material substrate, the computer-based communication media left this notion behind. Also being a successor to earlier media that achieved point-to-point connectivity, such as mail systems, the telegraph, or the telephone, the computer-based media transcended all of these influences, reintroducing their paradigms whenever a social situation required them.

The musical pieces offered on the websites and profile pages and in the performances at cultural events in the field helped facilitate the communicational situations I described by limiting the amount of fresh information they imported. The main factor was the absence of vocals, which ensured that the music did not interfere directly with spoken word communication. This was especially important for the continuity of interaction at the performance events, but it could also help when music was to be listened to as a stream from a website in an everyday situation. In addition, the music pieces also displayed a relatively high amount of repeating elements, e.g. sampled loops or recurring patterns played on acoustic and electro-acoustic instruments. This meant that there was not too much fresh information to be processed once a track was underway, as most of its internal structure could be seen to fit the expectations listeners had towards a piece by a specific artist known to them. This allowed the visitors at a performance event to switch into and out of audiences. Another factor contributing to this was the publics' knowledge of production methods used in recording or performing the musical pieces. As a result, audiences in the field were hard to surprise, as many of their members had technical categories of understanding for any element they perceived in the music. Thus, it was possible to leave the audience and reengage at a later point in time without the impression of having missed something relevant. This made the dynamic of switching back and forth possible and attractive.

The music played at the events I observed clearly belonged to the realm of electronic culture. Its main sources of inspiration seemed to be techno and house music in its various styles, where the notion of arranging in layers and loops played an important role. In terms of rhythmic structures, some performers separated their style from the mainstream Berlin techno culture, which was built upon the foundation of a straight bass drum on each quarter note, by importing beats from hip hop culture. Notably, techno and house, as well as hip hop, were known as very body-centric genres, with their rhythmic structures serving as functional elements to accommodate dancing. This function was almost completely absent in the performances I observed. There were no straight bass drums, and the hip hop beats were changed by the sounds selected for their elements, so that they were much more percussive and toned down, without the aggressiveness that could often be found in hip hop. Therefore, the sort of nonverbal communication possible in dancing was not accounted for at these events.

5.3 Interaction and Disciplines

The case studies have shown the prevalence of interaction systems as the dominant form of social action among visitors at the performance events. Engagement in actual listening or other forms of perception of the performed artistry ranked second, far behind interaction in its function as social activity. I have already mentioned some of the benefits and risks interaction holds for its participants. Interaction made accessible a multitude of contexts that would not have been available to non-interactional communication. This is especially interesting since, as we can see in the analysis of information flows in the field, non-interactional communication was the rule rather than the exception in the social process.

Accessing different contexts for communication in interaction systems means switching between narratives of different network domains, and everybody participating in communication in this context assumed certain roles in those areas. Thereby, new ties could be created among the participants, who embedded their action into communicational topics and narratives which other participants in the ongoing interaction could relate to. This relation created new ties, either as fresh connections between roles assumed by participants where there had been none before, or as additional connectivity extending the contexts of already existing relations. Adding further ties or enriching existing ones with more contexts increased the overall connectivity in the network. As I have laid out in the analysis of the observed network structures, they were not made from identities with an equal distribution of ties, but rather span several network domains, distinct areas of increased internal connectivity with only a few ties connecting them together to form the overall network structure which I could then describe as the field of my research. At the performance events analyzed in the case studies, several different network domains were represented among the visitors. Interaction at the performance events allowed participants who fulfilled roles in these different areas to establish, re-establish, or enrich connections to other network domains. Since such connections were scarce, this process could be observed as being of particular importance to the integrity of the wider cultural network. At the performance events I observed, interaction among members of different network domains did not form automatically, but many times had to be instigated by one of the overarching connections. Such a connection could have been an already established acquaintance between two members. From this, a joint interaction system could form, and participants who did not share ties could work on establishing them.

The sometimes radical shifts between communicational contexts in interaction assumed that participants actually could fulfill a role in that particular context. This underlines that participants in interaction mutually and recursively saw themselves as a multiplicity of roles, or indeed, as multi-faceted persons. This notion of personhood is perhaps the most visible departure from the mostly functional roles the participants usually fulfilled in their respective network domains.

Network disciplines as I have described them in section 3.4.3 operated outside of interaction systems. The processes that led to the establishment or change of certain valuation orders among identities were sometimes distributed, and sometimes hidden away from the network publics. The number of page visits an artist profile on MySpace received was the result of a process distributed among certain publics, where knowledge of that particular artist's identity was spread, while the selection of a label's artist roster was usually an internal process where certain parts of the label organization acted as a council, taking individual identity's offerings into consideration. The process was not completely internal, as the identities making the offers – of releasing new music material, for example – tried to influence the label council's decision. These disciplines were, however, not being discussed in the openness and uncertainty of interaction systems. Temporal decoupling seemed to be an important factor in social activity revolving around disciplines: Decisions were requested and communicated asynchronously as offer and acceptance or rejection were spread out over time. Processes of decision-taking in organizations or other functional network domains were often themes of communication in interaction, but they were never put at stake in any situation of interaction I observed.

5.4 Integration

I hope to have shown how the engagement in online publics and the organization of performance events complemented each other in the cultural and artistic practice of the participants in the field. As a practice that was largely native to the technological foundations of what has been called the Next Society, the opportunities offered by the online platforms for artists, labels, distributors, and the record stores to interact with their potential audiences were embraced and utilized without hesitation. At the same time, the deficit of the public communication on these platforms became clear as well:

The topics of communication were simultaneously very specific and very generalized. They were specific in that they usually kept the reactions to any communication offer very close to the original topic, while also focusing on the narrow realms of artistic production and its supporting lifestyle. And the topics were very generalized in that the reactions on MySpace and Facebook rarely added something of significance to an original post, other than creating a relation between the posting and the reacting participants. Often enough, reactions were reduced to a "great music!" or "thanks for the add!", with the "like" feature on Facebook marking the pinnacle of such generalized communication. Such reactions were more an echo from the network than the basis for a discussion. They were nevertheless reassuring, reminding the poster that, indeed, cultural practice did not proceed in a vacuum, but that there was interest to be met in the public situation. Contrast this with the diversity of topics at any of the performance events. There, the various different social contexts of the participants – including myself – became frequent topics of communication. Through the voluntary joint seclusion of the visitors at an event, these topics could be introduced by one participant, who could then, in the situation of mutual presence and synchronized observation, contain any unwanted reactions. The possibility to switch to such topics was gained largely in the continuous communication on online platforms, as well as in email. By taking part, field participants kept themselves and their peers up to date with all seemingly relevant information regarding the scene's core functional operation. That way, communication could quickly depart from these topics at the events. After all, many of the participants in the interaction at the events already had intimate knowledge of each other's recent activities in cultural and artistic practice. However, discussing other matters outside of this focused realm had been more or less suppressed in this online communication. As casual and intimate as it may have seemed, the posts and subsequent reactions given there appeared in a public situation, and one that lacked the possibility to immediately react to reactions. For this added level of perceived security, the synchronized, face-to-face communication of interaction systems still provided the better grounds. This integration is modeled as follows:

field publics =

Form equation 5.4.a: Publics of the field as public interaction in the context of public online communication, and public online communication in the context of public interaction, embedded in the publics of the network structure of the field, in the context of the wider cultural scene.

Substituting the terms "public interaction" and "public online communication" in form equation 5.4.a with their definitions from sections 4.1.1 and 3.4.7, we obtain the following equation:

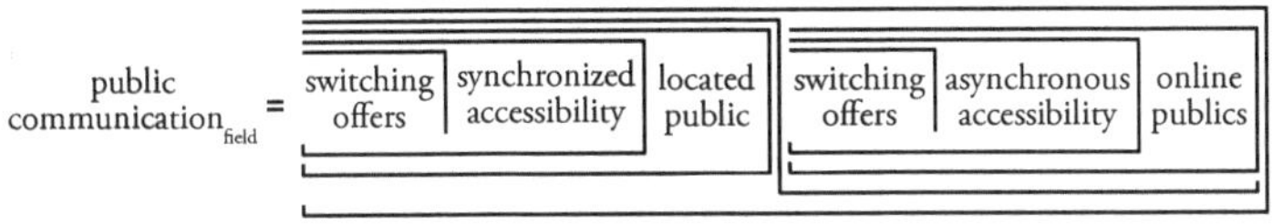

Form equation 5.4.b: Public communication in the field as switching offers observable in a context of synchronized accessibility, embedded in a situation of a located public, in the context of asynchronously accessible switching offers. All this in a situation of online publics, in the context of switching offers observable in a context of synchronized accessibility, embedded in a situation of a located public.

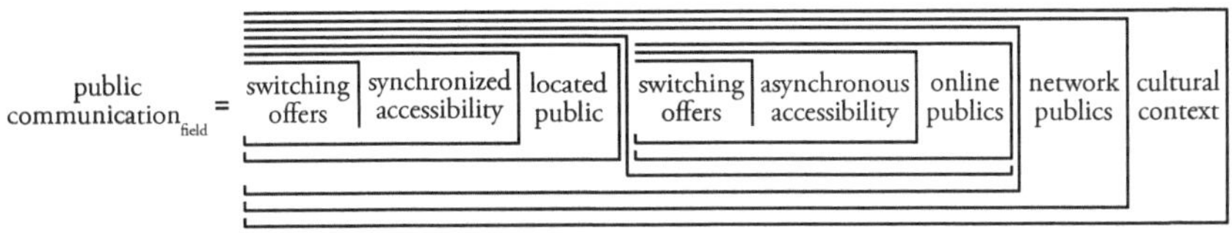

Form equation 5.4.c: Public communication in the field as switching offers observable in a context of synchronized accessibility, embedded in a situation of a located public, in the context of asynchronously accessible switching offers. All this in a situation of online publics, in the context of switching offers observable in a context of synchronized accessibility, embedded in a situation of a located public, embedded in the publics of the network structure of the field, in the context of the wider cultural scene.

The public communication in the field integrated the constant flow of information published through profile pages on online platforms with the sporadic, but intense and rich discussion of a diversity of themes at located performance events. The process of communication in the field oscillated between regular, asynchronous updates in a public situation I have described as casual intimacy and the synchronization of quick switchings between themes observing network domains in the situation of public interaction at performance events. Both cases highlighted the accessibility of switching offers. While their constant availability by using online media was convenient, their asynchronous nature brought with it the risk that misunderstandings could not be corrected right away, and thus have negative effects for the originator of a message. In interaction, this risk could be reduced via the ability to react on reactions in synchronization with the other participants. Also, the reactions happened among a known group and could be observed directly. If a conversation went in a direction that was undesirable for any of the participants, they could try to steer it away from that path. On the online platforms, this was much harder, or even impossible to do. Original statements could always be quoted, taken out of context, and forwarded to others. Thus, for any themes that could be delicate or overly ambiguous, such as discussing positions in companies, for example, participants in the field turned to public interaction.

This analysis hints at why the located performance events played such an important role in the field, even though it took much more effort to set them up than to simply upload some recorded music or video to MySpace or YouTube. In order to escape the casual intimacy of the public online communication and allow for the deeper change required to stay up to date and relevant in its cultural context, the scene had to bring participants together in the face-to-face situations offered by performance events. The form of the performance events was important as well, as it also lent a casual cause to the gatherings – one would just meet to listen to some music together –, yet also allowed for the complete disregard of this cause when visitors chose not to listen to the performance and instead focus on the discussions they found more interesting. Constructing spaces for a localized reality was a complex endeavor in the field, as it had to deal with, among other things, the "Zerstreuung" (Benjamin 1963) of attention in online publics, where it recruited its participants.

The heightened accessibility of different social contexts among network participants can be seen as the primary social function of the construction of space in the field. Spaces like the venues for concerts and label events facilitated interaction, disregarding any ulterior wishes of artists performing there. Their construction was the result of various control efforts by different participants and groups. The communication taking place in interaction was clearly informed by the online communication that had preceded it. Thereby, space limited and enhanced communicational freedom at the same time. It was limiting in that communication had to subject itself to very specific vectors in terms of time and location, with the addition of further control exerted by organizations and artists. Yet, through these limitations, communication gained a specific density that, for our field, increased social exchange across a broader range of topics than what would have been possible using the online communication I observed. However, in order to get to this situation, a cause was usually provided, such as a performance or the publication of a new music release. It became very clear in the analysis that the causes for an event given in advance were largely irrelevant for the actual course of that event. Instead, the causes served as a mechanism embedding the notion of the performance event in online communication, and it also served as a rationalization for the visitors to justify their attendance in their individual social contexts.

Online publics and the construction of social space were therefore closely interrelated in our field. None of the two areas could have operated the way they did without the other area, and both were embedded into the other, while at the same time retaining operational freedom. The area of online publics may already hint at structures of the Next Society, yet we have seen in our very limited example how such an area can change the construction and operation of other processes that would seem independent at first sight. Society, however, evolves as a notion, as an idea and a narrative, and even if some areas may appear to have a lead, they are forced to embed themselves into other areas and thereby find a communicational common ground to handle the complexity of everything that is social.

Bibliography

Aakerstroem Andersen, Niels (2010): The Semantic Analytical Strategy and Diagnostics of Present, in: John, René / Henkel, Anna, Rückert-John, Jana (Eds.): Die Methodologien des Systems: Wie kommt man zum Fall und wie dahinter?, VS Verlag, Wiesbaden, pp. 161-180.

Abbey Road (2012): Home Page, http://www.abbeyroad.com/, last access: 05/05/2012.

Ableton (2004): Ableton at Club Transmediale 2004, www.ableton.com/pages/2004/club_transmediale, last access: 05/05/2012.

Ableton (2011): Introducing Live Intro, http://www.ableton.com/live-intro?orig_ql=/live-intro, last access: 08/20/2011.

Ableton (2012): Company, http://www.ableton.com/pages/company/home?orig_ql=/company, last access: 05/05/2012.

Adelmann, Ralf (2011): Von der Freundschaft in Facebook: Mediale Politiken sozialer Beziehungen in Social Network Sites, in: Leistert, Oliver / Röhle, Theo (Ed.): Generation Facebook: Über das Leben im Social Net, transcript, Bielefeld, pp. 127-144.

Adorno, Theodor W. (1968): Einleitung in die Musiksoziologie, Rowohlt, Reinbek.

Adorno, Theodor W. / Horkheimer, Max (1969): Dialektik der Aufklärung, Fischer, Frankfurt a.M.

Ashdown Audsley, George (1988): The Art of Organ Building, Dover, Mineola.

Alexa.com (2011): Facebook.com, MySpace.com: Time on Site, http://www.alexa.com/siteinfo/facebook.com#, last access: 09/30/2011

All2GetherNow (2010): Schedule, http://a2n2010.sched.org/LoSo314/list/descriptions/, last access: 05/06/2012.

Amazon (2011): Recommendations: How Recommendations Work, http://www.amazon.com/gp/help/customer/display.html/ref=hp_13316081_how?nodeId=13316081#how, last access: 09/26/2011.

Anderson, Chris (2006): The Long Tail: How Endless Choice is Creating Unlimited Demand, Random House, London.

Apple, Inc. (2011a): Logic Studio: What is Logic Studio, http://www.apple.com/logicstudio/what-is/, last access: 09.25.2011.

Apple, Inc. (2011b): Garage Band '11: What is Garage Band, http://www.apple.com/ilife/garageband/what-is.html, last access: 09/25/2011.

Apple, Inc. (2011c): Mac 101: Automator, http://support.apple.com/kb/ht2488, last access: 09/26/2011.

Apple, Inc. (2011d): Logic Express, http://www.apple.com/logicexpress/, last access: 09/25/2011.

Apple, Inc. (2013): Logic Pro X, Mac App Store Vorschau, https://itunes.apple.com/de/app/logic-pro-x/id634148309?mt=12, last access: 10/05/2013.

Atteslander, Peter (2006): Methoden der empirischen Sozialforschung, 11th Ed., Schmidt, Berlin.

Avid, Inc. (2009): Avid 2009 Annual Report, self-published, Tewksbury, MA.

Bacon, Francis (1958): The Advancement of Learning, Dent, London.

Baecker, Dirk (1990): Die Dekonstruktion der Schachtel. Innen und Außen in der Architektur, in: Luhmann, Niklas/Bunsen, Frederick D./Baecker, Dirk (Ed.): Unbeobachtbare Welt: Über Kunst und Architektur, Haux, Bielefeld, pp. 67-104.

Baecker, Dirk (2001): Kopien für alle, in: Flender, Reinhard / Lampson, Elmar: Copyright: Musik im Internet, Kadmos, Berlin, pp. 51-72.

Baecker, Dirk (2003): Wozu Kultur?, 3rd Ed., Kadmos, Berlin.

Baecker, Dirk (2005a): Form und Formen der Kommunikation, Suhrkamp, Frankfurt a.M.

Baecker, Dirk (2005b): Kommunikation, Reclam, Leipzig.
Baecker, Dirk (2006a): Niklas Luhmann in the Society of the Computer, in: Cybernetics & Human Knowing, Vol. 13, No. 2., pp. 25-40.
Baecker, Dirk (2006b): Die Form der Kultur, in: Grant, Colin B. (Ed.): Risse im System, Issue 2, Stadtlichter Presse, Berlin.
Baecker, Dirk (2007a): Studien zur nächsten Gesellschaft, Suhrkamp, Frankfurt a.M.
Baecker, Dirk (2007b): The Network Synthesis of Social Action I: Towards a Sociological Theory of Next Society, in: Cybernetics and Human Knowing 14, no. 4, pp. 9-42.
Baecker, Dirk (2007c): Wozu Gesellschaft?, Kadmos, Berlin.
Baecker, Dirk (2007d): Communication with Computers, or How Next Society Calls for an Understanding of Temporal Form, in: Soziale Systeme, Vol. 13, pp. 409-420.
Baecker, Dirk (2008a): Zur Kontingenzkultur der Weltgesellschaft, in: Baecker, Dirk / Kettner, Matthias / Rustemeyer, Dirk (Ed.): Über Kultur: Theorie und Praxis der Kulturreflexion, transcript, Bielefeld, pp.139-161.
Baecker, Dirk (2008b): Systems, Network, and Culture, Presented at the International Symposium "Relational Sociology: Transatlantic Impulses for the Social Sciences", Berlin, September 25-26, 2008.
Baecker, Dirk (2009): Possen im Netz, Beitrag zur Tagung "Networking. Zur Performanz distribuierter Ästhetik", Ludwig-Maximilians-Universität München.
Baecker, Dirk (2010a): Culture Switch and Culture Brands, forthcoming.
Baecker, Dirk (2010b): Ein Freund fürs Leben: Facebook und die Folgen, in: Basler Zeitung, October 18, 2010, pp. 35, 37.
Baecker, Dirk (2010c): Das Theater als Trope: Von der Einheit der Institution zur Differenz der Formate, lecture held in the series "Die Kritik der Institution: Recherchen zum Stadttheater der Zukunft", Hessische Theaterakademie in cooperation with Theater Freiburg, Frankfurt a.M., May 20, 2010.
Baecker, Dirk (2011): Nur die Ähnlichkeit unterscheidet uns, in: Leistert, Oliver / Röhle, Theo (Ed.): Generation Facebook: Über das Leben im Social Net, transcript, Bielefeld, pp. 123-125.
Barabási, Albert-László (2003): Linked: How Everything is Connected to Everything Else and What It Means for Business, Science, and Everyday Life, Plume, New York.
Bateson, Gregory (1985): Ökologie des Geistes, Suhrkamp, Frankfurt a.M.
Beer, Bettina (Ed.) (2003): Methoden und Techniken der Feldforschung, Reimer, Berlin.
Beer, David (2008): Making Friends with Jarvis Cocker: Music Culture in the Context of Web 2.0, in: Cultural Sociology, Vol. 2, pp. 222-241.
Bell, Matt / Wherry, Mark (2002): Apple/Emagic Takeover: The Inside Story Of The Deal That Changed The Music World in: Sound On Sound Online, http://www.soundonsound.com/sos/Sep02/articles/emagic.asp?print=yes, last access: 09/25/2011.
Benjamin, Walter (1963): Das Kunstwerk im Zeitalter seiner technischen Reproduzierbarkeit, Suhrkamp, Frankfurt a.M.
Bennett, Andy (2000): Popular Music and Youth Culture: Music, Identity and Place, Palgrave, Basingstoke.
Bergmann, Jörg R. / Meier, Christoph (2007): Elektronische Prozessdaten und ihre Analyse, in: Flick, Uwe / von Kardorff, Ernst / Steinke, Ines (Ed.): Qualitative Forschung: Ein Handbuch, 5th Ed., Rowohlt, Reinbek, 429-437.
Berking, Helmuth (Ed.) (2006): Die Macht des Lokalen in einer Welt ohne Grenzen, Campus, Frankfurt a.M.
Berners-Lee, Tim (2006): Net Netrality: This is serious, http://dig.csail.mit.edu/breadcrumbs/node/144, last access: 05/19/2012.
Bierhof Rüdersdorf (2012): Kantine am Berghain, http://www.bierhof.info/, last access: 05/06/2012.
Blaukopf, Kurt (1996): Musik im Wandel der Gesellschaft. Grundzüge der Musiksoziologie, 2nd Ed., Wissenschaftliche Buchgesellschaft, Darmstadt.
Borio, Gianmario (1993): Musikalische Avantgarde um 1960: Entwurf einer Theorie der informellen Musik, Laaber-Verlag, Laaber.
Bourdieu, Pierre (1985): Sozialer Raum und Klassen, Suhrkamp, Frankfurt a.M.

Boyd, Danah Michele (2008): Taken Out of Context: American Teen Sociality in Networked Publics, Dissertational Thesis, University of California, Berkeley.

Boyd, Danah Michele (2011): Social Network Sites as Networked Publics: Affordances, Dynamics, and Implications, in: Papacharissi, Zizi (Ed.): A Networked Self: Identity, Community, and Culture on Social Network Sites, Taylor & Francis, New York, pp. 39-58.

Boyd, Danah Michele / Ellison, Nicole B. (2007): Social Network Sites: Definition, History, and Scholarship, in: Journal of Computer-Mediated Communication, Vol. 13, article 11, http://jcmc.indiana.edu/vol13/issue1/boyd.ellison.html.

Brand, Stewart (1988): The Media Lab: Inventing the Future at M.I.T., Penguin, New York.

Brice, Richard (2001): Music Engineering, 2nd Ed., Newnes, Oxford.

Brin, Sergey / Page, Lawrence (1998): The Anatomy of a Large-Scale Hypertextual Web Search Engine, in: In: Seventh International World-Wide Web Conference (WWW 1998), April 14-18, 1998, Brisbane, Australia, http://infolab.stanford.edu/~backrub/google.html.

Brown, David (2002): Mute records, home of Moby, sold to EMI, in: The Independent Online, May 11, 2002, http://www.independent.co.uk/arts-entertainment/music/news/mute-records-home-of-moby-sold-to-emi-650833.html, last access: 09/24/2011.

Bruch, Walter (1983a): Von der Tonwalze zur Bildplatte: Ein Jahrhundert Ton- und Bildspeicherung. Part I: Mechanische Tonspeicherung. Funkschau Sonderheft Vol.11/1983, Franzis, Munich.

Bruch, Walter (1983b): Von der Tonwalze zur Bildplatte: Ein Jahrhundert Ton- und Bildspeicherung. Part II: Tonbandaufzeichnung. Funkschau Sonderheft Vol.12/1983, Franzis, Munich.

Bundeszentrale für politische Bildung (2009): Die soziale Situation in Deutschland: Einkommensverteilung und Vermögen nach Zehnteln, http://www.bpb.de/files/7GSGVW.pdf.

Bunz, Mercedes (2012): Die stille Revolution, Suhrkamp, Berlin.

Cascone, Kim (2003): Deterritorialisierung, historisches Bewusstsein, System. Die Rezeption der Performance von Laptop-Musik, in: Kleiner, Marcus S. / Szepanski, Achim (Ed.): Soundcultures: Über elektronische und digitale Musik, Suhrkamp, Frankfurt a.M., pp. 101-106.

Connell, John / Gibson, Chris (2003): Sound Tracks: Popular Music, Identity and Place, Routledge, London.

Coy, Wolfgang (1998): Media Control: Wer kontrolliert das Internet?, in: Krämer, Sybille (Ed.): Medien - Computer - Realität: Wirklichkeitsvorstellungen und Neue Medien, Suhrkamp, Frankfurt, pp. 133-151.

de la Motte-Haber, Helga / Neuhoff, Hans (Ed.) (2007): Musiksoziologie, Laaber-Verlag, Laaber.

De:Bug (2007): Frontpage: 1989-1997: Die Asche, aus der die De:Bug stieg, in: De:Bug Online, http://de-bug.de/mag/4744.html, last access: 09/26/2011.

Dean, Jason (2007): The Forbidden City of Terry Gou, in: The Wall Street Journal, August 11, 2007, online version: http://online.wsj.com/public/article/SB118677584137994489.html?mo.

DeRidder, Daniela (2007): Vom urbanen Sozialraum zur telekommunikativen Stadtgesellschaft, Peter Lang GmbH, Europäischer Verlag der Wissenschaften, Frankfurt a.M.

Dhar, Vasant / Chang, Elaine (2007): Does Chatter Matter? The Impact of User-Generated Content on Music Sales, New York University, https://archive.nyu.edu/handle/2451/23783.

Discogs (2011a): Ostgut Ton, http://www.discogs.com/label/Ostgut+Ton, last access: 09/14/2011.

DJMag (2009): Top 100 Clubs in the World, Position 1: Berghain, in: DJMag Online, http://djmag.com/top100club/detail/101, last access: 05/06/2012.

Döring, Jörg / Thielmann, Tristan (Ed.) (2008): Spatial Turn: Das Raumparadigma in den Kultur- und Sozialwissenschaften, transcript, Bielefeld.

Dougherty, Heather / Fanelli, Marc (2008): Hitwise US Social Networking Report March 2008, self-published.

Douglas, Mary (2005): Grid and Group, New Developments, lecture held at the Workshop on Complexity and Cultural Theory, London School of Economics.

Drepper, Thomas (2003): Der Raum der Organisation - Annäherung an ein Thema, in: Krämer-Badoni, Thomas / Kuhm, Klaus (Ed.) (2003): Die Gesellschaft und ihr Raum: Raum als Gegenstand der Soziologie, Leske + Budrich, Opladen, pp. 103-129.

Drucker, Peter F. (2001): The next society: A survey of the near future, in: The Economist Online, November 1, 2001, http://www.economist.com/node/770819/print, last access: 05/06/2012.
Drucker, Peter F. (2002): Managing in the next society, St. Martin's Press, New York City.
Dünne, Jörg/Günzel, Stephan (Ed.) (2006): Raumtheorie: Grundlagentexte aus Philosophie und Kulturwissenschaften, Suhrkamp, Frankfurt a.M.
Entertainment Media Research (2007): The 2007 Digital Music Survey, Entertainment Media Research, London.
Esposito, Elena (2002): Virtualisierung und Divination. Formen der Räumlichkeit der Kommunikation, in: Maresch, Rudolf/Werber, Niels (Ed.): Raum - Wissen - Macht, Suhrkamp, Frankfurt a. M., pp. 33-48.
Facebook (2011a): Facebook Pages: Creating, administering and editing your Page, https://www.facebook.com/help?page=904, last access: 09/24/2011.
Facebook (2011b): Basics: Like, https://www.facebook.com/help/?page=773, last access: 09/24/2011.
Facebook (2011c): Help Center: Top Questions, https://www.facebook.com/help/?tab=top, last access: 09/24/2011.
Facebook (2011d): Basics: Wall: How to use the Wall feature and Wall privacy, https://www.facebook.com/help?page=820, last access: 09/24/2011.
Facebook (2011e): Basics: How to post and share content, https://www.facebook.com/help/?page=812, last access: 09/24/2011.
Facebook (2011f): Basics: How to create and manage events, https://www.facebook.com/help?page=829, last access: 09/24/2011.
Facebook (2011g): Basics: Sign Up, https://www.facebook.com/help/?topic=signup, last access: 09/24/2011.
Facebook (2012): Group basics, https://www.facebook.com/help/groups/basics, last access: 05/12/2012.
Faulkner, Robert R. (2003): Music on Demand: Composers and Careers in the Hollywood Film Industry, Transaction, New Brunswick, NJ.
Fischer, Hans (2003): Dokumentation, in: Beer, Bettina (Ed.) (2003): Methoden und Techniken der Feldforschung, Reimer, Berlin, pp. 265-294.
Foucault, Michel (2006): Von anderen Räumen, in: Dünne, Jörg/Günzel, Stephan (Ed.): Raumtheorie: Grundlagentexte aus Philosophie und Kulturwissenschaften, Suhrkamp, Frankfurt a.M., pp. 317-329.
Frey, Constance (2011): Mitgewachsen: In Berlin hat sich die Zahl der Hostelbetten mit dem Boom der Tourismusbranche binnen zehn Jahren verdoppelt. Davon profitieren Dienstleister, die diesen Häusern zuarbeiten, in: Berlin Maximal: Das Mittelstandsmagazin des Tagesspiegel Online, http://www.berlin-maximal.de/branchen/tourismus/art88,2246, last access: 09/15/2011.
Fuchs, Peter (1987): Vom Zeitzauber der Musik. Eine Diskussionsanregung, in: Baecker, Dirk / Markowitz, Jürgen / Stichweh, Rudolf (Ed.): Theorie als Passion. Niklas Luhmann zum 60. Geburtstag, Suhrkamp, Frankfurt a.M., pp. 214-237.
Fuchs, Peter (2005): Adressabilität als Grundbegriff der soziologischen Systemtheorie, in: Fuchs, Marie-Christin (Hg.): Peter Fuchs: Konturen der Moderne. Systemtheoretische Essays II, transcript, Bielefeld, pp. 37-62.
Fuchs, Peter (no date): DasWorldWideWeb – ohne Technik, in: http://www.fen.ch/texte/gast_fuchs_www.htm, last access: 06/19/2010.
Fuchs, Stephan (2009): The Behavior of Cultural Networks, in: Soziale Systeme 15, Vol. 2, pp. 345-366.
Funken, Christiane / Löw, Martina (Ed.) (2003): Raum - Zeit - Medialität. Interdisziplinäre Studien zu neuen Kommunikationstechnologien, Leske + Budrich, Opladen.
Future Music (2011): A brief history of Ableton Live, in: MusicRadar.com: The No. 1 website for musicians, http://www.musicradar.com/tuition/tech/a-brief-history-of-ableton-live-357837, last access: 09/15/2011.
Gearslutz (2011): Ableton Live Sound Quality, Discussion on Gearslutz Forum, http://www.gearslutz.com/board/music-computers/126945-ableton-live-sound-quality.html, last access: 05/06/2012.
Geertz, Clifford (1987): Dichte Beschreibung: Beiträge zum Verstehen kultureller Systeme, Suhrkamp, Frankfurt a.M.

Geisenhanslüke, Ralph (2007): Die ganze Stadt schreit "Party"!, in: Zeit Online, June 23, 2007, http://www.zeit.de/2005/03/Berlinbars_neu.

Gerlitz, Carolin (2011): Die Like Economy: Digitaler Raum, Daten und Wertschöpfung, in: Leistert, Oliver / Röhle, Theo (Ed.): Generation Facebook: Über das Leben im Social Net, transcript, Bielefeld, pp. 101-122.

Gerstein, Julie (2006): Morr Music: A label brokers peace treaties between the indie rock and electronic realms, in: Berlin Wasted Youth, XLR8R Vol. 101, October 2006, p. 44.

Gertner, John (2003): Social Networks, in: The New York Times Online, December 14, 2003, http://www.nytimes.com/2003/12/14/magazine/14SOCIAL.html?scp=12&sq=social+networks&st=cse.

Goffman, Erving (1959): The Presentation of Self in Everyday Life, Anchor, New York.

Goffman, Erving (1963): Behavior in Public Places: Notes on the Social Organization of Gatherings, The Free Press, New York.

Goffman, Erving (1979): Stigma: Über Techniken der Bewältigung beschädigter Identität, 3rd Ed., Suhrkamp, Frankfurt a. M.

Goldsmith, Jack / Wu, Tim (2006): Who Controls the Internet? Illusions of a Borderless World, Oxford University Press, Oxford.

Google (2011a): Google Trends Facebook.com, MySpace.com: Searches, http://trends.google.com/trends?q=facebook.com,+myspace.com&sa=N, last access: 10/06/2011.

Google (2011b): Google Trends Facebook.com, MySpace.com: Websites, http://trends.google.com/websites?q=facebook.com,+myspace.com&sa=N, last access: 10/06/2011.

Granovetter, Mark S. (1973): The Strength of Weak Ties, in: The American Journal of Sociology, Vol. 78 No. 6, pp. 1360-1380.

Greenberg, Reesa / Ferguson, Bruce W. / Nairne, Sandy (Ed.) (1996): Thinking About Exhibitions, Routledge, New York City.

Großmann, Rolf (2006): Die Spitze des Eisbergs: Schlüsselfragen musikalischer Laptopkultur, in: Positionen. Beiträge zur Neuen Musik, Vol. 68, pp. 2-7.

Grote, Florian / Klauer, Bernd / Thoma, Andreas / Werner, Jan St. (2011): Product Concept: Fluxpad, internal document, Berlin.

Günzel, Stephan (2009): Medienästhetik des Raums, in: Sachs, M. / Sander, S. (Ed.): Die Permanenz des Ästhetischen, VS Verlag, Wiesbaden, pp. 217-229.

Gutman, Robert W. (1999): Mozart: A Cultural Biography, Harcourt, Orlando.

Haaksman, Daniel (2007): Verschwende deine Jugend! Berliner Rave-Kultur, in: Spiegel Online July 14, 2007, http://www.spiegel.de/kultur/musik/0,1518,druck-494248,00.html.

Habermas, Jürgen (1990): Strukturwandel der Öffentlichkeit, Suhrkamp, Frankfurt a.M.

Hansa Tonstudio (2012): Home Page, http://www.hansatonstudio.de/, last access: 05/06/2012.

Häntzschel, Jörg (2007): Das Ende der Massen: Neue Grenzen im Internet, in: Süddeutsche Zeitung Online, March 6, 2007, http://www.sueddeutsche.de/kultur/493/406270/text/print.html.

Harenberg, Michael (1999): Virtuelle Instrumente – Von der Orgel zum Cyber-Instrument, Lecture given at the dvsm-Symposion „Musik im Spiegel ihrer technologischen Entwicklung", October 6-10, 1999.

Hargittai, Eszter (2007): Whose Space? Differences Among Users and Non-Users of Social Network Sites, in: Journal of Computer-Mediated Communication Vol. 13, No. 1, Article 14, http://jcmc.indiana.edu/vol13/issue1/hargittai.html.

Harper, Douglas (2007): Fotografien als sozialwissenschaftliche Daten, in: Flick, Uwe / von Kardorff, Ernst / Steinke, Ines (Ed.): Qualitative Forschung: Ein Handbuch, 5th Ed., Rowohlt, Reinbek, 402-416.

Hauser-Schäublin, Brigitta (2003): Teilnehmende Beobachtung, in: Beer, Bettina (Ed.) (2003): Methoden und Techniken der Feldforschung, Reimer, Berlin, pp. 33-54.

Hauser-Schäublin, Brigitta / Dickhardt, Michael (Ed.) (2003): Kulturelle Räume - räumliche Kultur: Zur Neubestimmung des Verhältnisses zweier fundamentaler Kategorien menschlicher Praxis, LIT Verlag, Münster.

Haver, Daniel / Galic, Mate (2010): Native Instruments GmbH Berlin: Jahresabschluss zum 31.12.2009, in: Elektronischer Bundesanzeiger, March 1, 2011.

Hegel, Georg Wilhelm Friedrich (1986): Enzyklopädie der philosophischen Wissenschaften im Grundrisse, Zweiter Teil: Die Naturphilosophie, Suhrkamp, Frankfurt a.M.

Heidegger, Martin (2001): Sein und Zeit, 15th Ed., Niemeyer, Tübingen 2001.

Heider, Fritz (1926 / 2005): Ding und Medium, in: Baecker, Dirk (Ed.): Fritz Heider: Ding und Medium, Kadmos, Berlin.

Henkel, Anna: Systemtheoretische Methodologie: Beobachtung mit Systemreferenz Gesellschaft, in: John, René / Henkel, Anna / Rückert-John, Jana (Ed.) (2010): Die Methodologien des Systems: Wie kommt man zum Fall und wie dahinter?, VS Verlag, Wiesbaden, pp. 181-200.

Herrmann, Thaddeus (2006): Dubplates & Mastering: Von der Festplatte aufs Vinyl, in: De-Bug Online, May 20, 2006, http://de-bug.de/musiktechnik/archives/179.html.

Hoffmann, Heiko (2010): Krise? Welche Krise? Zwei Berliner Unternehmen beweisen, dass es in der Musikbranche nicht überall bergab geht - ganz im Gegenteil, in: Zitty Berlin 12/2010, pp. 22-23.

Host, Vivian (2006): Panoramabar / Bergain: The life and times of Berlin's craziest underground mega-club, in: Berlin Wasted Youth, XLR8R Vol. 101, October 2006, p. 70.

Hünniger, Andrea (2009): Er ist der Härteste: Sven Marquardt ist der erste Türsteher mit Prominentenstatus. Als Fotograf dokumentierte er die Subkultur in der DDR, in: Zeit Online, August 8, 2009, http://www.zeit.de/2009/33/Portraet-Marquard/komplettansicht.

Hutter, Michael (2007): Are markets like protest movements? A theoretical appraisal of valuation systems, in: Soziale Systeme 13, pp. 32-45.

Hutter, Thomas (2012): Facebook: Der Unterschied zwischen EdgeRank und GraphRank, January 4, 2012, http://www.thomashutter.com/index.php/2012/01/facebook-der-unterschied-zwischen-edgerank-und-graphrank/.

Ikegami, Eiko (2005): Bonds of Civility: Aesthetic Networks and the Political Origins of Japanese Culture, Cambridge University Press, New York.

IMSTA (2011): Piracy, http://www.imsta.org/piracy.php, last access: 09/30/2011.

Jag, Nick (2007): MySpace Marketing: The Promotional Revolution, self-published, Orlando.

John, René / Henkel, Anna / Rückert-John, Jana (Ed.) (2010): Die Methodologien des Systems: Wie kommt man zum Fall und wie dahinter?, VS Verlag, Wiesbaden.

John, René / Henkel, Anna / Rückert-John, Jana (2010): Methodologie und Systemtheorie - ein Problemaufriss, in: John, René / Henkel, Anna / Rückert-John, Jana (Ed.) (2010): Die Methodologien des Systems: Wie kommt man zum Fall und wie dahinter?, VS Verlag, Wiesbaden, pp. 7-12.

John, René (2010): Funktionale Analyse - Erinnerungen an eine Methodologie zwischen Fixierung und Überraschung, in: John, René / Henkel, Anna / Rückert-John, Jana (Ed.) (2010): Die Methodologien des Systems: Wie kommt man zum Fall und wie dahinter?, VS Verlag, Wiesbaden, pp. 29-54.

Kant, Immanuel (1770 / 2006): Von dem Raume, in: Dünne, Jörg / Günzel, Stephan (Ed.): Raumtheorie: Grundlagentexte aus Philosophie und Kulturwissenschaften, Suhrkamp, Frankfurt a.M., pp. 76-79.

Karafillidis, Athanasios (2010): Soziale Formen: Fortführung eines soziologischen Programms, transcript, Bielefeld.

Katz, Bob (2007): Mastering Audio: The art and the science, 2nd Ed., Focal Press, Burlington, MA.

Kauffman, Louis H. (1987): Self-reference and recursive forms, in: Social Biological Structure, Vol. 10, pp. 53-72.

Kauffman, Louis H. (2002): Time, Imaginary Value, Paradox, Sign and Space, in: Computing Anticipatory Systems, CASYS - 5th International Conference (2001), AIP Conference Proceedings Vol. 627 ed. by Dubois, Daniel.

Kauffman, Louis H. (2005): EigenForm, in: Kybernetes Vol. 34, No. 1-2, pp. 129-150.

Kauffman, Louis H. (2009): Reflexivity and Eigenform: The Shape of Process, in: Constructivist Foundations Vol. 4, No. 3, pp. 121-137.

Kittler, Friedrich (1986): Grammophon Film Typewriter, Brinkmann & Bose, Berlin.

Klages, Thorsten (2002): Medium und Form - Musik in den (Re)Produktionsmedien, epOs Music, Osnabrück.

Konau, Elisabeth (1977): Raum und soziales Handeln: Studien zu einer vernachlässigten Dimension soziologischer Theoriebildung, Enke, Stuttgart.

Kossinets, Gueorgi / Watts, Duncan J. (2006): Empirical Analysis of an Evolving Social Network, in: Science, Vol. 311, pp. 88-90.
Kotler, Philip / Armstrong, Gary / Saunders, John / Wong, Veronica (2003): Grundlagen des Marketing, Pearson, Munich.
Krämer-Badoni, Thomas/Kuhm, Klaus (Hg.) (2003): Die Gesellschaft und ihr Raum. Raum als Gegenstand der Soziologie, Leske + Budrich, Opladen.
Krämer, Sybille (Ed.) (1998): Medien - Computer - Realität: Wirklichkeitsvorstellungen und Neue Medien, Suhrkamp, Frankfurt.
Kremp, Matthias (2006): Hausmusik: Das Studio im Wohnzimmer, in: Spiegel Online, November 28, 2006, http://www.spiegel.de/netzwelt/spielzeug/0,1518,druck-451141,00.html.
Kronemeyer, David (2009): Deconstructing Pop Culture: Things We Know to Be Indubitably True about the Music Business, in: Music Industry Newswire, May 5, 2009, http://musicindustrynewswire.com/2009/05/05/min1646_182956.php.
Krutter, Simon (2009): Verräumlichung von Komplexität: Zum Wandel gesellschaftlicher Raumsemantiken, MA Thesis, University of Vienna.
Kuhn, Johannes (2009): Strategie gescheitert: MySpace gibt den Kampf auf, in: Süddeutsche Zeitung Online, November 5, 2009, http://www.sueddeutsche.de/computer/117/493464/text/print.html.
Kusek, David / Leonhard, Gerd (2005): The Future of Music: Manifesto for the Digital Music Revolution, Berklee, Boston.
Lab.Oratory (2011): Events, http://www.lab-oratory.de/events/, last access: 09/14/2011.
Lakoff, George / Johnson, Mark (1996): Metaphors We Live By, University of Chicago Press, Chicago.
Lange, Bastian / Bürkner, Hans-Joachim (2010): Wertschöpfung in der Kreativwirtschaft: Der Fall der elektonischen Klubmusik, in: Zeitschrift für Wirtschaftsgeographie, Vol. 54, pp. 46-68.
Langlois, Ganaele / Elmer, Greg / McKelvey, Fenwick (2011): Vernetzte Öffentlichkeiten: Die doppelte Artikulation von Code und Politik in Facebook, in: Leistert, Oliver / Röhle, Theo (Ed.): Generation Facebook: Über das Leben im Social Net, transcript, Bielefeld, pp. 253-278.
Lau, Felix (2008): Die Form der Paradoxie: Eine Einführung in die Mathematik und Philosophie der "Laws of Form" von G. Spencer Brown, 3rd Ed., Carl-Auer-Systeme, Heidelberg.
Lederbogen, Jan (2003): Fotografie, in: Beer, Bettina (Ed.) (2003): Methoden und Techniken der Feldforschung, Reimer, Berlin, pp. 225-248.
Lee, Martyn (1997): Relocating Location: Cultural Geography, the Specifity of Place and the City Habitus, in: McGuigan, Jim (Ed.): Cultural Methodologies, Sage Publications, London.
Leistert, Oliver / Röhle, Theo (Ed.) (2011): Generation Facebook: Über das Leben im Social Net, transcript, Bielefeld.
Leistert, Oliver / Röhle, Theo (2011): Identifizieren, Verbinden, Verkaufen: Einleitendes zur Maschine Facebook, ihren Konsequenzen und den Beiträgen in diesem Band, in: Leistert, Oliver / Röhle, Theo (Ed.): Generation Facebook: Über das Leben im Social Net, transcript, Bielefeld, pp. 7-30.
Levi Martin, John (2009): Social Structures, Princeton University Press, Princeton.
Lewins, Ann / Silver, Christina (2007): Using Software in Qualitative Research, Sage, London.
Lido Berlin (2012), http://www.lido-berlin.de/, last access: 05/06/2012.
Lippuner, Roland (2008): Raumbilder der Gesellschaft. Zur Räumlichkeit des Sozialen in der Systemtheorie, in: Döring, Jörg / Thielmann, Tristan (Ed.): Spatial Turn: Das Raumparadigma in den Kultur- und Sozialwissenschaften, transcript, Bielefeld, pp. 341-363.
Löw, Martina (2001): Raumsoziologie, Suhrkamp, Frankfurt a.M.
Lovink, Geert (2011): Anonymität und die Krise des multiplen Selbst, in: Leistert, Oliver / Röhle, Theo (Ed.): Generation Facebook: Über das Leben im Social Net, transcript, Bielefeld, pp. 183-198.
Lüders, Christian (2007): Beobachten im Feld und Ethnogeographie, in: Flick, Uwe / von Kardorff, Ernst / Steinke, Ines (Ed.): Qualitative Forschung: Ein Handbuch, 5th Ed., Rowohlt, Reinbek, 384-401.
Luhmann, Niklas (1984): Soziale Systeme, Suhrkamp, Frankfurt a.M.
Luhmann, Niklas (1990a): Weltkunst, in: Luhmann, Niklas / Bunsen, Frederick D. / Baecker, Dirk (Ed.): Unbeobachtbare Welt: Über Kunst und Architektur, Haux, Bielefeld, pp. 7-45.
Luhmann, Niklas (1990b): Essays on Self-Reference, Columbia University Press, New York.

Luhmann, Niklas (1993a): Gesellschaftsstruktur und Semantik: Studien zur Wissenssoziologie der modernen Gesellschaft, Suhrkamp, Frankfurt a.M.

Luhmann, Niklas (1993b): Die Paradoxie der Form, in: Baecker, Dirk (Ed.): Kalkül der Form, Suhrkamp, Frankfurt a.M., pp. 243-261.

Luhmann, Niklas (1995a): Social Systems, Stanford University Press, Stanford.

Luhmann, Niklas (1995b): Die Kunst der Gesellschaft, Suhrkamp, Frankfurt a.M.

Luhmann, Niklas (1995c): Kultur als historischer Begriff, in: Luhmann, Niklas: Gesellschaftsstruktur und Semantik: Studien zur Wissenssoziologie der modernen Gesellschaft, Vol. 4, Suhrkamp, Frankfurt a.M., pp. 31-54.

Luhmann, Niklas (1996): Die Realität der Massenmedien, 2nd Ed., Westdeutscher Verlag, Opladen.

Luhmann, Niklas (1997a): Die Gesellschaft der Gesellschaft. Erster Teilband, Suhrkamp, Frankfurt a.M.

Luhmann, Niklas (1997b): Die Gesellschaft der Gesellschaft. Zweiter Teilband, Suhrkamp, Frankfurt a.M.

Luhmann, Niklas (2000): Art as a Social System, Stanford University Press, Stanford.

Magdanz, Fee / Hillmann, Jan-Rikus (2008): de:bug Verlags GmbH: Jahresabschluss zum 31.12.2006, in: Elektronischer Bundesanzeiger, May 7, 2008.

Magnet Club (2012), http://www.magnet-club.de/, last access: 05/06/2012.

Malsky, Matthew (2003): Stretched from Manhattan's Back Alley to MOMA: A Social History of Magnetic Tape and Recording, in: Lysloff, René T.A. / Gay, Leslie C. Jr. (Ed.): Music and Technoculture, Wesleyan U.P., Middletown, pp. 233-263.

Maresch, Rudolf/Werber, Niels (Ed.) (2002): Raum - Wissen - Macht, Suhrkamp, Frankfurt a.M.

Marqusee, Mike (2002): Come you masters of war, in: The Guardian Online, August 2, 2002, http://www.guardian.co.uk/music/2002/aug/02/artsfeatures.popandrock/print.

Millard, Andre (1995): America on Record. A history of recorded Sound, Cambridge U.P., Cambridge.

Miller, Daniel (2012): Das wilde Netzwerk. Ein ethnologischer Blick auf Facebook., Suhrkamp, Berlin.

Mörtenböck, Peter / Mooshammer, Helge (2010): Netzwerk Kultur. Die Kunst der Verbindung in einer globalisierten Welt, transcript, Bielefeld.

Müller, Karl-Josef (1988): Mahler: Leben - Werke - Dokumente, Schott, Mainz.

Münker, Stefan (2009): Emergenz digitaler Öffentlichkeiten: Die Sozialen Medien im Web 2.0, Suhrkamp, Frankfurt a.M.

MySpace (2009): Press Release: MySpace Launches Suite of Music Products for Artists and Fans, October 21, 2009, http://www.myspace.com/pressroom/2009/10/myspace-launches-suite-of-music-products-for-artists-and-fans/.

MySpace (2011a): How do I create a Myspace blog?, http://myspace2.custhelp.com/app/answers/detail/a_id/252/kw/blog, last access: 09/24/2011.

MySpace (2011b): How do I add kudos and manage comments on blog posts?, http://myspace2.custhelp.com/app/answers/detail/a_id/253/kw/blog, last access: 09/24/2011.

MySpace (2011c): How do I change or reorder my top friends?, http://myspace2.custhelp.com/app/answers/detail/a_id/1456/kw/top%20friends, last access: 09/24/2011.

MySpace (2011d): How do I control comments on Myspace?, http://myspace2.custhelp.com/app/answers/detail/a_id/271/kw/top%20friends, last access: 09/24/2011.

NAMM (2011): The NAMM Global Report 2010, http://www.namm.org/library/music-usa.

Noller, Peter (1999): Globalisierung, Stadträume und Lebensstile: Kulturelle und lokale Repräsentationen des globalen Raums, Leske + Budrich, Opladen.

Omahna, Manfred (2006): Plurale Räume: Mentale Stadterfahrungen als Instrument globaler Praktiken, Waxmann Verlag, Münster.

Olivarez-Giles, Nathan (2009): Recording Studios are being left out of the mix, in: Los Angeles Times Online, October 13, 2009, http://articles.latimes.com/print/2009/oct/13/business/fi-smallbiz-studios13.

Petroczi, Andrea / Nepusz, Tamas / Baszo, Fülöp (2007): Measuring tie-strength in virtual social networks, in: Connections Vol. 27, No. 2, pp. 39-52.

Pogue, David (2004): State Of The Art; Recording Studio In a Box, in: The New York Times Online, January 14, 2004, http://www.nytimes.com/2004/01/15/technology/state-of-the-art-recording-studio-in-a-box.html?pagewanted=print&src=pm.
Price, Jeff (2008): The Democratization of the Music Industry, in: The Huffington Post, March 24, 2008, http://www.huffingtonpost.com/jeff-price/the-democratization-of-th_b_93065.html.
Quantcast (2011): Facebook.com Audience Profile: Monthly United States People 6/2/07 - 7/30/11, http://www.quantcast.com/facebook.com, last access: 09/26/2011.
Rapp, Tobias (2009): Lost and Sound: Berlin, Techno und der Easyjetset, Suhrkamp, Frankfurt a.M.
Renner, Kai-Hinrich / Renner, Tim (2011): Digital ist Besser: Warum das Abendland auch durch das Internet nicht untergehen wird, Campus, Frankfurt a. M.
Renner, Tim (2004): Kinder, der Tod ist gar nicht so schlimm! Über die Zukunft der Musik- und Medienindustrie, Campus, Frankfurt a. M.
Richter, Klaus Peter (1997): Soviel Musik war nie. Von Mozart zum digitalen Sound: Eine musikalische Kulturgeschichte, Luchterhand, Munich.
Roads, Curtis (1996): The Computer Music Tutorial, MIT Press, Cambridge, MA.
Ruschkowski, André (1998): Elektronische Klänge und musikalische Entdeckungen, Reclam, Stuttgart.
Sacks, Harvey (1995): Lectures on Conversation, Paperback Ed., Blackwell, Cambridge, MA.
Schindl, Thomas (2007): Räume des Medialen: Zum spatial turn in Kulturwissenschaften und Medientheorien, Verlag Werner Hülsbusch, Boizenburg.
Schlehe, Judith (2003): Formen qualitativer ethnografischer Interviews, in: Beer, Bettina (Ed.): Methoden und Techniken der Feldforschung, Reimer, Berlin, pp. 71-93.
Schmitz, Stefan (2001): Revolutionen der Erreichbarkeit: Gesellschaft, Raum und Verkehr im Wandel, Leske + Budrich, Opladen.
Schönwälder, Tatjana / Wille, Kathrin / Hölscher, Thomas (2004): George Spencer Brown: Eine Einführung in die "Laws of Form", VS Verlag, Wiesbaden.
Schroer, Markus (2006): Räume, Orte, Grenzen. Auf dem Weg zu einer Soziologie des Raums, Suhrkamp, Frankfurt a.M.
Schroer, Markus (2008): "Bringing space back in" - Zur Relevanz des Raums als soziologischer Kategorie, in: Döring, Jörg / Thielmann, Tristan (Ed.): Spatial Turn: Das Raumparadigma in den Kultur- und Sozialwissenschaften, transcript, Bielefeld, pp. 125-148.
Schwanhäußer, Anja (2010): Kosmonauten des Underground: Ethnografie einer Berliner Szene, Campus Verlag, Frankfurt.
Scientific Software (2011): ATLAS.ti 6: The New Features, self-published, http://downloads.atlasti.com/newfeatures6.pdf.
Scientific Software / Friese, Susanne (2011): ATLAS.ti - The True Qualitative Tool, self-published, http://downloads.atlasti.com/library/friese_nl201108.pdf.
Seemann, Silke (2010): Organisationales Spielen in Form gebracht: Denkhilfen für dynamische Situationen in hyperkomplexen Umwelten, Kadmos, Berlin.
Seifter, Uwe / Kim, Jin Hyun / Moore, Anthony (2008): Paradoxes of Interactivity, transcript, Bielefeld.
Senatsverwaltung für Wirtschaft, Technologie und Frauen / Der Regierende Bürgermeister von Berlin, Senatskanzlei – Kulturelle Angelegenheiten / Senatsverwaltung für Stadtentwicklung (Ed.) (2008): Kulturwirtschaft in Berlin 2008: Entwicklungen und Potentiale, self-published.
Serrao, Marc Felix (2010): „Wie in einer Sekte": Studie zum Facebook-Entzug, in: Süddeutsche Zeitung Online, February 3, 2010, http://www.sueddeutsche.de/computer/810/502049/text/print.html.
Shannon, Claude (1963): The Mathematical Theory of Communication, in: Shannon, Claude / Weaver, Warren (Ed.): The Mathematical Theory of Communication, 1st Paperback Ed., University of Illinois Press, Urbana.
Siegler, MG (2010): I Think Facebook Just Seized Control Of The Internet, in: TechCrunch, April 21, 2010, http://techcrunch.com/2010/04/21/facebook/.
Simmel, Georg (1888 / 1983): Schriften zur Soziologie: Eine Auswahl, ed. by Dahme, H.J / Rammstedt, O., Suhrkamp, Frankfurt a.M.

Simmel, Georg (1992): Soziologie: Untersuchungen über die Formen der Vergesellschaftung, in: Rammstedt, Otto (Ed.): Georg Simmel: Gesamtausgabe, Vol. 11, Suhrkamp, Frankfurt a.M.
Simmel, Georg (1908 / 1995): Soziologie des Raumes, in: Kramme, Rüdiger / Rammstedt, Angela / Rammstedt, Ottheim: Georg Simmel: Aufsätze und Abhandlungen 1901-1908, Suhrkamp, Frankfurt a.M., pp. 132-183.
Simmel, Georg (1908 / 1995): Über räumliche Projektionen socialer Formen, in: Kramme, Rüdiger / Rammstedt, Angela / Rammstedt, Ottheim: Georg Simmel: Aufsätze und Abhandlungen 1901-1908, Suhrkamp, Frankfurt a.M., pp. 201-220.
Small, Christopher (1998): Musicking: The Meanings of Performing and Listening, Wesleyan University Press, Hanover, NH.
SO36 (2012), http://so36.de/, last access: 05/06/2012.
Sound On Sound (2012): Search Results "Abbey Road", http://www.soundonsound.com/search?PageSize=80&Keyword=abbey%20road&Year=%20&Month=%20&Words=All&Summary=No&Section=0&Subject=0&ShowResults=yes, last access: 05/06/2012.
Spencer Brown, George (1972): Laws of Form, First American Ed., The Julian Press, New York City.
Spencer Brown, George (1973): American University of Masters: Transcript Session One, http://lawsofform.org/aum/session1.html
Spencer-Brown, George (2008): Laws of Form, Fifth English Ed., Bohmeier, Leipzig.
Spinola, Julia (2009): Festspielhaus in ostdeutscher Brache: Fast wie Bayreuth: "Berghain", in FAZ.net, July 25, 2009, http://www.faz.net/aktuell/feuilleton/2.1781/fast-wie-bayreuth-berghain-festspielhaus-in-ostdeutscher-brache-1827273.html.
Stenton, Dave (2006): HardWax: The city's longest standing techno institution marches on, in: Berlin Wasted Youth, XLR8R Vol. 101, October 2006, p. 46.
Stichweh, Rudolf (2003): Raum und moderne Gesellschaft: Aspekte der sozialen Kontrolle des Raums, in: Krämer-Badoni, Thomas / Kuhm, Klaus (Ed.): Die Gesellschaft und ihr Raum: Raum als Gegenstand der Soziologie, Leske + Budrich, Opladen, pp. 93-102.
Stichweh, Rudolf (2005): Inklusion und Exklusion: Studien zur Gesellschaftstheorie, transcript, Belefeld.
Stichweh, Rudolf (2008): Kontrolle und Organisation des Raums durch Funktionssysteme der Weltgesellschaft, in: Döring, Jörg / Thielmann, Tristan (Ed.): Spatial Turn: Das Raumparadigma in den Kultur- und Sozialwissenschaften, transcript, Bielefeld, pp. 149-164.
Stichweh, Rudolf (2010): Theorie und Methode in der Systemtheorie, in: John, René / Henkel, Anna / Rückert-John, Jana (Ed.) (2010): Die Methodologien des Systems: Wie kommt man zum Fall und wie dahinter?, VS Verlag, Wiesbaden, pp. 15-28.
Stockfelt, Ola (2004): Adequate Modes of Listening, in: Cox, Christoph / Warner, Daniel (Ed.): Audio Culture: Readings in Modern Music, Continuum, London, pp. 88-93.
Stone, Brad (2009): Want to Copy iTunes Music? Go Ahead, Apple Says, in: The New York Times, January 7, 2009, online version: http://www.nytimes.com/2009/01/07/technology/companies/07apple.html?scp=1&sq=apple%20drm&st=cse.
Strauss, Anselm L. (1998): Grundlagen qualitativer Sozialforschung, 2nd. Ed., Fink, Munich.
Süddeutsche Magazin Online (2009): Im Reich des Wahnsinns: Falls Sie nicht reinkommen: Wir verraten Ihnen, wie der berühmteste und geheimnisvollste Club der Welt - das "Berghain" in Berlin - von innen aussieht, in: Süddeutsche Zeitung Magazin Online, http://sz-magazin.sueddeutsche.de/texte/anzeigen/28877, last access: 05/06/2012.
Tarde, Gabriel (1969): The Public and the Crowd, in: Tarde, Gabriel: On Communication & Social Influence, The University of Chicago Press, Chicago, pp. 277-294.
Taylor, Ken (2006): Native Instruments: A decade of tweaking, twiddling, and twerking, in: Berlin Wasted Youth, XLR8R Vol. 101, October 2006, p. 40.
Thomann (2011): Verkaufsrang: Sequenzersoftware und virtuelle Studios, http://www.thomann.de/de/prod_vrank-ncx.html?ar=226260, last access: 09/25/2011.
van Heur, Bas (2007): The Clustering of Networked Creativity: Between Myth and Reality, Center for Metropolitan Studies Working Paper Series No. 007-2007, Technische Universität Berlin.

Vincent, Fran (2006): MySpace for Musicians, in Electronic Musician Online, July 01, 2006, http://emusician.com/tutorials/emusic_myspace_musicians/.

Vogd, Werner (2007): Empirie oder Theorie? Systemtheoretische Forschung jenseits einer vermeintlichen Alternative, in: Soziale Welt, Special Edition Soziologische Systemtheorie und empirische Forschung, pp. 295-321.

Vogd, Werner (2010): Methodologie und Verfahrensweise der dokumentarischen Methode und ihre Kompatibilität zur Systemtheorie, in: John, René / Henkel, Anna / Rückert-John, Jana (Ed.) (2010): Die Methodologien des Systems: Wie kommt man zum Fall und wie dahinter?, VS Verlag, Wiesbaden, pp. 121-140.

Vogt, Sabine (2007): Clubkultur als Clubwirtschaft: Das Beispiel Berlin, in: Industrie-Kultur: Magazin für Denkmalpflege, Landschaft, Sozial-, Umwelt- und Technikgeschichte, May 21, 2007, http://www.industrie-kultur.de/modules.php?op=modload&name=News&file=article&sid=61.

von Foerster, Heinz (1993): Wissen und Gewissen: Versuch einer Brücke, Suhrkamp, Frankfurt a.M.

von Foerster, Heinz (2003): Understanding Understanding: Essays on Cybernetics and Cognition, Springer, New York.

Walker, Martin (1998a): Software Synth: Native Instruments Generator 1.5, in: Sound On Sound Online, September 2008, http://www.soundonsound.com/sos/sep98/articles/generator.html?print=yes.

Walker, Martin (1998b): PC Software Sampler: Nemesys Gigasampler v1.5, in: Sound On Sound Online, December 1998, http://www.soundonsound.com/sos/dec98/articles/gigasample.143.htm?print=yes.

Walker, Martin (2007): Multitrack Audio Recording & Editing Software for PC: Cockos Reaper DAW, in: Sound On Sound Online, June 2007, http://www.soundonsound.com/sos/jun07/articles/reaper.htm.

Walker, Michael (2006): Computer Software That Can Turn You Into a Songwriter, in: The New York Times Online, April 2, 2006, http://www.nytimes.com/2006/04/02/arts/music/02walk.html?scp=1&sq=Computer%20Software%20That%20Can%20Turn%20You%20Into%20a%20Songwriter&st=cse.

Waltz, Alexis (2009): Das Berghain, die Mitte der Welt, in: Rapp, Tobias (Ed.): Lost and Sound: Berlin, Techno und der Easyjetset, Suhrkamp, Frankfurt a.M., pp. 121-133.

Wanhoff, Thomas (2011): Wa(h)re Freunde: Wie sich unsere Beziehungen in sozialen Online-Netzwerken verändern, Spektrum Akademischer Verlag, Heidelberg.

Warnke, Martin (2003): Daten und Metadaten, in: zeitenblicke, Vol. 2, No. 1, http://www.zeitenblicke.de/2003/01/warnke/index.html.

Warnke, Martin (2004): Der Zeitpfeil im Digitalen: Synthese, Mimesis, Emergenz, Alcatel SEL Stiftung, Stuttgart.

Warnke, Martin (2008): Der Raum des Cyberspace, in: Zinsmeister, Annett (Ed.): welt[stadt]raum: Mediale Inszenierungen, transcript, Bielefeld, pp. 217-244.

Warnke, Martin (2011): Errechnet, gesteuert, vernetzt, in: Neue Zeitschrift für Musik, No. 1/2011, pp. 35-39.

Wenger, Christian (2006): Jenseits der Sterne: Gemeinschaft und Identität in Fankulturen: Zur Konstitution des Star Trek-Fandoms, transcript, Bielefeld.

Werber, Niels (2008): Die Geo-Semantik der Netzwerkgesellschaft, in: Döring, Jörg / Thielmann, Tristan (Ed.): Spatial Turn: Das Raumparadigma in den Kultur- und Sozialwissenschaften, transcript, Bielefeld, pp. 165-183.

Wherry, Mark (2006): Apple Notes: Apple & Emagic, in: Sound On Sound Online, August 2006, http://www.soundonsound.com/sos/aug06/articles/applenotes_0806.htm?print=yes.

Wherry, Mark (2007): MIDI + Audio Sequencer for Mac OS X: Apple Logic Pro 8, in: Sound On Sound Online, November 2007, http://www.soundonsound.com/sos/nov07/articles/logic8.htm?print=yes.

White, Harrison C. (1992): Identity and Control: A Structural Theory of Social Action, Princeton University Press, Princeton.

White, Harrison C. (1995): Network Switchings and Bayesian Forks: Reconstructing the Social and Behavioral Sciences, in: Social Research Vol. 62, pp. 1035-1063.

White, Harrison C. (2001): Markets from Networks: Socioeconomic Models of Production, Princeton University Press, Princeton.

White, Harrison C. (2008): Identity & Control: How Social Formations Emerge, Princeton University Press, Princeton.

White, Harrison C. / Fuhse, Jan / Thiemann, Matthias / Buchholz, Larissa (2007): Networks and Meaning: Styles and Switchings, in: Soziale Systeme Vol. 13, No. 1-2, pp. 543-555.

White, Harrison C. / Godart, Frédéric C. (2007): Stories from Identity and Control, in: Sociologica 3/2007, pp. 1-17.

White, Harrison C. / White, Cynthia A. (1993): Canvases and Careers: Institutional Change in the French Painting World, Second Ed., University of Chicago Press, Chicago.

White, Paul (1995): Mikail Graham: Emagic, in: Sound On Sound Online, September 1995, http://www.soundonsound.com/sos/1995_articles/sep95/emagic.html.

White, Paul (2003): MIDI + Audio Sequencer for Mac OS 9 & OS X: Emagic Logic Platinum v6, in: Sound On Sound Online, April 2003, http://www.soundonsound.com/sos/apr03/articles/emagiclogic6.asp?print=yes.

Ziemann, Andreas (2003): Der Raum der Interaktion - eine systemtheoretische und ihr Raum. Raum als Gegenstand der Soziologie, Leske + Budrich, Opladen, pp. 131-153.

MIX
Papier aus verantwortungsvollen Quellen
Paper from responsible sources
FSC® C105338

If you have any concerns about our products,
you can contact us on
ProductSafety@springernature.com

In case Publisher is established outside the EU,
the EU authorized representative is:
Springer Nature Customer Service Center GmbH
Europaplatz 3, 69115 Heidelberg, Germany

Printed by Libri Plureos GmbH
in Hamburg, Germany